"I remember the thrill of being published for the first time like it was yesterday. I was in the eighth grade and my poem, 'The Door to Escape,' appeared in the school yearbook. I kept running my fingers over the page, reading the poem again and again, feeling proud and scared in equal measure. Between you and me, the poem wasn't very good, but it didn't matter . . . It was the first time I was brave enough to put myself out there. I still think of that door to escape every time I hold a new book of mine that has managed to find its way into print. I feel proud and scared each time, but now with the balance maybe— just maybe—tipping in favor of pride. So I love that Girls Write Now gives young writers an opportunity to experience that thrill—that pride—and, through thoughtful mentoring, helps them to push past the fear."

—TARA ALTEBRANDO, author of *The Leaving*

"There is no greater proof of the power of writing—and reading— than Girls Write Now. They create space for a diverse range of young, female voices—but by giving us the opportunity to read them, we emerge changed as well."

—CHLOE BENJAMIN, author of *The Immortalists*

"These girls will create the feminism of the future. It is our job to listen to and support these young women. I'm very grateful that Girls Write Now is helping us do just that."

—ROWAN HISAYO BUCHANAN, author of *Harmless Like You*

"When I sit down to write, I'm boldly proclaiming that I like spending time with myself, that I am interested in my own mind, ideas, fantasies, and inner life. For girls and women, it's a radical act to say, *my mind is a fascinating place*. This is what we do every time we sit down to create."

—NAIMA COSTER, author of *Halsey Street*

"Stories are history, aspiration, consolation, and survival. For most of history, girls have been the objects of storytellers. It's time for them to write their own stories."
—**MOLLY CRABAPPLE**, author of *Drawing Blood*

"Young women deserve and require mentorship from adult women who've been successful in their fields of interest. That's exactly what Girls Write Now does: creates a bridge young women can use to move toward their goals. I love that."
—**CAMERON ESPOSITO**, cocreator of *Take My Wife*

"Throughout their lives, women are told that they need to be empowered. That creates the message that someone else owns a female's power and that it can be given and taken away. The incredible voices of girls collected in *Generation F: The Girls Write Now 2018 Anthology* proves this whole status quo about empowerment wrong. Girls don't need to be empowered, they need to be enabled to use their own power. The Girls Write Now program makes me so excited for the future, one where all voices matter, not just some. Now, that is power."
—**DR. PATTI FLETCHER**, cofounder, PSDNetwork, and author of *Disrupters: Success Strategies from Women Who Break the Mold*

"The work that Girls Write Now does, giving young women the tools to better express their ideas, opinions, and experiences, is vital. These girls' stories should be required reading for anyone hungry for hope in a world that feels increasingly complex and unsteady. These are the changemakers with the power to shape our future."
—**NEHA GANDHI**, editor in chief and COO of *Girlboss*

"Girls Write Now is the kind of powerful, lifelong experience I wish I'd had growing up. Young artists doing wildly creative work!"
—**N. K. JEMISIN**, author of the Broken Earth trilogy

"This anthology gifts us with the passionate voices of the next generation. You'll be inspired by the knowledge that the written word will far more than endure, it will shine."
—**WALLACE KING**, author of *Edenland*

"Girls Write Now is essential reading and essential writing. For a world that tells women and girls to be quiet, Girls Write Now is giving them the chance to make noise. Listen."

—JILL KOLONGOWSKI, author of *Life Lessons Harry Potter Taught Me: Discover the Magic of Friendship, Family, Courage, and Love in Your Life*

"When I was a young immigrant, struggling with language and acceptance, I wish I had had an organization like Girls Write Now to help me find my voice. It is truly humbling to see the eloquence and power that can be unleashed in young women with the right touch—and to hear the strength in a chorus of newly discovered voices that have been granted the training and opportunity to reach their full potential."

—MARIA KONNIKOVA, author of *The Confidence Game* and *Mastermind*

"The courageous and heartfelt stories that shape this anthology serve to remind us all that one of the most powerful things in the world is a girl with a pen in her hand."

—LANG LEAV, author of *Sad Girls*

"To speak in one's own voice—and to be heard—is a right as unalienable as the preservation of life, liberty, and the pursuit of happiness. Girls Write Now gives young women the means to exercise that right. This anthology brings the reader back, again and again, to one fundamental purpose of language itself: deliverance."

—RACHEL LYON, author of *Self-Portrait with Boy*

"In an age that requires activism in the everyday, the Girls Write Now community of shared experience, mentorship, and creativity has become indispensable. Through story, our understanding of others grows; when we are the ones writing the story, our understanding of self also blooms. These pages are alive with the strength and self-reflection that is born when women work together. *Generation F* is officially required reading!"

—KELLY McMASTERS, coeditor of *This Is the Place: Women Writing About Home*

"Our world is desperate for fresh voices and new ideas from unconventional sources. The wealth of stories, creativity, and bravery in this collection gives me hope that this next generation will thrive on opportunities to break the mold, challenge the status quo, and let their individuality shine ever brighter."

—NILOFER MERCHANT, author of *The Power of Onlyness: Make Your Wild Ideas Mighty Enough to Dent the World*

"Hooray for the courage of these young writers, for the grace of their mentors, and for the transforming power of story. Reading these young writers will make you stand up and cheer!"

—SY MONTGOMERY, author of *Walking with the Great Apes: Jane Goodall, Dian Fossey, Birute Galdikas*

"Writing has been a tremendous help for me in finding my voice and finding myself. I love that Girls Write Now is helping girls from all walks of life find that power and truth within themselves."

—BETH NEWELL, editor and cofounder of *Reductress*

"Few things can shape our future as vitally as empowering young women to become storytellers. Girls Write Now brings us yet another generation taking ownership of their narratives: bright and daring, past and present, now and always."

—TÉA OBREHT, author of *The Tiger's Wife*

"It isn't the meek who will inherit the earth—it's the young. Thank goodness these young writers, resisters, and boundary-pushers are anything but meek. Their powerful words will inspire you and give you hope for our future."

—CAMILLE PERRI, author of *The Assistants* and *When Katie Met Cassidy*

"This triumphant collection folds its arms around readers, letting us know that none of us is alone. That our voices are real, vital, and urgently needed. Thank you to all the girls who are brave enough to share their truest selves on these pages. You give rise to hope through your storytelling gifts. Your emergence is keenly felt."

—ANDREA DAVIS PINKNEY, *New York Times*–bestselling author of *The Red Pencil*

"Hearing someone start to find her voice is thrilling. I want to be there as these girls do just that, then stand back as their voices grow stronger and stronger until they're unstoppable."
—**KAYLEEN SCHAEFER**, author of *Text Me When You Get Home: The Evolution and Triumph of Modern Female Friendship*

"Writing is a powerful act that lets the writer articulate her thoughts and feelings directly, fluently, openly, and originally; and in doing so, the writer forges a connection with that other important half of the equation: the reader. These young writers are working hard every day to describe their inner lives and take them outward; to forge that essential, beautiful connection."
—**MEG WOLITZER**, author of *The Female Persuasion*

"These young girls are the real visionaries of tomorrow and we are beyond lucky to read their stories today."
—**JENNY ZHANG**, author of *Sour Heart*

Generation F

THE GIRLS WRITE NOW 2018 ANTHOLOGY

GENERATION

THE GIRLS WRITE NOW
2018 ANTHOLOGY

FOREWORD BY

Ashley C. Ford

INTRODUCTION BY

Samhita Mukhopadhyay

Published 2018

Printed in the United States

Print ISBN: 978-0-9962772-2-8

E-ISBN: 9781936932528

Library of Congress Control Number: 2018903004

Cover design by Kaitlin Kall

For information, write to:

Girls Write Now, Inc.
247 West 37th Street, Suite 1000
New York, NY 10018

info@girlswritenow.org

girlswritenow.org

Foreword

ASHLEY C. FORD

Before I sold a book, wrote an essay, or even knew I wanted to be a writer, I was defiant. As a toddler, when I did not want to be held, I would not be held. In fact, when an adult would try to hold me, I would head-butt them until they let me go. When my mother, at her wits' end with my antics, would attempt to tame me by strapping me into my car seat, I would rock back and forth until the seat tipped all the way forward. Then I would walk around with the whole contraption on my back, continuing my path of destruction through whoever's home I happened to be in at the time. My grandmother started to call me "Turtle" because she thought the car seat on my back looked like a tortoise shell. She would smile when she'd tell me these tales.

"Ashley, you never liked doing what you were told. I guess you just knew yourself."

My grandmother was right. Few people like being told what to do, but it went deeper than that for me. I didn't like being told I didn't know my own mind. I didn't want anyone else feeling as though they had a right to touch me if I didn't want to be touched. And most important, I knew all my goals, dreams, and desires lived somewhere inside me that only I had access to. So when the adults in my life encouraged me to play it safe, I continued to resist them. I majored in English even when I was told I'd never make a living with that degree. I moved to Brooklyn with two bags, $400, and no permanent place to live. I started writing my opinions, first hesitantly, then with all the defiant fury I hadn't been allowed to express until then.

But that was only the beginning.

Almost one year to the day after moving to New York, I got to meet several young women through Girls Write Now. They were brilliant and creative. They read stories that lingered in my mind for months, and asked questions I hadn't even thought to ask myself. One young woman spoke of her mother, who had encouraged her to write the feelings she couldn't yet speak. Still, she found the courage to read her story aloud before us all, and in her eyes I saw something familiar: defiance. Not the kind of defiance that takes the place of what you can't or won't say, but the kind that allows you to say exactly what you mean. She'd found strength in her words, and I found inspiration in her.

Girls Write Now has put together a book of the young women who have something to say. The same young women we all are or have been before. I am so excited for you to find yourself in the pages of this book. We're all here, in every word, and in every story, connected by the inherent defiance of girlhood. Enjoy it.

Xo,

ASHLEY C. FORD lives and works in Brooklyn by way of Indiana, hosts a local news-and-culture show called *112BK*, and is currently writing her memoir, *Somebody's Daughter*.

Generation F

THE GIRLS WRITE NOW
2018 ANTHOLOGY

Fabulous. Ferocious. Fragile. Fresh. Female. *Generation F* is all of these things and more. It is anything and everything we want it to be. That freedom, that unlimited potential, is what Girls Write Now stands for and offers to its participants. These girls have the world at their fingertips and they dig in, examining their own lives, the state of their neighborhoods, and everything going on today while marching unafraid into the future and all it promises.

The sun streamed through the large windows that lined the Girls Write Now office on September 24, 2016, the day I first met my mentee. Kimberley was a soft-spoken, polite girl with long, dark hair and an air of hesitation. Neither of us knew that day what was to come, but I was hopeful. We began chatting in the room packed with other fresh or returning mentor–mentee pairs, the goals and ideas of these women and girls reverberating in the air. Kimberley said she loved dark fantasy and we agreed that we both appreciated constructive criticism. Each pair strung beads of different colors, signifying a different Girls Write Now value, on a string in order of importance. Kimberley's hesitation dropped away as we ordered the beads, and I thought, *This girl has opinions and isn't afraid to share them.* I liked that.

Kimberley writes dark fantasy about human girls crossing into magical lands, but there is so much more to her work. She also writes essays about yearning to travel and her relationships with family and friends, and poems about experiencing womanhood and the inner lives of dolls. In the Girls Write Now workshops, she and other mentees learn about and write magical realism, plays, intergenerational memoir, and more.

We come, mentors and mentees alike, to Girls Write Now because we want to learn, grow, and share as writers. We come for the community we build and for ears that are always willing and eager to listen. We come to be seen and heard—to be reminded: "You, your thoughts, and your words are valuable. Never stop writing and exploring the world's potential." We can't stop and we don't want to.

In preparation for Girls Write Now's CHAPTERS Reading Series and QWERTY Digital Media Exhibition, mentees must attend a performance tech workshop. Each mentee stands to deliver her piece, looking up at her listeners and back down at her paper, then awaits critique. I watch their faces and I see: uncontainably broad smiles that only widen as they receive thoughtful praise and feedback from peers, mentors, and program staff. Sharing their work doesn't just thrill them, it sets them on fire, lighting them up from within.

So if you do one thing for us, do this: Free these words and see what happens. Let these stories ignite a flame in your mind. Know it makes us glow that this book is in your hands and you are turning the pages. Sharing our work is our greatest joy, and we welcome you into *Generation F* with open arms.

—ROSALIND BLACK, Anthology Committee Co-Chair

Anthology Editorial Committee

Molly MacDermot
Editor

Rosalind Black
Meg Cassidy
*Anthology Committee
Co-Chairs*

Keciah Bailey
Nan Bauer-Maglin
Laura Buchwald
Alexis Cheung
Elena Coln
Megan Elmore
Hermione Hoby
Linda Kleinbub
Erica Moroz
Kate Mulley
Livia Nelson
Hannah Nesbat
Cynthia-Marie O'Brien
Carol Paik
Nikki Palumbo

Leslie Pariseau
Emily Present
Rachel Shope
Lenna Stites
Maryellen Tighe
Shara Zaval
Maria Campo, *Director of
Programs and Outreach*
Naomi Solomon, *Assistant
Director of Programs*
Sierra Ritz, *Senior Program
Coordinator*
Marsha Bernstein, Muneesh
Jain, Maggie Muldoon,
Jessie Roth, Richelle Szypul-
ski, Paolo Villanueva,
Photographers
Maya Nussbaum, *Founder and
Executive Director*

Contents

THE GIRLS WRITE NOW
2018 ANTHOLOGY

Introduction

SAMHITA MUKHOPADHYAY

In the fall of 2017, I had the privilege of speaking with you—this year's class of mentees from Girls Write Now, and the authors in this anthology. You were bright and rigorous. As I spoke of my journey to becoming a writer and the obstacles I overcame—familial pressure, going broke, stereotypes, and fear—you nodded, recognizing your own journey in mine. It was an honor to speak to you, and after the event, several of you asked me how I got the courage to do what I do. Like me, many of you experience pressure to conform to certain ways of being, whether from your families or from the people around you. Use the art of writing to figure out who you really are—and use the support of the extraordinary mentors at Girls Write Now to take all the creative risks you can.

Shyness. Fear. Shame. Humiliation. Sadness. Ridicule. Social pressure. These are all feelings that stop women from writing, especially young women. Generations of women have held back their real feelings and experiences for fear of what could happen should they speak their truths both large and small. Women's interiority has historically been obscured by society's expectations about what it means to be a woman.

Not anymore. You are Generation F—the latest generation of girls using words to speak truth to power, share your experiences, and change the world. After the 2016 election, there was a sea of change across the world: We saw some of the largest public demonstrations in history and they comprised women, mothers and their daughters, daughters and their grandmothers, sisters, wives.

The marches were multigenerational, but it is the young women, the girls, who are carrying the torch. Generation F—perhaps F for "fuck" or "feminism" or "future"—you are asking the difficult questions that are leading movements to fight against gun violence, sexual assault, and police brutality.

What a time to be alive. You are navigating what it means to have the most freedom of any generation before you while also recognizing that sexism, racism, and other -isms still hold hostage your sense of self and your futures.

These confusing times call for self-reflection, and for sharing, and there is no better way to do that than through the written word. Girls Write Now is revolutionary in confronting the reality that women's voices are often overlooked, forgotten—or, worse, silenced. While the writing industry can continue to feel like an ivory tower, Girls Write Now creates space for diverse girls to workshop ideas, and by being a part of this organization, you are able to tell your stories.

So what happens when you find the space to express your inner lives? Fabulous transformation. It is through the telling of our stories that change happens, that our existence is written and our lives begin to matter to forces bigger than ourselves.

I'm beyond excited and privileged to introduce this ground-breaking collection of voices in *Generation F: The Girls Write Now 2018 Anthology*.

SAMHITA MUKHOPADHYAY is currently the executive editor at *Teen Vogue*. She is the coeditor of *Nasty Women: Feminism, Resistance and Revolution in Trump's America* and the author of *Outdated: Why Dating Is Ruining Your Love Life*.

Generation F

THE GIRLS WRITE NOW 2018 ANTHOLOGY

RACHEL ABEBE

YEARS AS MENTEE: 1

GRADE: Junior

HIGH SCHOOL: High School of American Studies

BORN: Bronx, NY

LIVES: Bronx, NY

MENTEE'S ANECDOTE: *Working with my mentor has been such a great experience not only because we get a lot of work done, but because our meetings truly inspire me to write more. We have explored new genres and forms, and it makes me feel very lucky to be in a community where creativity is celebrated.*

MARYELLEN TIGHE

YEARS AS MENTOR: 3

OCCUPATION: Assistant Editor, Debtwire Municipals

BORN: Council Bluffs, IA

LIVES: New York, NY

MENTOR'S ANECDOTE: *So much of Rachel's work is inspired by, or written for, people she knows and loves, which is inspiring in its vulnerability. Writing with her reminds me how important my friends and family are and how much they have shaped me. I am glad she feels so connected to her community, and I cannot wait to watch her build on that foundation and continue to excel.*

Tribe

RACHEL ABEBE

This piece is about friendship—specifically, the power of female friendship.

Singing through the halls and dancing in the rain
Navigating through uneven terrain
Having them makes you feel a little more sane

Painting eyes and tying laces
Giggling loud and pulling faces
All the things that friendship encases

When you are with them
You will always feel the sun
Because a girl in the arms of friends
Is a girl who has won

A Collection

MARYELLEN TIGHE

Rachel and I were discussing how much we appreciate our female friends, and we had a goal of writing more poetry this year, so this is how these two ideas came together for me.

From skinned knees to class
from soccer to grad school and
weddings, growing up.

Promise to never
play "Jai Ho!" again. Though, I
miss the dinosaurs.

Have you considered
watching *The Golden Compass*
while in Baltimore?

Hurricane-zone life:
sun, beaches, cruise, everglades,
evacuations.

Science fiction and
writing. The formation of
the first planets, stars.

Starting with bikes to
origami, hikes. Sharing
stories, patterns, time.

JISELLE ABRAHAM

YEARS AS MENTEE: 4

GRADE: Senior

HIGH SCHOOL: Edward R. Murrow High School

BORN: Queens, NY

LIVES: Brooklyn, NY

MENTEE'S ANECDOTE: *For the past four years, Girls Write Now provided me with a community of girls like me to share our feelings. Even if I didn't share at workshops, it was good to hear what goes on in other people's heads when they write. Thanks to Girls Write Now, I have a different perspective, and I have learned that every writing genre is a different outlet that can help express other sides of me. I want to thank the Girls Write Now community and my mentor for helping me move forward with writing. It will always be a part of me everywhere I go.*

HEATHER STRICKLAND

YEARS AS MENTOR: 4

OCCUPATION: Senior Manager Internal Communications, American Express

BORN: Philadelphia, PA

LIVES: Brooklyn, NY

MENTOR'S ANECDOTE: *Over the last four years, I have watched Jiselle grow tremendously, from a quiet, shy girl to a strong, opinionated woman. In turn, Jiselle has challenged me to explore new genres and always asks me how my writing is going, reminding me to put words on the page. We have become especially close this last year, opening up to each other and sharing personal stories to strengthen our bond. The Park Slope Starbucks (our regular meeting spot) will always have a special place in my heart, as will Jiselle. I am so excited to see what the future holds for her!*

White and Blue / Outta Luck

JISELLE ABRAHAM

I wanted my final anthology pieces to illustrate the feelings that people of color might feel. Everybody's experience is different, but we all have a universal understanding of what it can be like.

White and Blue

Simple in blue
Plain in white
Living in my world
Is a brownish delight
I can see your eyes
Judge my fate
Based on my skin
And based on your hate.

Heavy in power
Low in fear
You think my world
Is too much to bear
That's where you're wrong
And that's ok
How can you feel a statue
When it says "Do Not Touch"
In the display?

I cope with my problems
I live on strong
I live my life with passion
And in faith too
Your life may be pearls and diamonds
But mine is ruled by White
And scared of Blue.

Outta Luck

I had so much patience for you
I let you back in
And that's the stupidest
I've ever been
I should've just stopped
I should've just listened
To the blocked-out voices that told me
You were no good
I never thought that you could do this to me
How stupid could I be?
I was too busy
Blocking out the voices
When it should've been you
I asked you
What I was to you, and you said
you didn't know.
Six months for an
i don't know.
I waited six months to hear that none of it existed
That I just pictured
All the kissing
All the missing
You've got to be fucking kidding

You dragged me
All this way
To tell me I didn't matter
And in that moment
My whole body shattered
But you didn't give a fuck
And if I had a buck for every fuck you gave
I'd be outta luck

Faux Feminist

HEATHER STRICKLAND

Generation F means the power to be fierce. The power to be strong enough to publish something that makes me feel vulnerable and points to an example of the faux feminism we deal with daily.

My rapist is a feminist.

He went to the Women's March on Washington one year after we broke up—a year after he raped me. There were pictures of him, smiling, happy pictures. Pictures with captions calling for equal rights.

A sign behind him read "My body, my choice."

I wonder if he remembers how, the night we met, he walked me home, even though it was right around the corner. I thought it was sweet that he wanted to spend that extra forty-seven seconds with me. At the door to my apartment, he asked to use the bathroom.

Even though it took me longer to unlock my door than it would have taken for him to walk back to the bar in the first place, I let him inside.

He asked if he could stay the night. I told him I wouldn't sleep with him.

"That's okay," he'd said. "I just want to lie down next to you. I just want to cuddle."

I wonder if everyone's definition of cuddling includes repeated attempts to remove my pants.

I wonder if I should have paid more attention to that. I

wonder if paying more attention would have kept all of this from happening in the first place.

My rapist is a feminist. He posts links calling out television shows with all-male creative teams, telling them to "do better," calling for a boycott of the Hollywood professionals who aren't treating women with the respect they deserve.

I wonder if he remembers how, the last time we slept together, he argued with me about using a condom. I wonder if he remembers saying that I was overreacting when I told him he had a problem with consent.

I wonder if he is as ashamed of me as I am of myself for sleeping with him one more time, after he raped me.

My rapist is a feminist. He hosts events focused on equality and queer love. He attends future feminist dance parties and reposts articles on intersectional feminism.

I wonder if he remembers the night that it happened. If he remembers me telling him to stop. If he remembers pretending not to hear me. If he remembers pretending to be sorry. If he remembers the email he sent me, confessing and apologizing for all of the pain he caused me. If he remembers what a good showman he was.

My rapist is a feminist.

I wonder if he knows what that word means.

CRYSTAL ADOTE

YEARS AS MENTEE: 1

GRADE: Sophomore

HIGH SCHOOL: School of the Future

BORN: Queens, NY

LIVES: Queens, NY

MENTEE'S ANECDOTE: *Working with Girls Write Now and Arielle has been a great experience. They have taught me new writing techniques, confidence, and optimism. Something I like about the program is the speakers that they bring in for the workshops. It is interesting and exciting to listen to other writers' work and their histories. I also enjoy how we can write about anything we want and let our creativity run wild. I am particularly proud of my Column Writing piece—it taught me to state my opinion while being open to other people's as well.*

ARIELLE BARAN

YEARS AS MENTOR: 2

OCCUPATION: Account Supervisor, Derris

BORN: Los Angeles, CA

LIVES: Brooklyn, NY

MENTOR'S ANECDOTE: *When we started the Girls Write Now year, my mentee and I embarked on Intergenerational Memoir writing. I learned about her family and story as a friend, writer, niece, and daughter. It was an opportunity for us to share and learn about each other. Six months later, we have built on that experience of learning through our writing.*

Dela's Dream

CRYSTAL ADOTE

My aunt is my role model—she inspires and motivates me. She's an independent woman who came to this country with nothing and made her way up with the help of some friends along the way.

In Togo, the public schools had small rooms—the students were crammed into hot, mosquito-infested spaces. The parents were uninvolved. As a result, the teachers fed off the feeling that the parents didn't care that much about their children's education and just needed them to get out of the house. The private schools were different, with better learning environments.

The private school teachers were nuns. As they walked around the school, the extreme heat from the Togo sun left the nuns hot and sweaty under their wool habits, but they never complained. They had dedicated their lives not only to God but also to nurturing the next generation to excel. After a long day of teaching, they went home to their beds in the church and awoke the next morning, doing it all over again. Their lives revolved around the school.

One of the lovely children whom the nuns taught was a girl named Dela. Even though private schools were expensive, Dela's father insisted that all of his children attend a good school where the teachers and administrators cared more about education. Dela was a small girl who laughed a lot; she enjoyed the time she spent with her friends. While she wore khaki skirts and long black stockings to school every day, she dreamt of wearing shorts or pants and letting her legs breathe! Dela always dreamed of being a fashion designer and going to school in America. Whenever Dela's mother visited her family, she would find her sewing machine and fix or make new clothes. Dela always knew in the back of her mind that her father did not agree with her dream, but that didn't stop her.

While she had big dreams, she needed to face reality and middle school first. Dela didn't grasp things that easily or quickly, so her dad found tutors to help her. Her first tutors were her brothers, but they weren't that helpful. They would make fun of how slow she was, saying things like "This is so easy, how do you not get it?" or "Only a dummy would get this wrong." This did not help Dela. Her dad saw that she wasn't growing—she wasn't learning to believe in herself at the hands of her brothers. So he got her a new tutor, a close family friend. There was a massive change in her learning, and she started doing better in school.

Dela's father, proud of how well Dela was excelling, wanted her to be a teacher. He sent her to a boarding high school that focused on language. There she learned how to speak English, and she was very grateful for the opportunity. There were many people living in Togo who didn't have the privilege to go to school and get a good education or any nurturing. Sometimes strict nuns were available only to the few who could afford it. Many children had to stay at home to take care of their siblings and clean the house while their parents were at work. Others would have to go to work to make some money to support their family.

The boarding school gave Dela many opportunities, including being able to attend university. After she graduated from college, she joined a program that connected her with some summer camps in the U.S., and she traveled there for the first time to work in Massachusetts. When she arrived she didn't want to leave—she loved it there. The people were nice and accepting. They didn't judge her or make fun of her accent like her brothers would. She made many friends quickly, many who have helped her to get to where she is now. Every day she is grateful and blessed for the people she has met along the way.

GRANDmother

ARIELLE BARAN

My grandmother passed away a week before Trump's inauguration. While I missed the Women's March to celebrate her life, she is my guidepost for strong womanhood today. She is my Generation F.

One month before she passed away, my grandmother condemned me for not wearing lipstick. I was sitting at the edge of her hospital bed, running my fingers through her beautiful gray hair, when she pointed to her purse on the nightstand. She pulled out her beaded makeup case and placed it in my hand, motioning for me to gloss a layer of red lipstick over my heartbroken smile. There was no one quite like her. Even as she suffered from Parkinson's and dementia, my *tiwa* never stopped being the fierce, lipstick-wearing grandmother who helped raise me.

She was one of a kind. She was known to place hexes on any driver who dared to cut her off. She always kept her nails long and manicured with a bright, orangey-red polish. She never left the house without her elegantly layered pearls or diamond earrings. She always set the table according to etiquette expert Emily Post and taught each of her grandchildren the purpose and preferred placement of each fork. She owned and managed a Western clothing store with cunning and business savvy. She placed hundred-dollar bills in plastic Easter eggs and hid them around the house during the holidays for her grandchildren, and later great-grandchildren, to find and save for college.

I grew up surrounded by strong women; my grandmother sat at the helm of our tribe. From my mom to my teenage cousins, my grandmother taught each of us how to define our own fierce version of being female. Sometimes the fierceness collided with big opinions and large personalities crescendoing at one of our large family dinners, but at least, because of her, the women in our family have big opinions and personalities to share with the world.

SOLEDAD AGUILAR-COLON

YEARS AS MENTEE: 2

GRADE: Junior

HIGH SCHOOL: Beacon High School

BORN: Bronx, NY

LIVES: New York, NY

PUBLICATIONS AND RECOGNITIONS: Scholastic Art & Writing Award: two Silver Keys, Honorable Mention

MENTEE'S ANECDOTE: *These past two years with Linda have been eye-opening! There was this one particular Monday when Linda and I met at our usual spot, the Atrium in Manhattan, and did what we always do, talk. But this time, Linda and I decided to go further in our discussion. Instead of discussing politics or daily life frustrations, we talked about family. From then on, I felt a shift in our relationship and that reflected itself in the topics that we wrote about because we felt more open and comfortable with each other.*

LINDA CORMAN

YEARS AS MENTOR: 8

OCCUPATION: Freelance Editor and Writer

BORN: Newton, MA

LIVES: New York, NY

PUBLICATIONS AND RECOGNITIONS: Community Preservation Corps, Underwriting Efficiency

MENTOR'S ANECDOTE: *Sole had given clues that she wanted to discuss her sexuality on a number of occasions, but I did not know how to respond. One day, she talked candidly about her displeasure with the sex-education course at school because it ignored same-sex couples. This was the beginning of our ability to talk more openly about sexuality. For this, I am infinitely grateful to Sole. It really felt like Sole was the adult in creating this opening.*

Who Is Ozzie?

SOLEDAD AGUILAR-COLON

This piece began as an exploration of masculinity through the lens of a young Afro-Latino boy but became an exploration of my own struggles with my identity through this character, Ozzie.

Who is Oscar Rosario? What does he look like? No—what *should* he look like? Ozzie was already familiar with his own face. The same brown skin, brown eyes, and curly-almost-kinky fro sitting on top of his head like a lion's mane. Wild and free. *Como el espíritu de Puerto Rico*, his mom used to tell him as she pulled and yanked at the tangled knots forming at the back of his head. Every damn morning he saw the same person in the mirror, intently studying the tiny mole on the left side of his cheek, or the slight widow's peak that only could have been inherited from his grandfather, whom he had never met, and heard from only occasionally. Every year on March 16, his *abuelo* would call from Puerto Rico to sing him a *feliz cumple* and remind him of the protests in New York to Free Oscar Lopez from incarceration. *"Siempre pa'lante negrito"*—always go forward—he would say, and Ozzie would picture his *abuelo* sitting on a plastic lawn chair in front of his little red *casita*, drinking rum and wearing a white *guayabera* with the socialist flag swaying behind him.

Sometimes when Ozzie stared at himself for too long, his image started to dissolve into the features of his ancestors: his nose resembling that of his defiant *abuelita* as she would cook *maduros* in hot oil during the day and teach the other *campesinos* (farmers) how to read at night. Or his infamous, untamable fro resembling that of his cigar-smoking black grandfather, who chased chickens during the day and held secret radical meetings with the neighbors about the revolution in Cuba by night. But he never just saw *Ozzie*. It was as if his face carried the reminder of *only* the oppression and poverty of the Puerto Rican people.

As Ozzie finished rubbing leave-in conditioner through his hair, he could see the ghosts of his heritage flickering inside the reflection of the mirror. Clapping and hip-bumping. Dipping and swaying. The colors before him flashed like a memory across his mind: the red, yellow, and blue skirts of the local women dancing to the beat of the conga drum. *"That hijito is Bomba y Plena,"* his mom had whispered as they watched the Puerto Rican Day Parade pass by. He had never seen so many coffee, cream, and brown faces like his own, all crammed into one place, eating and drinking together as if they had never left the island to begin with. He was so captivated by the movement of the parade that he let go of his little sister's fingertips and ran right into the heart of the crowd. His mother's urgent calls for him to come back were quickly drowned out by the throaty sound of what Ozzie would later learn was a *guirro*.

The older man next to him looked down at Ozzie and offered him the toffee-colored instrument. At first Ozzie just stared, perplexed by its oval shape and strange marks indented in the middle. Finally, he took the small instrument into his even smaller eight-year-old hands and ran his fingers along its body. "Put it to your ear and you'll hear the ocean waves from Puerto Rico," said the man, gesturing to the hole at the top, and then held his hand up to his ear like he was holding a cell phone. As Ozzie was just about to put the delicate instrument to his ear, he felt a hand grip his *Star Wars* shirt tightly and yank him away from the man. The instrument fell with a clunk onto the ground and as he was dragged away by his mother yelling words she had banned him from saying, Ozzie wondered if he would ever get the chance to hear the sound of Puerto Rico's ocean.

Now the memories swirling in his mind blinded him to his surroundings as he tried grasping for . . . for what? Every day Ozzie walks past the posters plastered across the 191st Street train station entrance doors, wondering if that's what he should look like . . . like a light-skinned rapper with triangles tattooed on his shiny bald head and fake, gleaming gold chains hanging from his neck. This year the new Latino icon was Bad Bunny, but only a couple of years ago Pitbull had taken over the radio, rapping about naked girls in Spanglish. So when he couldn't find himself in the posters, Ozzie tried rummaging through the old comic editions at St. Mark's Comics bookstore, searching for a brown face and kinky fro dressed in a Spider-Man suit. And yet, even after searching New York's most famous comic book store, Forbidden Planet NYC, Ozzie always left with his money still in his wallet and disappointment hanging over him like a thick cloud ready to pour. Ozzie couldn't tell anymore if what he saw every morning in the bathroom mirror was him or a reflection of years of searching through the city he calls home and always feeling like a lion swarmed by a crowd of eagles.

A Gen F'er Meets Her Great-Great-Grandparents

LINDA CORMAN

The novel I am working on is about the impact of one generation on the next. So, when thinking about the meaning of Generation F, I immediately considered it in relation to preceding generations.

What would my grandparents think of Generation F? (And what, by the way, should their generation be called? Generation Sh, for *shtetl*? Generation S, for survivors? Generation TR, for Teddy Roosevelt?)

I picture my great-niece, the Generation F'er Madeline, at her great-great-grandmother's dining table. My grandma's head is shaking, as it has at least since my generation gathered at this same table for matzo ball soup and matzo sandwiches of haroset and bitter herbs.

Madeline is peeking at her iPhone beneath the white embroidered tablecloth, under which my generation ducked to sneak sips of sweet and sticky Manischewitz.

Madeline knows this shaking may be Parkinson's. Her generation knows these things. It's the beneficiary of the gradual ending of the hush around so much—illness, sex, race, gender.

My generation, Madeline's grandmother's generation, when it sat at the same table, thought the shaking was an expression of disapproval. Grandma, we thought, was onto us and the Manischewitz.

The shaking, as we saw it, was an incessant reproach for our wayward thoughts, for whatever we secretly did that the grown-ups didn't want us to do.

But this, Madeline's generation, isn't prey to that. It's been brought up to be unashamed, proud of whoever they are. They live by their beliefs and values; they don't compartmentalize to make their way under present circumstances.

Madeline's parents, too, would know the shaking was probably Parkinson's. But they retain some of the fear of being disapproved of by earlier generations. Possibly the shaking had something to do with the contrasting colors of their skin.

"*Shvartze,*" the great-great-grandfather had been heard to say—a racist Jews' word for a person of color. All succeeding generations had cringed when the offending word had come out of the family patriarch's mouth, and they were glad the great-great-granddaughter had never heard him say it.

And if she had, what would she have said?

Whatever it was, it would have been forthright. It would have been impossible to mistake for a degenerative disease. It would be thoughtful, devoid of rancor and not intended to shame. It would respect her great-great-grandfather's experience. But it would give him pause.

NAZERKE AKILOVA

YEARS AS MENTEE: 1

GRADE: Senior

HIGH SCHOOL: International High School at Lafayette

BORN: Almaty, Kazakhstan

LIVES: Brooklyn, NY

PUBLICATIONS AND RECOGNITIONS: Scholastic Art & Writing Awards: Silver Key

MENTEE'S ANECDOTE: *At a cozy coffee shop, Leslie and I started discussing my personal statement for college applications. It was a rainy and miserable day. Anxiety triggered me every time I looked at the 1,000-word essay. The more we sat there, sipping our tea, the easier it was for me to confidently share my thoughts. Not only did Leslie pave a path toward an effective personal statement, she listened, empathized, and helped me polish emotionally raw ideas into a beautiful and solid piece of writing. This day was an integral part of realizing how soulful and sincere my mentor is.*

LESLIE PARISEAU

YEARS AS MENTOR: 1

OCCUPATION: Writer/Editor

BORN: Findlay, OH

LIVES: Brooklyn, NY

PUBLICATIONS AND RECOGNITIONS: *The New York Times, Saveur, PUNCH, New York* magazine, *SPRITZ* (2016); 2017 James Beard nominee; 2014 *Forbes* 30 Under 30

MENTOR'S ANECDOTE: *On a cold, rainy fall day, Naze and I got to talking about her college essay. We were looking for a solution to writing the essay in a way that might tick college admissions' boxes while communicating the breadth of her personal journey—and letting her creativity sing. Eventually, I saw Naze recognize how it could come together without sacrificing the passion she'd woven into the piece. Fast-forward several months, and she's got her pick of colleges, no doubt in part because she's a killer writer who can make the world listen to what she has to say.*

A Gift from My Mom

NAZERKE AKILOVA

My mom's strength, passion, and kindness became my main inspiration for writing this piece. Her rush for freedom and feminism became my main definition of Generation F.

It was 11 p.m. in Almaty, Kazakhstan. My mom, fourteen years old, was trying to rub away a smudge on her little sister's beige satin blouse. She was recalling the memory of her fifth-grade performance in front of a whole school when she wore the same lucky shirt.

Suddenly, a rageful voice from down the hall pierced through the flashback. It was her father. She knew the sequence of events like the back of her hand. First, her mother would nervously walk on eggshells. Then he would start diminishing his wife, my grandmother. It would turn into a fight. It would turn into a standard demonstration of Kazakh male dominance. And, in a while, her mother, anxious and afraid, would run to her, saying, "Please, talk to him, he listens to you!"

And so it went. Legs shaking, my mom went to the kitchen. And though she had dealt with this very situation before, every time was like the first. She never knew what to expect. She would have to choose her words carefully so that this highly sensitive human, this avid drunkard, would finally back away from the edge and just go to sleep. Her father thought himself a philosopher, and alcohol a way to open his *chakras*. He drank until he reached deep contemplation. She sat in front of him like this. She was strong and resolute, but her childhood happiness had been annihilated by responsibility. She should have been charged only with juvenile cares, anxiousness for tomorrow's test. Instead, she had to rescue her mother from her father's rage and battering. The oldest of five, she had to look after four sisters and get them ready for school.

For her entire life, my mother survived while carrying a huge burden. My grandmother, too, carried a burden. Her husband constantly took "breaks" from his duties, disappearing into intoxication to find "enlightenment." Her simple state of mind was a symbol of stupidity in his eyes. He saw her as the root of all evil. She was closed-minded in his eyes, and his dissatisfaction manifested as dark purple bruises across her face. My mother never understood what my grandmother was guilty of.

My grandmother was a strong woman, but the tradition of patriarchy in Kazakhstan insisted that she had an inability to disagree with men. Like millions of Kazakh women before her, she was punished for his inadequacy and forced to support her family alone. She passed this quiet strength on to my mother, who became even more determined—set on changing the path for her daughters to come.

Where my grandmother frequently gave up, exhausted from her husband's onslaughts, my mother worked to build a wall to keep this terror at bay. She protected us from experiencing the same violence. Every horrible situation we heard about our relatives—many of which could have been prosecuted by law—was just a scary story. We have never had to see violence, oppression, or neglect. My dad had nothing but love toward my mom and his three daughters. My mom was strict and disciplined because she knew it was best for us. All three of us were raised with love and were encouraged to embrace our individuality. Even when my mother made the brave step to immigrate to the USA when I was only five years old, I tried to remember her as a real, strong woman. My mother violated the age-old Kazakh tradition of patriarchy where women are seen only as a mothers and servants. In fact, my core values are based on her reform and have become the basis for forming my own self-respect as a woman.

Ghost Geography

LESLIE PARISEAU

When Naze wrote her piece, I thought about what I have done to change so that my kids' lives (re: Generation F) might be better. At its most essential, it started with leaving where I'm from.

I'm from a small town in rust-belt Ohio. I won't bother telling you its name because you have never heard of it. I have never met a person in the larger world who has.

But if you are interested in visiting, it can be found by following a county road lined with cornfields and big white grain silos slowly oxidizing from the inside out. Once, a devout woman said she saw Jesus in one of the tankard's rust stains, and for days cars lined up along the shoulder to catch a glimpse, their passengers peering and nodding at the blood-colored blotches like they knew something blessed had occurred there. Follow the signs advertising once-prosperous, long-shuttered glass factories and sparkplug plants. You'll know you've arrived when you smell the soybeans cooking hot and earthy like boiling beer.

This town sits amid a triangle of train tracks over which slow-moving, graffiti-tagged boxcars whistle at all hours, a lullaby and an alarm clock. Since the railroad ties were laid, kids who live along them have put pennies on the smoldering silver rails, waiting for the CSX line to flatten them into smooth copper ovals. Ghost stories about headless conductors and ladies in white dresses lingering over country crossings have always been recited, eerie warnings to always look both ways.

For decades, nothing has changed. People have left and died, industry has left and died. And yet nothing has changed.

There is a part of my mind imprinted with the geography of this town—its decaying neighborhoods and abandoned grain elevators. It's the part that reminds me of where I'm from, and yet exists apart from it, so that I might not stay the same—so that I might shift and change and change and change.

SADE ANDRE

YEARS AS MENTEE: 1

GRADE: Junior

HIGH SCHOOL: Millennium Brooklyn High School

BORN: Brooklyn, NY

LIVES: Brooklyn, NY

MENTEE'S ANECDOTE: *I remember the first time I read my poem to Keciah. I was filled with pressure because I usually don't share my writings with anyone. I've also never written much poetry before meeting her. But while she was reading it her face slowly became filled with joy, and she loved my writing. Since I hold her opinion very dear, knowing that she likes my writing makes me more comfortable with sharing and makes me more willing to write more even if it's out of my comfort zone.*

KECIAH BAILEY

YEARS AS MENTOR: 1

OCCUPATION: Communications Associate, Hebrew Public

BORN: Kingston, Jamaica

LIVES: Brooklyn, NY

PUBLICATIONS AND RECOGNITIONS: *Canarsie Courier*

MENTOR'S ANECDOTE: *I think of Sade as "the lion and the lamb." At first glance, she is this shy and unassuming teenage girl. Then she writes, and someone fierce, bold, and powerful emerges. She is so strikingly self-aware with a perspective on life that is far beyond her years. While I can never craft a perfectly written poem in twenty minutes (which she does effortlessly), she is exactly who I was in high school. It is truly rewarding to take this journey with her yet offer her a wiser, more evolved version of myself as a mentor and as a writer.*

(F)ear

SADE ANDRE

"(F)ear" is about my outlook on how life should be perceived. I know many teenage girls who sometimes take life too seriously. At this age, we should think of life as more of a big picture that is still unfolding, rather than as a micro-moment.

Taught from young that the pit in her stomach, the sweat on her hands, and the pain in her chest will always be there no matter what. The feeling of being lost in a place full of people who already have their opinions and intentions for her. They'll all hurt and destroy her, adding more things to her demise. Although she's remained strong through mental, physical, and sexual abuse—she knows that it's coming.

The strength is dwindling
The light at the end of the tunnel is
No longer twinkling.
For it is pitch black, cold, and she's numb.
She is sweating and shuddering
Because everything is out of her control.
Yet, inevitably, she endures a breakthrough
And the blue devils become invisible
Like gravity, her infelicity into the galaxy . . .

Taught from experiences, she knows that even though these experiences may be dark, she must go through them. Not because she's terrible or deserves the worst—but because these hardships, sufferings, are nothing but lessons and experiences. The scars and burns are stories to tell someone who needs it.

From this she learned a lesson—maybe even a philosophy—that without fear there would be no function, no motivation to get out of where she is. But we must pull positivity from our experiences because we don't know our expiration date.

So why live in the darkness and not chase the light? Why take everything while we're young as such burdens and not lessons? There's no need to view teenage years as if they are negative times, because this time we have is for lessons. Shaping. To formulate the best versions of ourselves. Generation (F)ear is the generation of hope and strength.

Freedom

KECIAH BAILEY

Quite often, it's the story we tell ourselves about our past and our experiences that keeps us bound. Through my own inward journey, I've found that the path to true freedom is to revisit the past, reconcile the good with the bad, then redefine our identities so we can fully embrace the promise of the future. Generation F is Freedom.

I went back into my past and planted a garden there—
The memories were dead and dried.
And all along the fields
Where dreams laid buried,
I gathered up their bones
And prayed them back to life.

In an old shed I found a bucket of tears,
Locked up in frustration and failure.
With it, I watered my garden
Parched with regret and shame,
And sowed seeds of faith,
Where there grew weeds of fear.

Now when I revisit the memories are sweet
Fragrant with life, laughter,
Hope and promise.
The dreams are alive,
Singing and dancing with praise,
And the grains of faith are ripe for the harvest.

I went back into my past and planted a garden there . . .
Now as the future blooms eternal—
She rejoices.

ASSATA ANDREWS

YEARS AS MENTEE: 2

GRADE: Senior

HIGH SCHOOL: Hillside Arts and Letters Academy

BORN: Queens, NY

LIVES: Queens, NY

MENTEE'S ANECDOTE: *At first, I was afraid to start all over with a new mentor because it is tough for me to meet new people. However, Kate was able to take all of my worries away and I am able to talk to her about topics that I wouldn't with my friends, making me enjoy meeting her every week. She gives me criticism that gives me the ability to think about what I want my work to become. Also, Kate makes sure that I understand my goals. I appreciate her hard work and the good atmosphere that she brings every week.*

KATE BRYANT

YEARS AS MENTOR: 1

OCCUPATION: MFA Candidate at Queens College

BORN: Marietta, OH

LIVES: Queens, NY

MENTOR'S ANECDOTE: *Assata's creativity is really inspiring and I've been impressed and amazed with how she plans out her stories. I have learned a lot from talking to her about time management and relating about our shared perfectionist tendencies. We've both been juggling lots of deadlines this year, so we are really ready to plan something fun. I think often about how much braver she is than I was when I was her age and how clear she is about her writing goals, and I'm really excited for her to continue expanding her writing horizons in college and beyond.*

Dear Black Women,

ASSATA ANDREWS

*I came up with this piece once I began to think about the problems
African American women face when it comes to being dehumanized
and looked down upon by the world and our own community.*

To those with large, dark lips, nappy kinks, and midnight
    skin—
sorry to say that we amount to nothing
We are nothing but the loudmouthed, dumb, jealous, ugly,
    and bitter roaches that everyone is ready to step on
Even our own are prepared to do it
We are the female dog, the garden tool, and that is all we'll
    ever add up to be
Our beauty is nonexistent
We hold no power or resilience
When someone says we deserve better, prepare yourself for the
    rants:
"No! All women deserve better!"
Feeling pretty?
Well let's prepare ourselves to be bashed against the head and
    spat on by our own men
Skin color will separate us because light is *always* better
Bodies drooled over, but when finished being used
are thrown out like trash or dragged through the mud no
    matter what we do
Portrayed as hoodrats, poor, and ghetto is an inevitability

Attitudes holding us back because we are the worst kind of
woman

Imagine believing that?
Imagine that we aren't the glue that is holding this world
together
Imagine that we haven't influenced others,
despite never having been given any credit that we deserve
Imagine thinking that our sun-kissed skin is an abomination
to society unless it is as light as a brown paper bag like
Beyoncé's
Imagine that we aren't one of the most educated
demographics
Imagine that we can't come together and grow

We are powerful, resilient, and beautiful
And we do deserve so much more.

Even though I know how very far

KATE BRYANT

When I wrote this I was thinking about some of the things Assata and I have been talking about this year: our hopes and fears about the future, and how to share the reality of our experiences through words.

The eclipse made me think of
two cartoon mice singing to one another
Fievel and his sister, whose name you might not remember
but it's Tanya Mousekewitz
And later a steel drum band covering the song
someone sending it to me before the reality problem chasmed
    between us
And later, quite recently, two celestial bodies converging along
    their paths
the way they do from time to time
Their pace is leisurely and relentless, a way I'd like to be
A momentary awareness of the shared sky and then we're back
wrestling strong theories and donating to GoFundMe
Money sent to strangers for any and every thing
A meditation made material, without the pause or the peace
All year I have been tired and awake
or asleep with my mind racing
There's a story that keeps reoccurring
where we're not seeing the same thing
even if we're in the same place, looking in the same direction
I'm trying to say what it looks like over here

and I want to know what it looks like where you are
The future depends on us speaking precisely
so that's what we are learning to do

JANEIN BROOKES

YEARS AS MENTEE: 2

GRADE: Sophomore

HIGH SCHOOL: Success Academy High School of the Liberal Arts

BORN: New York, NY

LIVES: Bronx, NY

PUBLICATIONS AND RECOGNITIONS: Scholastic Art & Writing Awards: two Silver Keys

MENTEE'S ANECDOTE: *As a free-verse poet, committing to a sonnet, a structured writing style, was not easy. I remember being frustrated with counting the vowels of each word, and that annoyed feeling in the pit of my stomach whenever Cynthia asked me to choose a different word. Still, when I wrote the last word, even though there was no drastic world change, I felt like the entire world had tilted on its axis. Despite my clammy hands and throbbing migraine, I felt a rush of pride and overwhelming self-worth, like a great breeze had blown the clouds out of my sun's way.*

CYNTHIA-MARIE O'BRIEN

YEARS AS MENTOR: 2

OCCUPATION: Copy Editor, Queens Library

BORN: New Haven, CT

LIVES: Queens, NY

PUBLICATIONS AND RECOGNITIONS: *America, The Literary Review, U.S. Catholic*

MENTOR'S ANECDOTE: *After the Structured Poetry workshop, Janein was initially reluctant to use forms. She even told me that she hates structure. I challenged her to use form—a sonnet—to focus her ideas—and she did! The resulting poem won a Scholastic Art & Writing award. I was so proud of how she stretched herself as a writer and moved the judges.*

Soar

JANEIN BROOKES

"Soar" is a sonnet, and my first structured piece. As a poet, I prefer to write free verse. "Soar" is personal because, while I don't know the boy, I watched him grow up.

Go on and fly little chocolate boy, fly! Won't you fly?
Will your wheels roll fast enough for you to get along
In a world that doesn't protect little chocolate boys?
Tell the world that your moving body is not a toy. Fly!

Your stare is patient enough to hide insanity
within dark eyes that have borne witness to travesty.
But how long can you avoid the restriction of your blue
jacket? Just remember that people can catch up to you.

I'm up here, little chocolate boy, watching the moving
form of you, wondering if you expect someone to swoon
at your little tricks. Because you have skin they want to peel
and with your valiant resistance, they'll make the perfect

example of you, soon enough. Little boy, you'll have to fly
when the airplane of tomorrow's resistance soars above.

Lunchtime by the Bay

CYNTHIA-MARIE O'BRIEN

I wrote this lighthearted piece for our Structured Poetry workshop. The sounds are meant to convey and conjure up vivid memories of enjoyable afternoons. Generation F is connected to earlier generations, celebrating their example.

Mary's at the seat of her truck
Thinking that with some good luck
For her lunch today
She'll eat at the bay.

The sun shines hot through the windshield
And she thinks that she will yield
To her appetite for a sandwich
Before she gets up to boogie bandwidth.

She drives to Kettle Cove
Where often she's known to roam
Whoopie pie in her hand
She thinks of one demand:

We love our Amato's
So full of tomatoes.

NATHALIE CABRERA

YEARS AS MENTEE: 1

GRADE: Junior

HIGH SCHOOL: A. Philip Randolph Campus High School

BORN: New York, NY

LIVES: New York, NY

MENTEE'S ANECDOTE: *Being with Deb means having meaningful, much-needed conversations. We talk about everything about life in our weekly meetings. Every time I meet her we just feed off each other's knowledge and we transform this into ideas that become part of our writing as well. Our space has turned into one that is safe and has no filters because no one else gets to judge. It is just us. I love having the opportunity to talk and write and create and have the chance to do things that we love the most.*

DEBORAH HEILIGMAN

YEARS AS MENTOR: 3

OCCUPATION: Author of Books for Children and Teens

BORN: Allentown, PA

LIVES: New York, NY

PUBLICATIONS AND RECOGNITIONS: *Vincent and Theo: The Van Gogh Brothers* (Henry Holt); YALSA Excellence in Nonfiction winner, Michael L. Printz Award Honor Book, *Boston Globe*–Horn Book Award winner for nonfiction, SCBWI Golden Kite Award winner for nonfiction

MENTOR'S ANECDOTE: *The first time I met Nathalie, she hugged me, and I knew we were going to be a great pair. And we are. From our very first weekly session, we have been able to talk deeply and truthfully about a range of subjects, from the personal to the political. We talk so much sometimes we realize we haven't written—yet. And so we write, and when we do, it is magic, the words flowing out of us, into the space of safety and comfort we have created together. I am so grateful to have this opportunity to work with Nathalie.*

Mirror

NATHALIE CABRERA

*I wanted to write about self-love, about a woman realizing her full
potential.*

The sky had rose-pink and gold hues woven through it as the
wee hours of the morning began to fade away. I walked home,
my hands bunched up in my pockets, the cold air numbing my
face as I breathed it in. I headed toward a worn-down, tan-
colored building, its paint chipping off like LEGO pieces, and
an entrance door that often failed to close.

I climbed the stairs to the third floor, and as I unlocked
apartment 3C I smelled stale coffee and lavender disinfectant. I
sighed wearily at my apartment's living room: two chocolate-
brown couches, a coffee table, and a television. This home lacked
any life, it seemed as if no one cared to live in the boring four-
white-walled room. I strode to my bedroom, which had sunlight streaming through a crack in the window, illuminating the
room with warm kisses.

Peeling the clothes off my body, I reached for my towel. In
the bathroom, I stepped into the shower and turned on the faucet. I let the warm water run over my chest, my breasts, and my
navel. I turned my back to let the water pound against it.

As the water streamed along the hills and mountains of my
body, I sighed deeply in a state of sheer peace. This peace is not
something I have grown accustomed to. I have been tormented
for many years with my own belittling thoughts. I thought I

didn't deserve to be strong and happy. I told myself I was weak, incapable of being loved or accepted.

This vicious scrutiny terrified me. As the water ran over my body, I realized I was tired—too tired of the violent destruction within me. A destruction that I knew would lead me to lose myself and all I could be.

But this time I allowed myself to be free of those thoughts. I let my mind, for once, be empty.

I reached for a honey bar soap and lathered it on my skin and I rinsed.

When I was finished, and felt clean and ready, I stepped out of the shower and wrapped myself in the warm, soft towel.

And—

There was a girl staring at herself in a long, narrow rectangular mirror, reflecting her entire body.

I didn't know who she was or why she was in my room, but I suddenly didn't have the ability to speak or move. I stood there motionless, in a dreamlike state, almost as if I were part of an audience waiting for a show to unravel. I closed my eyes and then pried them open again, but she was still there. *This is real*, I told myself, *there is a girl, a stranger in my room.*

She was completely naked. She stood there admiring her caramel skin, the stretch marks along her wide hips and arms. She admired her small breasts, her lips, and her broad tipped nose.

She was admiring it all. All of herself.

She began to play music on her phone and I recognized the song but couldn't quite remember the lyrics, just how it made me feel.

She wasn't a good dancer, but that didn't matter to her, as she moved and sang along with the song's fast tempo and rhythm.

As the song began to fade away, she came to a stop and

returned to the mirror. She looked at herself, but this time she spoke to her reflection.

"I will learn to accept myself."

"To forgive myself."

"To learn how to be my own muse."

"To learn that my beauty comes from within despite what anybody else may think."

"To learn that everything will be okay when I reach rock bottom because I will rebuild as much as I have to."

"I will learn how to finally love myself and become superior to the girl I was yesterday."

The girl looked in my direction with a softness in her eyes as she slowly walked toward me. She extended her arm and interlaced her hands with mine. We stood there for a good few minutes looking at each other when she said:

"Don't you recognize me?" A smile spread across her face as she saw my empty eyes.

She then gently cupped my face in her hands and planted a kiss on my forehead. I remained motionless, unable to move or to speak.

My eyes traveled to her face once more and only then it dawned on me that something seemed familiar in the way she carried herself, the energy she exuded.

And only then did it hit me that this girl was me. A better version of me.

Then she was gone. I was alone. And I could move again. I let the towel drop to the floor.

I turned on my music and I told myself:

I am worthy.

I am strong.

I am beautiful.

This is the mantra that I will carry through the rest of my life. It is a reminder that all I need is within myself.

I am worthy.
I am strong.
I am beautiful.

Ashes of Hope: A Prayer

DEBORAH HEILIGMAN

When I sat down to write something for this anthology, all I could think about was apologizing to these girls for the world we're giving them. My apology turned into a prayer.

Dear Nathalie,
(and Kiana and Cleo and all the young women I know and
  don't know in Generation F),
I wanted to write you a poem.
This is not a poem.
This is an apology.
I wanted to write you a poem of hope and praise and
  encouragement.
Not this.
This is not what I meant to write.
This is not what I meant to say.
But it is what I have to say, right now, in 2018.
I am sorry.
"Sorry" was not the word I had planned to use
when I wrote to you.
When I wrote to you I was going to use the word
PROMISE.
I was going to say:
The future holds promise.
Go for it.

Go for it with all of your might and heart and goodness of
purpose.
But might and heart and goodness of purpose—these are only
a fraction of the qualities you need now.
What you need now is might—and more.
What you need now is tenacity and anger and fury and rage.
Rage for the good, rage against the bad.
Those of us who came before you, with hope and idealism, we
are angry and sad and mostly we are tired.
We have lost the
fierce spirit we used to have.
Or maybe, I hope, just misplaced it.
I have, I know I have.
I don't have the right to speak for my whole generation.
I will speak for myself:
My heart is filled with grief.
I am exhausted most of the time.
When I am not exhausted, I am frustrated, my impotence
exploding into volcanic flames of fury,
bursting from me, too-hot-to-touch
erupting continuously . . .
I know, I hope, that the eruptions of fury will cool,
turning to ashes and
please, Generation F, let us hope that
from the ashes the phoenix will rise.
May there be a rebirth of hope for me, for all of us.
So this, after all, is not a poem, or an apology, but a prayer:
May there be a rebirth of hope.
Hope for a better world.
Hope for the world you will make.
May there be a rebirth of promise.
A promise that the world can be better, can be yours to
shape.

Make the world yours.
Shape it for good.
This is a prayer.
A plea.
To you.

SAONY CASTILLO

YEARS AS MENTEE: 1

GRADE: Sophomore

HIGH SCHOOL: High School of Art and Design

LIVES: New York, NY

MENTEE'S ANECDOTE: *Sarah introduced me to new genres such as playwriting and screenwriting. She made me outlines of screenwriting stage directions on Starbucks napkins, which were both helpful and confusing. She always made me laugh. We are pretty weird and talked about the plot of the horror movie* The Human Centipede *for like forty-five minutes today.*

SARAH CONGRESS

YEARS AS MENTOR: 1

OCCUPATION: Executive Assistant to the Deans and Faculty Services Coordinator, Columbia University School of the Arts

BORN: Alexandria, Virginia

LIVES: New York, NY

PUBLICATIONS AND RECOGNITIONS: *No Knowing Where We're Rowing*, produced by the UP Theatre

MENTOR'S ANECDOTE: *Saony and I quickly learned that we both have a deep love for* Pretty Little Liars *on ABC Family, and one day we did a TV writing prompt for an episode of our favorite show! Which was very funny and our scripts should totally be produced ASAP.*

Because He Liked It

SAONY CASTILLO

My mentor and I share a love of dark humor. We also have been try-ing to explore power and gender roles . . . while still having fun. I think this piece does both and I definitely had a lot of fun writing it.

A wife's serial killer was happy as can be, now that he was free.

He did not have to hear any whining or have any fighting. He could go to a bar and look at another woman's boobs and not get slapped across his beautiful face. 'Cause, boy, was he handsome. At least, he'd like to think so. He could also watch baseball without having the channel changed because it was "too boring."

Over time, this happy state started to fade. He missed the whining and the fighting. Because, apparently, it is really hard to talk to people buried in your backyard! Turns out, they're no fun. He wanted someone to change the channel because base-ball is, actually, really boring. He no longer wanted to stare at another woman's boobs because none were as good as his late wife's . . . so this sad and depressed "widow" husband decided to go out and get himself a new wife.

And he did. She was a maid who he once paid to clean his house. She had beautiful brown hair, green eyes, and the red-dest lips he'd ever seen. Her beauty was incomparable to any-thing or to anyone. He made sure that she wasn't close to anyone so they wouldn't interfere. He hated when people "in-terfered." He was so in love he thought, *You know what? I might keep this one. This gorgeous woman.*

But he soon realized that it wasn't because of beauty or bad habits or personality. It had nothing to do with her at all. It was simply because he liked it.

Love Bite

SARAH CONGRESS

Saony and I love horror movies. So one day, during a weekly meet-up, we decided to write a Generation F–inspired horror fiction prompt— a piece of writing that would explore feminine power and sexuality. These were our results.

Tanya awakes with a start. Her blond hair cascades over her sore and sweaty body as she looks at her phone, which reads 3:03 a.m. A strange man's arm hugs her waist close to his chest. "Who the hell is that?" She gazes at his pale, white skin, perplexed.

This wasn't like her. Tanya did not have one-night stands. Tanya did not get drunk. She was pragmatic. She was disciplined. She was a law student, after all.

She gets up and stumbles to the bathroom, "Oh Christ," she quietly roars, she'd stubbed her right toe on a heavy textbook. "I must still be drunk," she whispers.

In the bathroom her red eyes looked back at her. Hauntingly. *Odd*, she thinks. *Is that a bite mark on my neck?* She peers back into her bedroom, where the strange man rolls over to one side and drags a cigarette from a pack of Marlboro Reds on the nightstand.

With a switch to the left, the shower faucet turns on and out comes steamy, hot water. She jumps in and puts her face under the faucet, letting the water wash off her mascara and her eyeliner and "What on earth?" She looks to her ankle and sees a fresh tattoo of a vampire bat staring back at her. "Impossible . . . it can't be . . ."

Suddenly the shower door slides open and the strange man stares back at her, cigarette dangling from his fangs . . . his fangs . . .

"It can't be," she says.

"Move over, babe, let me get a chance with the hot water."

She catches sight of her reflection in the shower door—a pair of matching fangs stare back at her.

"It just can't be."

He winks at her.

"You look pretty without makeup, Tanya. I like you this way."

"It can't be."

"Let's go hunt after this, what do you say?" He kisses her on the cheek.

She looks at him, at his fangs, at the tattoo on her ankle. "I am never drinking margaritas again," she declares, decisively, and turns off the shower.

REBECCA CEDENO

YEARS AS MENTEE: 1

GRADE: Junior

HIGH SCHOOL: H.E.R.O. High School

BORN: Bronx, NY

LIVES: Bronx, NY

MENTEE'S ANECDOTE: *I didn't know what to expect from a program like this. It is a little more than what I have expected. When I first met Lucy, it was during this icebreaker game, but I did not know that she was my mentor yet, and I was so surprised because it was a cool coincidence. I have bonded a lot with her and she helped me grow more in my writing. I really appreciate her as a friend and a mentor and I am going to miss her and being in Girls Write Now.*

LUCY FRANK

YEARS AS MENTOR: 2

OCCUPATION: Writer

BORN: New York, NY

LIVES: New York, NY

PUBLICATIONS AND RECOGNITIONS: *Two Girls Staring at the Ceiling* (Schwartz & Wade, 2014), 2011 PEN/Phyllis Naylor Working Writer Fellowship recipient

MENTOR'S ANECDOTE: *The very first time we met, Rebecca showed me her notebook, filled with stories. Even so, I came to our first session with a bunch of writing prompts. It was instantly clear Rebecca does not need writing prompts. She is always writing, always has another idea. I have pushed her to take each piece further, deeper, and each week her voice gets stronger, more confident, more daring. And more funny, which makes working with her even more fun. She is inspiring me to be more daring in my writing, too. Thank you, Rebecca. I cannot wait to see what you come up with next!*

I Wanted to Be Cool

REBECCA CEDENO

I always thought that writing was about writing something that makes you feel vulnerable. So I wrote about how I was tormented in middle school about my appearance. I think that anyone can relate to this, female or male. I hope this helps. Be yourself, fuck everyone else.

Okay, so here is the thing. In middle school, I bought Jordans. The shoes, those retro 13s, or whatever number they were, but I don't really care because I honestly hate Jordans. They are just really ugly to me. (For all the sneakerheads reading this, please don't slit my throat. I just think it is a really overrated kind of shoe.) Every time I think about how I actually went and got those shoes, it just makes me cringe so hard. They are literally the same style with different colors and the cycle goes on. They are not really new shoes, just a new color. They were pretty pricey. I think for my size they cost $120. Worst of all, I bought them only to be accepted by people I don't even like.

I got these Jordans because I wanted to be cool. I wanted the bullying to stop, too. A lot of kids in my class would always spit insults at what I wore, especially my shoes. Like, fuck you, I can wear whatever I want. (Of course, I only said that in my head because why cause even more conflict, ya know?) I wanted to be unbothered. Also, I wanted friends, but that did not turn out well for me because they still made fun of me. A waste of money, right?

I was made fun of for having hair on my arms. It was very noticeable, so a lot of kids in my class called me "wolverine" or "werewolf." So I shaved my arms because I wanted to be cool. I shaved them anytime I saw the hairs growing back at a certain length. I could not risk being made fun of. But all in all, it did not work. But clean arms, right?

Everyone's favorite thing to make fun of about me was my forehead. So everyone and their mom decided to call me "Megamind." They basically compared me to the blue guy with the really huge forehead. I cannot lie: It is pretty big. I swear it reached the sky. I could not do much about it, but I did wear my hair down more instead of putting it in a ponytail or anything else that shows my forehead even more. And . . . you guessed it! That didn't work, either.

I could not name a worse period in my life than middle school. When I finished middle school, I hoped for things to be different, especially the bullying part. When I got to high school, things did change eventually. Although I still considered high school to be a failed experiment in preparing adolescents for the adult world, I have met a few good peeps here and they are all right. I have also started to love myself more, I guess. Hey, at least I'm trying.

SPEAK

LUCY FRANK

I've titled this piece "Speak" in honor of Laurie Halse Anderson's novel about a young woman who went silent after she was raped.

I thought I was numbed out. Thought, after months of one famous and powerful scumbag after another getting taken down (or not), that I had reached outrage overload. But a few days ago, a story appeared in *School Library Journal*, and then in *The New York Times*, about sexual harassment in the children's literature world. Some prominent, powerful, esteemed, and beloved male writers have been accused of preying on aspiring young women writers at children's-lit conferences.

What? Writers, too? Aren't we the good guys, the sensitive ones, the progressive ones, the empathic ones? I write novels for middle-grade kids and teens. I have been a proud part of the children's literature world since the '90s. I spent the morning yesterday compulsively reading the hundreds of comments in response to the *SLJ* revelations, getting more and more bummed, thinking, *Yeah, right, classic power imbalance.* Same old story. Bummed, but still somewhat numb. Then I came across a quote from prizewinning author Laurie Halse Anderson about her "volcanic anger about rape culture and toxic masculinity." It was not the "toxic masculinity" that made my blood roar and my eyes blur. It was the words "volcanic anger."

When the Harvey Weinstein story broke last fall, I spent some time working on a poem I called "Coming Forward." About how I did not. How it never dawned on me I could. In the almost fifty years since I was raped, I have come to know it was not my fault. Even so, I could not bear to put myself back there, in the fear and helplessness. The paralyzing shame. Could not bear to use a word that I did not realize still carries so much power over me. Even now, writing it, my blood pounds and I can hardly see.

I have been practicing these past few months, though. Telling other women, saying the word "rape" out loud to try to strip it of its shame. And it is astonishing, the number of women whose eyes have filled with tears, who have said, "Yes, it happened to me, too."

My anger is volcanic. For all of us. Though, what a huge relief, thanks to the #MeToo movement and the countless women who have dared to come forward, dared to feel pure rage instead of that confusing mix of rage, humiliation, fear, and shame.

I have been looking for a way to tie this piece to this year's theme, *Generation F*. But what is in my heart is last year's: We are not helpless. Rise. Speak. Make them change.

JORDAN CHE

YEARS AS MENTEE: 1

GRADE: Sophomore

HIGH SCHOOL: Hunter College High School

BORN: Queens, NY

LIVES: Queens, NY

PUBLICATIONS AND RECOGNITIONS: Scholastic Art & Writing Awards: Silver Key and Honorable Mention

MENTEE'S ANECDOTE: *Being paired with Maria was more than a stroke of luck. From the first day we met, I already found it easy to talk to her. Our pair sessions went swimmingly as we bonded over bubble tea, horror movies, and the creepy guy who cannot sit still at the Queens Crossing mall every Friday. Seven-minute intervals and Reddit writing prompts made our sessions productive as well as fun, and we would always leave with a new (yet unfinished) story in our notebooks. But on top of everything, her enthusiasm and endless support are the best parts of our weekly meetings.*

MARIA WHELAN

YEARS AS MENTOR: 1

OCCUPATION: Assistant Literary Agent, InkWell Management

BORN: Dublin, Ireland

LIVES: Brooklyn, NY

MENTOR'S ANECDOTE: *The first time I went to Flushing, Queens, was to meet my wonderful mentee, Jordan. It was there where I had my first taste of bubble tea. The location and drink immediately became staples of our weekly sessions, along with Jordan's incredible creativity and compelling sense of humor. In the loud, brightly lit food court in Queens, Jordan never ceased to impress me with her vivid imagination, radiance, and sharp wit. While no meet-up was the same, these are the threads that make up the tightly knit tapestry of our friendship!*

Mirror Image

JORDAN CHE

When you can't even turn to the person in the mirror for answers, you end up looking within yourself, instead, in order to figure out what you believe is right despite everyone else saying otherwise.

Calla Reyes sits in front of the full-length mirror on the shaggy carpet, curling her toes as the person wearing her skin curls them back. She breathes in the sweet silence of an empty house on Valentine's Day. With her parents out making new memories over a candlelit dinner and Melody in a mysterious stranger's arms after swiping right for an Eros-filled fling, Calla has the pleasure of having the whole house to herself—at least for now. Running a hand through her knotted hair, she inches closer to the mirror until she and her impostor are noses apart. *The person in the mirror isn't me*, she thinks to herself for the fifth time today. We share the same drifting eyes, chapped lips, and nervous smiles, but she isn't me. It's 5:50 p.m. She glances at the clock, tearing her eyes away from the impostor. Zenia said she would be here at six. Following an intent glare outside her door, Calla dashes to the bathroom as if her feet are on fire, despite the emptiness of the hallway.

Squeezing out a dollop of cleanser and scrubbing at her face until her impostor shares the same frothy white mask, she tries not to think about how she was in the exact same location just a week ago, except for the fact that she wasn't the only one in the bathroom. She tries to dismiss the memory of her parents barging into the room, interrogating her about the mysterious crewneck sweater hidden poorly under her bed with a bold "Z" on the back. The bathroom walls suffocated her as they argued and screamed until Calla's lungs shriveled up. Between the vigorous shakes of her head, she stole a glance in the mirror and came face-to-face with a total stranger whose pupils were dilated, afraid, and filled past the brim with tears that rolled down her dry face.

Calla closes her eyes and lets the water run down her face and disappear in a spiral into the sink, along with memories of her impostor that she had sworn to put aside, at least for today. She is not going to let the person in the mirror ruin what would soon to be the best Valentine's of her life. She waits before swiping the cream-colored concealer wand, and ultimately decides to turn away from the mirror.

It is six o'clock. Calla slips on the crewneck sweater, hidden securely in the nooks and crannies of her underwear drawer. She had definitely learned her lesson. Running her fingers through her freshly brushed hair, she turns to the window's reflection as a makeshift mirror instead. She had always been fond of how the dual view of her bedroom and the outside world came together at a certain angle in the window, distorting her own face and masking it with shades of the night sky. As she presses her nose against the cool glass, a quick tap on the windowsill shocks her out of her stupor. Looking into the window again, the face she sees isn't her own, but it isn't her impostor's, either. She allows a grin to surface as she opens the window enough for a gloved hand to lift it open, and makes room for Zenia on her bed.

"Hey, you." Zenia's light voice, still partially muffled behind the glass, reaches Calla's ears, already making her feel lightheaded. "Hey, yourself." They sit on the bed and wordlessly embrace, sharing each other's warmth without a single sound. Zenia murmurs, focused on Calla's brushed hair and face masked with concealer, "You dressed up today." "Yeah, I guess I did,"

Calla stammers, caught off guard. Zenia smiles softly, moving closer. "You know you didn't have to." "I know." Calla's feelings of being scrutinized are short-lived as she moves closer as well, closing the gap between the two. "They'll be home soon," she mutters, whispering into Zenia's neck. "There's no way your parents can finish a large fettuccini alfredo that quickly. Knowing them, we have at least thirty minutes to ourselves. So might as well make the most out of it." Zenia beams, radiating confidence and affection. "Already one step ahead of you." Calla mischievously grins, and before Zenia can even question it, she is ambushed in a bear hug tight enough to break her ribs—not that Zenia is complaining, of course. And as the two lay together, limbs and hearts intertwined, the full-length mirror resting against the opposite wall is finally forgotten.

Refraction

MARIA WHELAN

No two generations are the same, but each is informed by the ones that have come before. In order to secure a brighter future, we must strive to create a society of inclusion and tolerance by sharing experiences with those around us.

Man feeding a tiger, man drinking a Slurpee, man on a motorcycle, man holding a gun—swipe left.

Man cradling a guitar—swipe right.

Man holding freshly baked bread—swipe right and it's a match!

Calla slinks into my room and I notice she has that mischievous glint in her eye.

"What are you up to?" I ask her reflection in the mirror, as I am too caught up in trying to shove a silver hoop into my hot, pulsating lobe.

I can sense that she has something to say but is just dithering. When I turn around I notice that her eyes are studying my tacky snow globe, which imprisons a miniature Taj Mahal. She is deliberately avoiding my quizzical glance.

"Why are you so dressed up, Melody?" she asks, and now it is my turn to squirm.

I am still on the fence about dating apps. Growing up, I had to look no further than the schoolyard or library to get my kicks. Depressingly, now, in my mid-twenties, I look to my phone to find love.

"Got a date," I say nonchalantly while clamping my spider eyelashes with a curler.

Calla brightens. "Who is he?"

She could take for granted it was the guy who had the pleasure of seeing me later. It was in that moment I realized I could not always presume the same for her. As of a week ago this was a new revelation for my parents, but I had an inkling. I was caught in the crossfire.

"Did you know about Calla and Zenia?" my parents demanded.

"I don't understand why they are so shocked," Calla whimpered, puffy-eyed, following their confrontation.

"Oh, just some guy from Tinder," I say, then add, "It's grim out there in the dating world. Take it from your wizened older sister, you're lucky to have found someone you genuinely like and who likes you back."

I notice her flinch for a second. It is all still so new and scary.

"Anyway . . . what have you planned?"

Calla puffs out her cheeks and shrugs.

"It's Valentine's Day—you better be doing something with Zenia! Mom and Dad mentioned that they are going to that fancy new French restaurant downtown, so they'll be out late."

Calla smiles, appreciatively.

"Now get out so I can put on this little black dress," I say, closing the door with a wink.

MAGGIE CHEN

YEARS AS MENTEE: 1

GRADE: Senior

HIGH SCHOOL: High School for Health Professions and Human Services

BORN: Manhattan, NY

LIVES: Brooklyn, NY

MENTEE'S ANECDOTE: *My meetings with my mentor, Hannah, are really enjoyable. Every week, I anticipate our sessions, as not only do I have someone to talk to about my life, but also she gives me the biggest support in starting my novel! So far, my favorite meeting was when Hannah took me to her own favorite place to eat and talk about my work: Molly's Cupcakes. Because we go to different places, hang out together, and get to sit and talk about our progress, I'm really grateful to have been able to work with Hannah this year.*

HANNAH NESBAT

YEARS AS MENTOR: 1

OCCUPATION: Marketing Coordinator, Penguin Random House

BORN: Belmont, CA

LIVES: Brooklyn, NY

MENTOR'S ANECDOTE: *Where we meet: Brooklyn Roasting Company, one hour before closing, often their last customers of the day; Starbucks, for a late-afternoon coffee (me) or a Frappuccino (Maggie); Molly's Cupcakes; the Chobani café. What we write: college essays, the first fifteen pages (!) of a novel (Maggie); feedback, free-write exercises (me). What we bond over: YA books and specifically swoony boys in YA books (a recent favorite: Hideo from* Warcross*).*

Korean Pop Highlights Are Their Own Flaws

MAGGIE CHEN

As a recent Korean Pop fan, the column idea that popped into my head was writing about my new obsession. I also wanted to discuss how exactly K-pop came to be, as well as the bad side that is overshadowed by the trend's popularity.

Korean Pop. Pop that is exclusive to South Korea. An expanding trend that I never had thought would come to America. When I had just discovered the movement, I was struck with the fact that most of my favorite idols had plastic surgery done. I remember how I analyzed the trending K-pop videos on YouTube and realizing how unnaturally perfect some of the stars were. For example, G-Dragon is one of the most talented singers and rappers that I've ever known, and it was revealed from his childhood photos that he had plastic surgery done on his nose. In old pictures, G-Dragon had a round face and a nose with wide nostrils. But in his famous music videos, he has a smaller nose that makes his face look more slender. Of course, many entertainment agencies such as SM Entertainment recognize his talent, but how he is viewed is based on looks. A K-pop star's popularity depends on how pretty or handsome they are.

G-Dragon's exquisite transformation was only a small example. According to an article in *Wasabi Now* by Crystal Tal, South Korean stars have had rhinoplasty, eyelid surgery, facial contouring, and even body contouring. Rhinoplasty is favored the most out of the categories. With the ability to change the face image entirely, most male and female idols alike can have their idealized vision of themselves. From the scraping of their jaw and chin, they can alter their facial proportions to those that are considered best for their careers.

Now, of course, there is a certain controversy over this. Plastic surgery can be both good and bad depending on one's opinions. Sure, I totally understand the effects of admiring good-looking people; it is definitely more powerful to see a face that leaves you starstruck than one that leaves you with nothing. Also, the idols themselves can benefit from their altered looks. Society generally accepts those who are pleasing to the eye. Thus, it is natural for them to change their look to further their career. We are bound to look at those people who are unquestionably more beautiful than others.

There is also a bad side to all of this. South Korea's use of plastic surgery can also be its weakness. To become accepted into their society, one is forced to choose whether they can do more to their natural-born face. Expectations will be held a lot higher in terms of being pretty or being handsome. Those who are not enough are left to pursue nothing just because they aren't good-looking. You have to be aesthetically pleasing or be shunned for life.

In addition to career reliance, the actual health risks of plastic surgery are simply outrageous. According to the website Health line.com, risks such as scarring, organ damage, infections, and even death itself are part of plastic surgery. Simply changing one feature on a face can astonishingly become fatal. Plastic surgery may be a total game changer for the faces of South Korea, but one should really consider sacrificing one's looks because of the chance of an ugly effect. According to a friend of mine, it is rumored that plastic surgery can severely damage your face as you age. Skin and proportions might become distorted, and the results might look far uglier than even your previous state before taking the surgery.

I would not trust my face with a complete stranger when the chances of health risks are far greater than they are without surgery. However, the fact that almost every entertainment agency out there in South Korea pressures their idols to confront these dangers is actually terrifying. Society, of course, can give influence and grant success once you pander to their preferences, but on the other hand, having faith in yourself and believing you are talented is also a crucial factor in being a K-pop idol. Only an individual can decide to become an idol, but unless he finds his own way to succeed, that individual will be nothing more than a puppet—not just to the entertainment agencies but also to South Korea, and to the world.

The choice of doing plastic surgery is certainly controversial. In the end, plastic surgery is only a step closer to being accepted into society, but South Korea idols have to learn, in my opinion, that one does not have to rely on looks to be successful in life.

The Personalities Are Political

HANNAH NESBAT

Maggie writes about plastic surgery and K-pop stars—something she debates with her friends regularly. I love a passionately held pop-culture opinion, and wrote my column about why it's important we keep treating them as serious.

Before the 2016 election, I used to Keep Up with one specific family I have never even met, the Kardashians, like it was my job. I would keep a live text chain with my friend as every episode would air on Sunday and follow each family member gleefully on social media. No development was too small to catch my notice. After November 2016, it's all seemed a little less fun. Our weekly watch dates petered out. It was hard to bring ourselves to care when there were so many other things to care about. And reality TV had lost some of its escapist sheen, coming a little bit too close to reality.

And then: *US Weekly* was sold to American Media Inc., the publisher of the *National Enquirer.* They started putting Trump children on their covers, writing about them like fun celebs you should know. Women wore black on the Golden Globes red carpet and started a legal fund for victims of sexual harassment and assault. Oprah has been floated as a presidential candidate. Celebrity culture is as political as it ever has been—and I would argue it always has been.

Anyone who wants to say that caring about celebrities is dumb is buying into a sexist narrative. Celebrity, like any cultural interest that primarily belongs to women—cooking, interior design, romance novels—is often sidelined and belittled. Sports? Import-ant and valuable to our discourse. But, of course, sports are widely thought of as by and for men.

And there's something to be said for caring about something political but with littler nuclear-war-level consequence on our immediate lives. It's cathartic to get into an argument about Kylie Jenner's pregnancy at a party. Or about plastic surgery in K-pop with our close friends.

To talk and write and read about celebrity is to think criti-cally about our culture: about the press and social media, about what privacy means and who we grant it to, about who holds power and why; about global standards of beauty, about popu-larity and mass appeal—and about politics. Who we like, what we care about, who we choose to represent that.

MARYCLARE CHINEDO

YEARS AS MENTEE: 3

GRADE: Senior

HIGH SCHOOL: Bronx Lighthouse College Prep Academy

BORN: Bronx, NY

LIVES: Bronx, NY

PUBLICATIONS AND RECOGNITIONS: Scholastic Art & Writing Awards: Gold Key, Silver Key, and Honorable Mention

MENTEE'S ANECDOTE: *Morayo is like my big sister. She gives great advice; she's funny and amazing. She pushes me to write outside of my comfort zone and write about things I normally wouldn't write about. Whenever I need help with something that's not writing-related, she's always willing to help. For example, once she pretended to be a college interviewer to help prepare me for an interview. Her flexibility and patience are why I'm able to grow as a writer and as a person. She's such a great mentor and I am very grateful to have had her.*

MORAYO FALEYIMU

YEARS AS MENTOR: 6

OCCUPATION: Senior Program Manager, Peer Health Exchange

BORN: Miami, FL

LIVES: Elizabeth, NJ

MENTOR'S ANECDOTE: *Wow! I can honestly say it's been a pleasure watching Maryclare gain confidence in her voice and sense of humor. Over the past three years, I've watched her experiment with different genres, tackle real-world issues through satire, and think critically about how she wants to use her voice as a storyteller. I can't wait to see her work added to the canon.*

Maryclare Yesterday vs. Maryclare Today

MARYCLARE CHINEDO

Generation F stands for Finally. I finally speak my mind and can be unapologetically me. This piece is about my finally being straight with myself and reflecting on who I was versus who I am now.

Maryclare Yesterday
Maryclare Today
Shy and passive
Funny and full of life

I hate putting my ideas out there. They're horrible!
Yes, you are speaking to a 2018 Gold Key winner. Holla!
I'm not good at anything but watching Netflix
Class of 2018 valedictorian baby! Talk to me nicely.

Is that something out of my comfort zone? Yea . . . I'll pass
Wow. What's that strange cool thing? I wanna do it!
Uhm . . . I think I'm okay with only speaking English.
Yo no hablo ingles! Lo siento, chica

If my mom wants me to be a doctor, so be it.
Girl, you know I love dance. Minoring in dance it is!
Should I enroll in AP Spanish? Nah. It's too challenging
Yea, I'm with you on that one. Let's take AP Calc instead

I'm not African. I'm, uhm . . . Native American and Latina
Girl, please! You're Nigerian all the way, baby!
Is that a protest about women's rights? I'll just walk past.
"Pro Choice! My Body!" Oops, am I protesting too loud?

Before I do anything, I have to think of the What-Ifs
No you don't. Be a free spirit! Stop being so paranoid!
I need to delete my Netflix account. It's distracting
Should I get Hulu and HBO Go? Eh, the more the merrier!

Maryclare Yesterday
Maryclare Today
Shy and passive
Funny and full of life

Bechdel Tests

MORAYO FALEYIMU

The Bechdel test measures women-centered narratives. To pass the Bechdel test, a work must feature two women who talk to each other about something other than men. These narrators try with little success. I think a crucial part of being a member of Generation F is centering the experiences of women.

Test #1: Betta Fish

My b——— kept a betta fish in a huge glass tank. It swam in brisk, uninterrupted circles that my knocking did not disturb. It ignored me, much the same way that D——— ignored me in science class, even though I sat *directly* in his line of sight. And yet I could not imagine being angry at D. It wasn't that he was ignoring me: It was that he could not yet see me.

Back at home, I dug out a compact mirror from my mother's purse. It was marbled purple and gold. The mirror was dusty with powder, but I could still see my own face through the stipple. I turned it toward the tank. The betta swam by once, unbothered. I flicked the mirror back and forth until I caught its attention. It hesitated, taking in the new interloper on the other side of the tank. Then it charged. Again and again, it hurled itself at the glass. The interloper responded in kind. Mesmerized, I watched until the sound of the doorbell startled me out of my reverie. The compact fell from my hand into the tank. The betta went belly up a few hours later.

My mother fished them both out that evening and replaced the betta before my b——— got home from his overnight game. The new betta fish swam in a languid, confused circle. Poor thing: trapped in a tank, not knowing a single thing about girls.

Test #2: Lipstick Theory
We are reading the labels and deciding who to be tonight. A dusky English Rose. A lurid Tropical Sherbet. A slash of red in Sultry Siren. Or one, dark purple, simply titled Mistress.

Test #3: Last Night
I dreamt of a gate tied shut with two pink ribbons.
    I dreamt of a world without men.

BRIANNA CLARKE-ARIAS

YEARS AS MENTEE: 1

GRADE: Freshman

HIGH SCHOOL: Hunter High School

BORN: New York, NY

LIVES: Bronx, NY

PUBLICATIONS AND RECOGNITIONS: Scholastic Art & Writing Award: Silver Key

MENTEE'S ANECDOTE: *Meeting with Rachel has led to many breakthroughs in not only my writing, but in my views of myself as a writer. I have become more conscious of my role as a constructor of worlds simply through the sharing of my lenses of my surroundings and experiences. This act of openness had always seemed daunting to me before, and through a closer and continuous relationship with a mentor who is a writer herself, I can feel myself becoming braver and more bold.*

RACHEL SHOPE

YEARS AS MENTOR: 1

OCCUPATION: Associate Editor, CB Insights

BORN: Chapel Hill, NC

LIVES: New York, NY

MENTOR'S ANECDOTE: *I always look forward to meeting with Brianna, because it's magical every time. Whether we're tucked in a corner at the public library or sharing red-velvet cupcakes in a café or snagging chairs at a random Whole Foods, we connect as writers and friends. I am constantly struck by her talent and brilliance. I leave each of our pair sessions with a renewed sense of creativity and hope for the future. Being her mentor has made me a stronger editor, a more disciplined writer, and I think just a more positive person overall.*

Musings from a Lost New York Native

BRIANNA CLARKE-ARIAS

This poem explores the process of getting to know oneself when given the freedom to do so. More recently, I've noticed aspects of myself mirrored in the city, and I want my work to reflect that.

I don't want to put on a hat.
My ears are so cold
they burn.
But I won't do it.
I can't.

Warmth feels unnatural now.
Let the air prick and my hair
run loose in the
wind,
slipping into my eyes,
out from behind my ears.

I left my scarf at school. I'll
probably never see it again. The cold
bites into my skin as I gaze skyward,
to the tops of the buildings that
I pass.

The night swallows every
building I pass. They are
frigid and invisible in the dark, only

light can unfreeze them.
My hair could stand on end in this cold . . .
it feels like it is.

It's late now,
and only the top of
the Empire State Building
matters anymore.
The bottom half of my head
stays cold and forgotten too.

The dark wanders along beside me
in this big city.
It's a larger than life
kind of town, so many eyes to watch
what belongs to me,
let them see.

I don't want to put on a hat.
Let the air prick and my own hair
bite into my skin as I gaze skyward.
My hair could stand on end in this cold,
but only the bottom half of my head
belongs to me.
Let them see.

From Ellis Island

RACHEL SHOPE

This poem is about finding your place, and feeling so strongly that you belong there that it seems like you've been there before. It is about the connections we share to our past, previous generations, and the homes that we choose for ourselves.

Standing in the Great Hall,
I know
I have been here before.

I heard the echoes
when they were voices.
Smelled the ink and the anxiety
of the stamp poised to grant entry,
to give permanence.
Or something like it.

I had a different face then.
A different posture.

I was carried in the blood
of my great-great-grandparents,
tucked between
the fibers of their coats,
folded into the spaces
left by the letters they erased and
the new ones written in,

making them blend,
making them American.

I am familiar with starting over.
That is a language I still know.
The assonance of your few possessions
in one trunk—they mean
everything and nothing.

You cling to them,
but wonder if you could bear that loss.
You are almost tempted
to pronounce it—to
let go of the handle and walk away.

Perhaps you would forget.
Perhaps you would carry that weight
forever, like you carry your great-great-granddaughter,
like you carry the letters cut from your name.
Silent. Heavy.

The city was different then.
And it is the same.

I was passing through.

But now, I let go
of the handle of my suitcase.
I open the trunk and unpack,
allowing myself to say the word—
Permanence.
Or something like it.

I look at the city
from this island, like they did.
My face is my own.
The letters spell a name wholly different
from the one in the book,
the one etched on the wall.

I trace the letters with my finger.
I say them aloud.

I have been here before.

LILA COOPER

YEARS AS MENTEE: 1

GRADE: Junior

HIGH SCHOOL: Institute for Collaborative Education

BORN: Brooklyn, NY

LIVES: Brooklyn, NY

MENTEE'S ANECDOTE: *Girls Write Now has helped me grow as a writer. It's taken me out of my comfort zone of plotless short stories and poetry. Even though I do a lot of poetry, I have learned there are other genres that I actually enjoy. I've appreciated Robin's critiques, because she makes me think in a different way about my writing. She helps me see what's working and what isn't; she gets it. Sometimes we both obsess over a single word. It's great to be able to do that together on Saturdays over a cup of tea.*

ROBIN WILLIG

YEARS AS MENTOR: 3

OCCUPATION: Chief of Staff, Center for Reproductive Rights

BORN: Far Rockaway, NY

LIVES: Brooklyn, NY

PUBLICATIONS AND RECOGNITIONS: Summer Residency, Writers Colony at Dairy Hollow, Eureka Springs, Arkansas

MENTOR'S ANECDOTE: *I never studied poetic forms and I was struck, in the Girls Write Now session, by the many rules. Lila and I talked a lot about "Garland Cinquain." Wasn't he an informant on an SVU episode? She and I share a love of words and often our time is spent dissecting and rebuilding. At the end of the Poetic Forms workshop, the girls read their pieces aloud and each chose to ignore the rules. I appreciate that about the mentees, and Lila especially—their willingness to explore. Generation F indeed: freedom, flouters of rules, and, likely, founders of a better way forward.*

In Memory of Ma

LILA COOPER

This poem is a recollection of the time I spent in India as a child.

God slipped in between the gauzy white sheets last night
she pulled at the bottom of my slip separating me from the
    warm sun that enveloped my barely there body
Begging for my attention
she was dressed in red like fire and roses and watermelon in July
Like the man who took a bite out of a pomegranate like it was
    an apple
she wore marigolds around her neck like I did when I was five
Like my mother did on the day she got married
she wore the ones in the Kainchi garden where I sat and tasted
    the sweetness of mangoes for the first time with my best
    friend
Where we chased each other into the terra-cotta pagoda
    hearing the faint chants of kirtan wallahs and cow bells
In monsoon season we would venture down the unpaved road
    in our bright pink rainboots to get toast from the Tawaris
piled up to my head and wrapped in crinkled tinfoil
She was blue like the dye from my skirt that would run into
    the river
She had warm hands like the milk she gave me in her garden,
    my hands have always been cold

I am in a house without her while it's snowing outside and all
    I have is a child's blanket to keep me warm

I miss you
I hope you're doing ok
I can't wait to see you again
Talk soon,
Lila

Her hair was always white like the temple walls

The ones I was a devi under

The ones I ate halwa and basin ladus out of a banana-leaf bowl
under

She always reminded me of the trees during monsoon season,
so big and full of life, the kind of life I didn't see in New
York

that's probably what I remember the most about India how
comic book green all the trees were and when we were
driving around a bend and I looked down all I could see
were those Technicolor trees for miles and miles

Sometimes I wonder when I'll go back and how it will feel
now that she's no longer there

Poetic Forms and Dance Steps: A Sonnet

ROBIN WILLIG

This attempt of a Shakespearean sonnet was started in the Poetic Forms workshop at Girls Write Now, in which I was challenged to follow the rules. I was inspired by the freedom with which those rules were rejected by our fearless mentees.

Surely men made up the poetic forms
Sonnet, sestina, villanelle, cinquain
Like boys and drinking games in college dorms
How 'bout: Five tercets and then a quatrain

Repeat this word, third stanza, second line
How low can you go, can you go down low?
So I chafe and resist those rules assigned
Who counts the syllables? And also: no.

It's not the words with which I so quarrel
But arbitrary, patriarchal rules
The art confounds me. Wherefore the laurels
Would women create such confining tools?

You and I, let's create our new bounty
Let's write lines as if no one is counting

Lawless. Unburdened. Free.

MEDELIN CUEVAS

YEARS AS MENTEE: 3

GRADE: Senior

HIGH SCHOOL: H.E.R.O. High School

BORN: Bronx, NY

LIVES: Bronx, NY

PUBLICATIONS AND RECOGNITIONS: Scholastic Art & Writing Awards: Silver Key

MENTEE'S ANECDOTE: *When I first met Rakia, I knew that she was the perfect fit for being my mentor. She is smart, talented, and genuine when it comes to my writing and other life events. When I told her about NYU, she was ecstatic! It is great to share your biggest dream with someone who watched you grow, and Rakia has been the greatest mentor for me.*

RAKIA CLARK

YEARS AS MENTOR: 2

OCCUPATION: Senior Editor, *Beacon Press*

BORN: Atlantic City, NJ

LIVES: New York, NY

MENTOR'S ANECDOTE: *I remember when Maddy showed up to our weekly session more excited and bubbly than usual. She had just received her first admissions letter to college—NYU, of all places. I was so proud of her, I could barely stand it. I have seen Maddy work incredibly hard to make herself a great candidate for college, all while balancing a busy home life. More acceptance letters quickly followed, but that first one was the sweetest.*

A Letter to My Unborn Daughter

MEDELIN CUEVAS

For me, Generation F stands for freedom, fearless, and faithful. Going through high school, I never thought I was "free enough" to do certain things. This piece holds a sentimental value to me because I cover things I want my future daughter to know and to take away.

Dear Daughter,

I was not the type of girl who hung around with girls. Like, girls who played with Barbie dolls all day long or pretended to be princesses. I was not the girl who was into skirts and Twinkle Toe shoes as a kid. Your uncle was too big of an influence on me for that sort of thing. Instead, he and I played first-person shooter video games on the computer, and I was wide receiver to his quarterback when we played football. You could say l colored outside the lines.

Baby girl, when you come into this world, you will be going through a lot of bumps and cracks and learn a lot of fascinating things. You will learn what you like, set your biggest dreams, take your first steps, and learn how the world works and who you are as a person. I hope you see the world in the most blissful way any child would see it: blue skies, sunny rays of sunshine beaming on your beautiful skin, and happy moments.

However, life will not be all gumdrops and rainbows. You are going to experience people who do not want to see you prosper. You will encounter evil serpents called bullies who will tease you for characteristics that you should cherish, like your big imagination and your beautiful curls, and the butterfly birthmark that you share with me, your *tia* and your *abuelita*.

You are what Alicia Keys describes as "A girl on fire" or "a superwoman," which means a woman with potential and high hopes—a woman who has a high level of charisma, competence, and optimism. With these talents, I hope you think like a revolutionist who seeks to change the world for the better and make a positive difference. Baby girl, shine! Shine like Celia Cruz, Sonia Sotomayor, Michelle Obama, Ilia Calderon, Angela Davis, and even me, *tu madre*. Whatever you experience, more than likely, when I was younger, I experienced it, too. Bullies doubted me and my talents. But you know what your *mami* did? I still kept on shining.

When I was growing up, I was pretty lost knowing what I wanted to do when I grew up. I didn't know how to get a boyfriend, and I was pretty antisocial until high school, where I met a few good people. When I befriended them, they became a part of my support system and life. They were my friends not only because they did support me, but because they taught me how to enjoy life and gave me wonderful experiences to cherish. I learned then that, with friends, it is about quality, *not* quantity.

My advice for you, *mi hija*, is that it is okay to ask for help. When I was at my lowest points, I talked to a guidance counselor at school. When there was a problem and I wanted someone to just hear me out, I went to my mom or my best friends. There's nothing weak about assistance. It does not mean you are a failure. It just means that you are juggling so much and it is starting to go out of hand. Additionally, there will be tests that will stress you out. You might get a score you are not satisfied with. It does not mean you are dumb. It just means you have trouble understanding something. So figure out a way to understand. Never let anyone or anything determine how much potential you have. That number you get on your test will not reflect how much effort and hard work you have done.

So always remember the fire that is inside of you. It is there for a reason. Add more fuel to it and do not let anyone put it out. You are going to do big things, baby girl, and if you ever feel hopeless or you feel that you can not take the pressure anymore, *Mami* is here to support you.

With love,
Your mother and number-one fan

What I Wish My Younger Self Knew

RAKIA CLARK

Hindsight really is 20/20.

When I was a teenager, I worried about everything. The way I looked, my grades, my friends, my clothes, whether or not anybody could see the pimple beneath my bangs. I went to the restroom between each class at school, smoothing my hair with a small comb from my back pocket and reapplying Vaseline to my lips. Like most teenagers, I wanted to fit in.

I wish I had known how much cooler it is to stand out! The kids who stood out had way more fun than I did. By not letting other people's opinions guide their decision-making, they ended up doing more of what they really wanted to do. I didn't understand how important that was for a long time.

As far as I know, the life you're living right now is the only one you get. Why let someone else call the shots? This is a lesson I learned well in adulthood. But, boy, do I wish I'd have realized it sooner.

BERNA DA'COSTA

YEARS AS MENTEE: 2

GRADE: Junior

HIGH SCHOOL: Stuyvesant High School

BORN: Goa, India

LIVES: Bronx, NY

MENTEE'S ANECDOTE: *The end of last year was brutal to me; I was dragging myself out of it in pieces. I stopped writing for a long time, I stopped reading, I stopped going to Girls Write Now workshops, and I stopped meeting my mentor, wonderful, wonderful Jamie. Not everything has subsided completely yet, but I push through each week and wait to sit at the little mint-green booth stuffed into the corner of Financier Patisserie, eat too many hazelnut macarons, freak out about rain sometimes, and write with Jamie.*

JAMIE SERLIN

YEARS AS MENTOR: 2

OCCUPATION: Director, West Wing Writers, LLC

BORN: Philadelphia, PA

LIVES: Brooklyn, NY

MENTOR'S ANECDOTE: *Whether she is writing poetry or prose, memoir or fiction, Berna writes in a voice that is unmistakably her own. She refuses capital letters. She is fond of parentheses. She has the gift all great writers possess—the ability to find meaning, and humor, and wonder in the ordinary, like missing your bus stop and walking the rest of the way home. Reading Berna's work is like taking a trip inside her head. I feel lucky to peek around inside her world.*

acknowledgments . . .

BERNA DA'COSTA

I believe that life creates a writer. My life, the people around me, the things I've loved, the places I've been to, the happy days, the crappy days, have turned me into the type of writer I am. It's given me my style, my voice.

for a book i will probably never write

p.s. (in the beginning because i never follow the rules when it comes to writing anyway) this is going to be long because i have a lot of people to give my love to. BUT BUT BUT if you're just a reader and not someone who expects themselves to be included in my acknowledgments, just read the first few sentences. if you've already flipped past this page and closed the book . . . you're not going to see this anyway . . . . sooo . . . . this is awkward for me.

to the reader, thank you thank you thank you in every language of the world for picking up my book and actually finishing it. if you loved it, you get a free puppy (not really). if you didn't, i'm not going to say thank you for pushing yourself through, i'm going to say sorry.

to my mother, you will always be the first person i thank for any success in my life, and this book is probably also dedicated to you even though you might never read it. that's okay. thank you for your patience—it is the strongest thing in the world. for your kindness, for always loving me (because i make it so hard sometimes). you have always believed in the best of me. i've hurt you, and no mother should be hurt, especially you. i've screamed and yelled and fought with you and it breaks me a little how easily you hug me after everything. thank you for reminding me to cry. you have shown me the greatness of a mother's love, the invincibility of it. i'm growing up and slowly realizing you are the world growing from underneath my feet. thank you for staying awake with me until i finished my homework. thank you for the lemon tea, for the papaya. i love you.

to my publisher, for releasing this monster out of its cage. i've spent a majority of my life with this story in my head, and maybe i should say that this story is for the readers, for every lovely person who is willing to turn pages and bury their nose in new books (i hope my book smells good). but it's not. this is for me. i have written every word with the most selfish intentions because i needed to let this story go.

to my editing team, thank you for whipping my manuscript into readable and publishable shape. i am the biggest disgrace to grammar. sorry for all the commas (i know i use too many of them), sorry for all the run-on sentences (unfortunately i can't bother with proper punctuation), sorry for never knowing how to use one of these "-" or one of these "–" or one of these ";" or one of . . . well you get the point.

to production, thank you for designing the cover of this book. you've added to the beauty of (i hope) many bookshelves.

to my father, thank you for teaching me how to use my words carefully. you're the reason i write.

to my sister, thank you for showing me that i am capable of loving someone too much. thank you for being everything i'm not. thank you for your heart and the space you let me reserve in it. thank you for being the stronger one. i want to give you every sunrise, every sunset, every rainy day. you are stars and moons, an explosion of light every morning. my little moju, always finding you on the other side of the bed, waking up with limbs and jungle hair, i can't leave you alone. keep on drawing. uwu.

to the community, thank you for giving me memories, for making me laugh harder than i do with anyone else, for making me feel like something more is possible, for the weirdness, the craziness, the insanity of us together in a room dreaming like fools. we need more paper plates.

to the stars,

to the moon,

to the rain,

i will never stop writing about you.

to goa, the only place that feels like coming home.

to all the books that let me wander around in their world for a while.

to all the songs that melted my heart.

to all the poets,

to all the authors,

to all the writers,

who found the words that i couldn't, arranged them into a tangible thought, gave me that moment of yes,

god yes,

this is what i meant.

to words, i love them so much.

to the moments of silence, i appreciate them.

to every person who understood me, thank you, give them an award please.

to every person who told me to write, write, write, you are wonderful human beings who believe in the magic of this world, in extraordinary things, like me using a semicolon correctly.

to me, you wrote a BOOK!

(this book will never exist.)

Ode to an aspiring author...

JAMIE SERLIN

This is a true story of how I let a grumpy old man derail my novelist dreams. I still hope I write my book one day—but I know for sure Berna will write hers.

I am nine and he is half a century older. He is a local celebrity—a nationally renowned children's author. I am a voracious reader and an inconsistent diarist. I dream of writing my own novels. He has published more than twenty.

When I find out he is coming to my fourth-grade career day, I can't believe my luck. The day's second-most-exciting presenter is a preowned car salesman. Every student is allowed to pick four tables to visit. I am the first to sign up for the author's booth.

The morning of career day, I slip a copy of his most celebrated book into my book bag before I leave for school. He arrives in the auditorium looking mussed and fussed, collared shirt misbuttoned, gray hair slightly askew. I imagine he is so busy churning out masterpieces, he does not have time to concern himself with unimportant things like combs and shirt buttons. When the time comes, I make my way over to his table, stomach fluttering.

He talks about the book in my bag, which won the Newbery Award. I listen intently to every word. When he pauses for questions, my hand shoots up.

"What is it like to write a book?" I ask him. "I want to be a writer, too."

His bushy brows furrow. "You want to know what it's like? You'll have an idea you think is pretty good. You'll work day and night, for years, to write the perfect manuscript. When you finally complete it, you will send it off to agents and publishers. And when it arrives they will dump it in the trash without ever reading it."

I wait for the "but" I know must be coming. "*That's* what it's like," he finishes with a shrug.

I decide I need a new career.

Two decades later, I meet a high-schooler in a mentorship program. I am a speechwriter. She is an aspiring author. I am still afraid of rejection. She is clever, and brave, and sharp as a tack.

She talks about the book she will never write (though she has already written the acknowledgments). I assure her that she can and she will.

GIA DEETON

YEARS AS MENTEE: 3

GRADE: Senior

HIGH SCHOOL: Baruch College Campus High School

BORN: New York, NY

LIVES: New York, NY

PUBLICATIONS AND RECOGNITIONS: 2018 Scholastic Art & Writing Award, Honorable Mention for Writing Portfolio

MENTEE'S ANECDOTE: *I really want to know the algorithm that Girls Write Now uses to pair mentors with mentees, because Lindsay and I couldn't be a better match for each other. Whether we're working hard at our favorite café, the Hungry Ghost, or wandering around the Brooklyn Botanic Garden just for fun, our conversations are always enjoyable and inspiring. After three years together and many hair color changes between the two of us, we've developed a friendship that will surely last beyond my graduation from Girls Write Now.*

LINDSAY ZOLADZ

YEARS AS MENTOR: 3

OCCUPATION: Staff Writer, *The Ringer*

BORN: Washington Township, NJ

LIVES: Brooklyn, NY

MENTOR'S ANECDOTE: *The Generation F topic has led to so many enlightening conversations between Gia and me. Because of media stereotypes, I am used to thinking of the word "millennial" as synonymous with "young person"—and, let's be honest, often "entitled, lazy young person." One day Gia and I had a long conversation in which I asked her what "millennial" means to her, and her empathic viewpoint made me feel a little more comfortable embracing the word. We are not sure yet what the media will end up calling her generation, but regardless, I feel optimistic about what it will come to stand for.*

85 White Street

GIA DEETON

Despite profound differences among several generations of family members, they are all connected by a shared location: 85 White Street. The address is fictionalized, but all the other details are true to my family's experience.

Imagine a time when one of the busiest streets in Manhattan was deserted enough for kids to roller-skate in the middle of the road on the weekends. Believe it or not, this was the reality for my mom when she was growing up, before Canal Street became infamous for its ability to attract crowds of tourists with counterfeit bags and great restaurants. It's even harder to picture Canal Street as an actual canal in the early 1800s, surrounded by towering bluffs, which also have streets named after them now. In 1850, my great-grandfather's grandfather lived on White Street, just a few blocks south of Canal, peddling goods such as shoe polish, fabric, and kitchenware before leaving for the Gold Rush. Just down the street from where he'd lived, a new cigar warehouse was built in 1868. To this day, my family still lives there.

I've always lived at 85 White Street. Although it's been converted from a warehouse to a residential building, the building's five floors still seem unfinished and not really meant for human life. I learned to crawl up the four flights of stairs to my apartment before I even knew how to walk. When the ten-foot-tall crimson doors at street level are opened, you're greeted by a steep mountain of seventy-eight steps that stretch all the way to the back of the building. Unlike the other buildings in the neighborhood, it has unprofessionally installed plumbing, no elevator, and a threat of giving you a splinter from the floorboards.

My grandparents purchased the top two floors of 85 White in 1969 for a relatively cheap price, and the building has increased in value in more than just monetary ways. My mother was nine years old when she first moved in, and we've shared some of the same childhood experiences of falling down the treacherous stairs and picking splinters out of the soles of our feet. Unfortunately, though, I don't think Canal Street will ever again be empty enough for me to try roller-skating there like she did. Her father was a painter, so choosing a house with lots of space to work on his vast canvases came first, and comfort came second. The loft still smells like oil paint and sawdust, because just like my mom's dad, my dad is a painter. My dad's abstract paintings often compete with the large sizes of my grandfather's figurative paintings, and these enormous works can be found hanging side by side under twenty-six-foot-high skylights.

The house has become a relic of my family's history. For three generations it has remained the home and workplace for many of my family members, and for me and my sister, it's the only home we've ever known. Not everyone has the experience of having lived in only one house, and it's even rarer that I'm able to grow up in the same house where my mother did. People often move to New York City to escape their hometowns and live in pristine apartments that offer a fresh start. There have been times when I wished our house had less clutter and looked more normal, but that was before I realized that a lot of our knickknacks have important meanings. We don't necessarily need to hold on to my grandfather's cassette collection since nobody owns a cassette player anymore, but it's always a nice reminder of the times he'd blast loud music while painting. Some days he'd play Mozart, other days he'd play the Sex Pistols. Now that we have the Internet, we don't really need my grandma's old cookbooks, but getting rid of them isn't worth the price of losing her best recipes.

I'm lucky that I live in a home saturated with reminders of people I love. My maternal grandparents passed away when I was young so I didn't get to spend that much time with them, but their presence lives on in the objects and furniture that I see every day. Growing up in this house has given me valuable intergenerational experiences, and I have gained an appreciation for my family and our value for authenticity over perfection. Although it isn't as polished as a lot of other apartments, I bet those apartments wouldn't be able to hold two generations' worth of paintings and endless family memories. Our house may look peculiar and incomplete, but it tells a story that is truly priceless.

85 White Street

LINDSAY ZOLADZ

Is it possible to define a generation in a single word?

> "A lot of people are nervous. I have heard some people say that at 12:00 all the money will come out of the ATM. A lot of people don't want to be in a plane at midnight. Still, I don't think it will be so bad." —the December 2, 1999 entry from the "Y2K Journal" I was asked to keep in my seventh-grade English class.

I hate the word "millennial." By the time I was in my early teens, it already felt retro-futuristic—a leftover remnant of fruitless Y2K anxiety or, even worse, a reminder of Will Smith's novelty album *Willennium*. I'm not sure what I would have chosen had I been given the opportunity to name my generation. I just know I wouldn't have chosen "millennial."

The media has been even less creative in deciding what to call the generation after us: I've heard some say "Generation Z," some say "postmillennial," some even combine those first two into the cringeworthy portmanteau "zillennial." (Ugh.) But over the past year or so, the bright, optimistic cohort that makes up this demographic has proven that, no matter what we call them, they're out to change the world. When it comes to gun laws, environmental activism, dismantling racism, and so much more, this as-yet-unnamed generation is leading the charge to a more humane world.

My mentee, Gia, and I have had some enlightening talks about the similarities and differences of our respective generations. Because of media stereotypes, I am used to the word "millennial" being used to generically connote "young person" (or, especially if it's coming from someone of an older generation, "entitled, lazy young person"). My conversations with Gia, though, remind me that youth is temporary and that my generation has a more specific identity—and responsibility to those coming up behind us.

I asked Gia how she'd define her generation (and what she thought they should be called) and she told me she wasn't yet sure. I then remembered myself at her age, seventeen, and it made me realize how few of the phenomena that we now associate with millennials even existed at that point. Smartphones didn't exist yet, nor did social media as we understand it today. I'd argue that we had more trust in institutions—from the economy to the real estate market to Social Security—before 2008. The world we inherited and the concepts we are commonly associated with had not yet taken shape. It reminded me that, in defining generations, we must be patient. I'm in no rush to name the one coming up behind us. But, now that I think of it, *Generation Girls Write Now* has a nice ring to it.

SOPHIA DEMARTINO

YEARS AS MENTEE: 1

GRADE: Senior

HIGH SCHOOL: Susan E. Wagner High School

BORN: Staten Island, NY

LIVES: Staten Island, NY

MENTEE'S ANECDOTE: *Elle is the absolute sweetest person you can ever meet, and I am forever grateful to have gone through my first and last year with Girls Write Now with her by my side. We have laughed, cried, and so much in between because of how strong our relationship has grown since day one. Although our writing is very different, our stories, our experiences, and even more have brought us together and have only proven how strong this relationship really is. I am sure that our relationship will continue after I get shipped off to college, and even beyond.*

ELIZABETH ROY

YEARS AS MENTOR: 1

OCCUPATION: Global Sales Operations Manager, Spotify

BORN: Peachtree City, GA

LIVES: Brooklyn, NY

MENTOR'S ANECDOTE: *Sophia and I hit it off from the beginning. Even though we have different backgrounds, we speak a common language. We can spend hours talking, laughing, and having fun. Sophia's bravery to speak her mind and live her unique life has given me the courage to make bold choices both professionally and personally. I have no doubt that our friendship will continue when the program ends and she goes off to college. I'm eternally grateful to Girls Write Now for bringing two kindred spirits together.*

silenced

SOPHIA DEMARTINO

Life is precious, and I am sorry that it took this long for us to recognize and realize it. Now we are here to fight, and we are here to stay.

They say what they are doing is right, it is the will of the gods that control them, that they are saving the lives of so many innocent children because they are not able to speak up for themselves. They call their protest bravery, their March for Life a symbol of hope and defiance because a child has the right to life no matter how the child was conceived. These pro-life supporters will often forget that the mother herself deserves the same right to life but is not granted that right because she has an unborn, voiceless child growing inside of her. Some pro-life supporters have gone as far to open fake abortion clinics to scare and terrorize pregnant women into not wanting an abortion. These mothers, no matter how old, are told that they should be happy they have the ability to bear children, even if it kills them or inflicts permanent physical damage.

Tamir Rice, a twelve-year-old boy, was shot within seconds of police officers arriving to the scene at a playground in Cleveland, in response to a 911 call. There was no further investigation, just immediate action taken by the police officials who responded to the call. The same people who had claimed to be pro-life began to state how a child should not play with toys that resemble guns, and how this was essentially the fault of the twelve-year-old boy. People began to speculate where his mother was, if he even had one. This incident came after recent events of police brutality against African American citizens across America, sparking a nationwide movement called Black Lives Matter. These members advocated for police training to include non-bias training, gun reform laws, body cameras, police accountability, and much more. This movement brought to light the many struggles an average African American faces, but because they were facing police brutality, many people silenced their movement with the counter All Lives Matter movement, which was based on blatant racism and ignorance against minority groups. And so his name, along with the movement, have been silenced and swept under the rug, even as similar cases rise in headlines again and again.

Four years after Tamir's life was taken, seventeen more children were executed on Valentine's Day—not by police, but by a former nineteen-year-old student. He was always a threat to the school and has been expelled and reported to the FBI and police because of his threatening behavior. By this time, it was too late to act because he had already done his worst. America has a unique gun problem that is unlike any other in the world, and it comes with deadly consequences that don't question "What if?" but rather "When will it happen again?" This time was different. Immediately, as the victims were carried out in black body bags, their friends had already created a movement that would ensure that these seventeen kids would be the last to ever die in a mass shooting by a weapon built to kill as many people as possible in the shortest amount of time. These mass shootings have become so common, these pro-life supporters began to testify and falsely claim that these survivors were actors hired by news outlets because the media loves the ratings. The supporters have continued to claim that "people kill people" and refuse to acknowledge that guns are a real threat to this nation. The All Lives Matter movement was painstakingly silent as teenagers, no older than I, took the stage and demanded immediate action.

As a generation, we call BS. We aren't even old enough to say the word "bullshit" in front of our parents, but we are still able to recognize that we are all potential targets for the very next mass shooting. We are still able to recognize that this government, that these supporters, do not give a damn about life because they are fighting for the total opposite of what it means to be alive. A strong movement like this has never taken place before and has forced the media to continually cover the Never Again movement as we advocate for the right to life under new pressures for gun reform. The adults that are supposed to be our role models have done nothing but give us a platform to voice our distaste for their ignorance, and this time is the perfect and only time we refuse to be just as silenced as everyone else. We will include and promote the livelihood of every person, of every identity and of all backgrounds, because it has come to the point where no one is safe as long as semiautomatic rifles are available to the public. After that, we have an even bigger agenda to accomplish, and if you think we'll stop, think again. We are the change and the heroes that we have been waiting for, and we call BS.

silence

ELIZABETH ROY

The idea for my piece manifested itself after some texts Sophia and I exchanged about the Parkland school shooting. Sophia's bravery and boldness in her piece inspired me to step outside of my comfort zone and write a poem from the perspective of a person who suffers from mental illness. Our country turns its back on these people. Let's end the silence.

silence

thoughts in my head swirl endlessly

voices

yours or mine?
yours, never directed at me
mine, echo louder than a cannon
sorrow

envelops me like an avalanche I can never outrun

trouble

all around me, surrounding all of you

fear

I am afraid . . . of you, of him, of her, of them
of myself

anger

the rage inside of me might swallow me whole

loneliness

deep inside myself like the bottom of an endless canyon

acceptance

this is me. this is who I am. this defines me.

ending

it's now. it's here. it's over.
silence

MANAR DIHYEM

YEARS AS MENTEE: 1

GRADE: Sophomore

HIGH SCHOOL: MESA Charter High School

BORN: Yonkers, NY

LIVES: Queens, NY

MENTEE'S ANECDOTE: *I've never had a mentor before, but having Annette as my first mentor is a pleasure. My first year in Girls Write Now has been quite a ride. I tried writing in new genres, which is a bit out of my comfort zone. I feel that I'm more confident in my writing. Taking on new challenges has allowed me to connect more with my readers.*

ANNETTE ESTÉVEZ

YEARS AS MENTOR: 2

OCCUPATION: Poet, Office Manager

BORN: Bushwick, NY

LIVES: Queens, NY

MENTOR'S ANECDOTE: *It's been a joy working with Manar, learning about her interests and beliefs, and "embracing awkwardness"—a mantra we came up with together when we first met. One of my proudest moments insofar as Manar's achievements this program year was when a column she wrote for her Girls Write Now portfolio was assigned as supplementary reading material in her high school English class. She continues to shine bright and grow as a writer and individual, and it is a gift to witness and be a part of.*

The Hijab—A Shield or a Threat?

MANAR DIHYEM

I wrote this column based on an assignment from a Girls Write Now Journalism workshop. I also wrote this piece to reflect upon issues currently occurring in the Muslim community.

Some people think that it is a choice for Muslim women to wear the hijab. Others say that it is a non-negotiable requirement. I am a follower of Islam and I am beyond proud of it. Therefore, I follow and agree with the words of the Qur'an—the words of Allah—as it reads that it is essential to wear the hijab if you are a Muslim woman. Unfortunately, due to misrepresentations of Muslims in movies, news reports, and social media, misconceptions are born and spread like wildfire. Despite the bigotry, I choose to wear the hijab, as it is a necessity: a sign of strength, courage, and devotion.

THE BEGINNING

I began to wear the hijab in the fourth grade. I hadn't even hit puberty yet. Mama told me that wearing a hijab is "a sign of strength." When I first entered school wearing the hijab, I thought people would make fun of me, but I was wrong. People thought I looked "cool," which I found confusing. I've had to answer a whole lot of intrusive questions like: *Do you sleep with that on? Do you shower with that on? Don't you get hot in that?* At the time, I was the only hijabi in school and was always told I was "unique" or "different." I never thought of removing my hijab, nor do I plan to.

ASPIRE TO INSPIRE

"The Qur'an actually tells women to cover themselves so that they can be appreciated for who they are as humans instead of being looked at lustfully. Men are also told to dress modestly and to lower their gaze in front of women so as to avoid looking at them lustfully, a sort of veil in itself."* Within a society that views Muslim women as oppressed, it's a sign of resistance to wear the hijab in spite of these biased perceptions. In fact, it's a source of empowerment. There are many role models in the Ummah (Muslim community) who publicly and proudly wear the hijab, such as the journalist Noor Tagouri. Tagouri appeared in one of my favorite TED Talks, "Calling on the 10,000," about Muslim identity. The two cousins, Yasmeena Rasheed and Fatima Abdallah, knowingly and intentionally motivate and inspire many through fashion content shown on their social media platforms. As the years progress, they've gained thousands of followers on their Instagram and YouTube, especially. They empower us to prove the bigots wrong, as Muslims are not animals who kill, abuse, and fight, as American pop culture often suggests.

FAKE NEWS

The media has dehumanized people of the Muslim community, and the president, Donald Trump, encourages this dehumanization. He has enacted unjust rulings, such as the Muslim ban, also known as the travel ban. This ban prevents Muslims from entering the U.S.A. In movies or on the news, non-Muslim actors are hired to say the phrase "Allahu Akbar" before a bombing or a shooting. What people can never seem to understand is that all the phrase means is "God Is the

* Syed, M., "What You Need to Know About Muslim Women, by a Muslim Woman," *Teen Vogue* (March 27, 2017).

Greatest"—simple and innocuous. These misrepresentations promote ignorance to what the Muslim religion truly is—peaceful. Muslims are to attack if being physically attacked. Despite that, harming others is beyond a sin; it is disgraceful. Such legislation and stereotypes affect Muslims' self-perception and others' perceptions of them, affecting their confidence and shattering their pride.

NOT BEHOLDERS OF GRUDGES

I don't blame people who are ignorant to the truth of Islam. They base their knowledge on what the media tells them—fake news. Those who are ignorant are fearful of how we dress and who they believe we are—monsters. When in reality, we fear ignorance. The Qur'an tells us to stay away from ignorance and those who follow it. "Pardon them and overlook—Allah loves those who do good" (Qur'an 5:13).

OVER IT ALL

The media continues to give off negative ideas about Muslims. On the news, when there are shootings or life-threatening accidents, eyes go on the Muslim. Politicians, like our current president, encourage these distorted ideas by passing unjust legislation affecting the Muslim community. People tend to be easily influenced by their leaders, causing them to be negative toward women who wear the hijab and making some Muslims insecure about wearing theirs. It would be a dream if we could vanquish ignorance. Then people would know the absolute truth they deserve. Nobody would give nasty glares to the old lady on the bus praying as she is wearing her hijab with pride. I've always been proud of wearing what is much more than a cloth, a hijab, despite the ignorance and hatred spread about my religion. There are many successful Muslim women who proudly wear the hijab and deliberately influence and inspire young Muslim women to champion their faith and confidently persevere wearing theirs, too. To some, the hijab may be a threat. To Muslim women who wear the hijab, it is a shield—the definition of courage.

Moonflowers

ANNETTE ESTÉVEZ

I wrote this poem to honor my best friends. This piece reflects Generation F, as it highlights the empowerment and strength in sisterhood.

For Jas and Leesah, my Bushwitches

Oye: *las lluvias que caerán sobre nuestros cuerpos*
y mojarán las flores que nos crecen por dentro

Our friendship—prayer
a sunset amethyst

I trust y'all, blindfolded
knowing only the sand and your hands -

the gift of ocean
in the absence of candles

We wish on waves
rising to meet our stars

We manifest constellations
This coming undone

becoming a garden
of teeth   of eyes   of *what if*

what if isn't always doom?
What if we are art as we are?

What if we believe ourselves
worthy of love this constant?

What if we don't? Then
soil   smoke   open doors

heartbeat-to-heartbeat-to-heartbeat
We: bass reverberating infinite

We shake thorns from our chests
feeding the earth with their seeds
We: shed exoskeletons of burden
We: harvest of possibility

Laughing ourselves out of ourselves, we bloom
night, unraveling all the space we need

LAILA DOLA

YEARS AS MENTEE: 1

GRADE: Sophomore

HIGH SCHOOL: Thomas A. Edison Career and Technical Education High School

BORN: Jessore, Khulna, Bangladesh

LIVES: Queens, NY

PUBLICATIONS AND RECOGNITIONS: "The Diversity Visa: A Ticket to a Better Life," *Gotham Gazette*

MENTEE'S ANECDOTE: *Ever since I met Megan, I've never seen her without a big smiley face. She always made my day better and inspired me to smile more often. Through Megan I learned that being an adult just happens and you slowly realize it, and that entering adulthood can be scary but I will slowly get the hang of it. I learned a lot through the experiences she shared with me. Megan never fails to find a happy approach to the things around her. She is AWESOME and BEAUTIFUL. Megan is changing the world with her beautiful smile.*

MEGAN ELMORE

YEARS AS MENTOR: 1

OCCUPATION: Assistant Production Editor, Penguin Random House

BORN: Rochester, NY

LIVES: Brooklyn, NY

MENTOR'S ANECDOTE: *From the moment I met Laila I was impressed and inspired by her outgoing personality and positive approach to life. Even when her schoolwork is overwhelming or when she feels like an outsider, she always manages to find the silver lining and the grace in every situation. She brings a sunny outlook and a determined work ethic to everything she does, whether it's her beloved Web design class or a Girls Write Now workshop. I have really enjoyed getting to know her and I have no doubt that she'll go forth to change the world.*

The Clouds That Smile

LAILA DOLA

This piece is inspired by my personal struggles and how I overcame them with the optimism that I had inside me and that other people brought to me.

As I sit by the window
I sense the sun looking at me,
Its neon red-orange vibes staring at my insecurities.
As I look up to meet its eyes,
I feel the sunshine lighten my spirit,
Making my dark brown eyes look like bright brown-red.

I can sense optimism rising in my soul,
But then, suddenly, the dark clouds surrounding the sun
Start to prevent the rays from meeting my heart.
Now I can sense the emptiness inside my soul,
As if pessimism has started to take control.

I can still see a little bit of optimism left inside me,
So I quickly smile at the clouds and wave them a hello
Because they say that a smile can brighten the darkest days,
And remove the clouds of fear and doubt.
But my intention was not to drive away the clouds,
Rather it was to embrace them and turn them into a positive
    crowd.
And as the clouds change their frowning face,

They smile back and grin as if someone has finally understood
    their grace.

You see, all my life I've felt misunderstood.
At home, at school, on the streets, or in nearby stores.
The desolation inside my heart is something I cannot explain,
But it's not like anyone wants to hear my pain.
By now I am used to comforting myself.
And I've learned to tell myself "I'm strong."

As I walk through the main entrance of my school,
Or sit there inside a classroom,
I feel like my body is on earth but my mind has flown away to
    Mars.
I feel judged based on my test scores,
And the flaming report cards that feel like a stamp classifying
    my future
It's as if they have the capacity to define who I am.
But I've learned to follow my heart and stop letting numbers
    define my potential.

As I walk on the streets,
I feel like a burden drowning this entire universe.
I pass by the lamppost and the humongous trees,
Feeling so little and invisible as if no one sees.
I feel a sudden force pushing me onto the ground.
And as I struggle to get up, no one reaches out a hand,
But that is how I learned to stand up on my own.

Everyone stares at me as if I am an alien,
As if I am a failure which no one deserves to look at.
As if I did something wrong every minute of my life,

And I have to justify all my actions and make sure everyone
    knows
that there's no bomb in my black plastic bag or inside my
    backpack.
I cannot fit in with society's terms.
I usually feel like an outcast.

I fail to formulate a reason for the sudden increase of my
    heartbeat,
And for the tears in my eyes that are overflowing.
I'm going crazy overthinking everything.
Yes, I sense the world in front of me,
The roads and pathways to many opportunities.
But sometimes it can be very intimidating.
So I taught myself to ask questions and figure out solutions.

But deep inside my heart,
I know that we're all the same in terms of being a human.
That we all sometimes feel rejected.

So if you feel like a dark cloud is storming inside,
I'm here to tell you that optimism still lies within you.
So don't give up and keep moving forward,
And turn those dark moments of your life into beautiful
    lessons to learn from.
And that is the power of positivity.
Within you lies humanity.

The Place We've Made

MEGAN ELMORE

Laila's relentless optimism inspired me to work through my anger and hopelessness I feel about our current political climate to find the simple goodness that we're all capable of bringing to the world.

on the days I most want to burn the world to ashes—
down to the charred detritus of men's unwanted touches,
    presidential tweets and YouTube comment sections—
I think of how much easier it would be
to go inside a warm, dark place
and wait for the halcyon days of spring to arrive
dripping wet with freshness and vitality and possibility.

how much easier to hide oneself away,
but how impossible,
how even inside the bear's closed den the fingers of frost
    creep.

to be safe in this world seems more impossible with each
    passing day;
and even the expectation of safety,
once unquestioned,
somehow rings naïve.

a girl fainted in front of me on the C train last year,
crumpling to the floor silently, without warning, and
all at once our sleepy train burst into action.

someone rolled the girl onto her side because she had started
    to shake;
two other women pressed the emergency call button to alert
    the train operator;
another man stood there shouting that she'd had a seizure and
    that she'd peed herself,
which was neither helpful nor accurate.

and I could do nothing
except kneel on the floor of the car with the girl's curly brown
    head in my lap,
so she wouldn't wake with her head on the filthy train floor.

in the end, that may be what matters most in this life,
doing what we can in the face of fear and uncertainty,
even when the lure of the warm, dark place beckons,
the lure of the safe place,
because increasingly we learn that these places are not
    inviolable
and because the only real place we have is the one that's right
    here,
and we must make of it what we can.

KIMBERLY DOMINGUEZ

YEARS AS MENTEE: 1

GRADE: Sophomore

HIGH SCHOOL: Academy of American Studies

BORN: Queens, NY

LIVES: Queens, NY

PUBLICATIONS AND RECOGNITIONS: 2018 Scholastic Art & Writing Award: Honorable Mention

MENTEE'S ANECDOTE: *My mentor has helped me explore new forms of writing, such as journalism. The sharing of her favorite articles has made me want to write and read pieces similar to those and also educate myself more on important and newsworthy topics. She also helped me develop more interests, such as art and new dystopian novels. Reading one of her favorite novels,* Brave New World, *changed my perspective on our current politics and social customs.*

ELIZABETH THOMAS

YEARS AS MENTOR: 1

OCCUPATION: Director of Content Strategy, New York Law School

BORN: Norfolk, VA

LIVES: Queens, NY

MENTOR'S ANECDOTE: *My mentee, Kimberly, has infected me with her passion for great poetry! As a result, it's a form I'm now exploring. She also encouraged me to read her favorite book,* 1984, *and I enjoyed the many conversations we had afterward about its themes and relevance to society. I have also loved discussing Kimberly's interest in art and the notion of who "owns" art, an idea she has explored in her writing.*

Dianthus

KIMBERLY DOMINGUEZ

*This piece follows a feminine figure as she encounters and accepts a
new companion. I was exploring and experimenting with different
ideas outside of my realm.*

A quiet walk down a solemn street
It slowly creeps around the corner,
And turns in the direction of the wind,
As it glides through the Night,
Seeking your Scent

It whispers in your ear
Tugs on your hair
Skims the side of your hip

It observes you from behind,
Its silhouette visible from the corner of your eye

It follows you home and slips through the doorway
It presses on your chest while you lay in bed

The next morning it stares at you through the mirror,
As you apply your mother's lipstick

It walks with you to the subway,
And sits beside you on the empty train car,
Your shoulder brushing against it

One day,
You followed it instead
Other days,
You left the door open

Its Warmth kept you close,
Its Breaths became your own,
As you inhaled its Dianthus Scent

Daylight Saving

ELIZABETH THOMAS

I have been inspired by Kimberly to explore poetic forms, and this piece is different from most of my writing. The narrator is a woman evaluating her decisions and contemplating change.

A soft drip from the upstairs pipe
is weakening my ceiling. And
behind the plaster of these walls,
the wood is aging in the dark.
And buried in the cabinets,
the baking pan is caked with crumbs.
The floor is soft, like spoiled fruit
unused but past its usefulness.

So many things I have ignored
in hours or days, I thought,
or weeks, I would repair them but
instead they waited months or years,
like dying trees in public parks
or beaches stripped of shells and sand
or lonely birds who perch on rocks,
as seasons changed and years rolled by like cars.

But I can feel a coming change
that seeps in through the window gaps,
and waits behind the closet walls,
and comes in vapors through the pipes,

and streaks the sky in rose and gold.
Another chance to start again
to leave the old things on the ground
to walk out of the room and close the door.

JOLI-AMOUR DUBOSE-MORRIS

YEARS AS MENTEE: 1

GRADE: Junior

HIGH SCHOOL: Benjamin N. Cardozo High School

BORN: Queens, NY

LIVES: Queens, NY

PUBLICATIONS AND RECOGNITIONS: 2018 Scholastic Art & Writing Awards: Honorable Mention, Silver Key

MENTEE'S ANECDOTE: *One time, Alex and I went to the Museum of the Moving Image, and something had happened to me the day before. My mood was quite gloomy. Being with Alex at the museum definitely did more than just inspire my writing, it uplifted my spirits as well. We sat at a table after giggling throughout the Muppets exhibit, and she bought this strange donut. We sat there for two hours and I shared with her the reasons behind my sadness. Alex enlightened me with words that eased my pain and reminded me that "people" come and go.*

ALEXANDREA KLIMOSKI

YEARS AS MENTOR: 1

OCCUPATION: Associate Editor, *Architectural Record*

BORN: New York, NY

LIVES: Queens, NY

PUBLICATIONS AND RECOGNITIONS: "Magazzino Italian Art," *Architectural Record* (March 2017)

MENTOR'S ANECDOTE: *In the room, before we met, Joli sat in the front row, and I a few behind her. I first noticed her from the back of her head. Her hair was adorned with dozens of beads—some wood, some with metal embellishments. Since then, she's donned several hairstyles, each uniquely her. Joli has cultivated a rich sense of style for a young person, and exhibits a strong sense of self. She isn't afraid to explore what's inside her. She is a brilliant artist. Her curiosity and dedication inspire me to push my own boundaries as a writer. Her spunk energizes me.*

Lonely, Womanly

JOLI-AMOUR DUBOSE-MORRIS

This piece is about existing, specifically as a soon-to-be woman. It is about approaching adulthood and womanhood, and accepting growing up, even if we feel unfit to exist.

THE WORLD IS SMALL, microscopic, dense, and it's intense. The cities aren't as big as one perceives them to be. Yes, there are streets, alleyways, and the buildings cave inward like pop-up cards on Valentine's Day. Except I've never received a card from anyone other than my mother.

THE PEOPLE ARE SO LARGE, I wish I could peel my skin off and try someone else on for a change.
     Yet that is not possible,
     I guess I'll have to grasp on to myself, and what's left of it, and grow into a woman to be, even if the small child beneath her isn't okay with where she is, and where she's supposed to be.

My eyes are burning, as if they are washcloths getting wringed out so tight.
     I still right my wrongs.
     Womanhood vastly approaches like the alarm clock
     we knock over when it dawns six and sleep has to be postponed because right now, morning calls.

The duties of human are to talk and socialize but I disguise myself in various hairstyles and teary eyes. I'm not acquainted with Womanhood but she sits at the table of adulthood and cocks her brow with a poise that I've always dreamed of having. Womanhood and I will never be friends because she holds a better résumé and is ready to perform her flirtatious repertoires.

I've said it before, I am afraid to grow up,
    yet it dawns on me that Womanhood is the first to show up, her hugs warm and motherly, but I don't need another mother, I just want more friends. I wander through the world like a solemn ghost with wild hair, and everyone sits next to everyone else while I'm that *one* that doesn't know what or who I belong to, unless I'm supposed to remain by myself.

No matter where I am,
    silence saunters sonorously around me
    and it weighs, and w
                    e
                 i
              g
           h
         s.
    The cities are so small, but the density comes from the intensity of the amount of people existing around one another. Then there's me. Somewhere in between being a kid and a woman, kind of lost, and kind of found, but unsure of what foot to step with next. Womanhood sits on the bus, and she sits beside me, and whatever comes after that,
    is unwritten history, perhaps.

Saturn Returns

ALEXANDREA KLIMOSKI

This piece is about being in limbo. It's a reflection on being in between a young person and an adult. It's about questioning my own femininity and what it means to be a woman. It's an observation of myself. It's a stream-of-consciousness about nothing.

It always takes me a while to leave the house. I like to be relaxed when I rush; to linger in the day's first thoughts of nothingness; to sit motionless in my most adult-looking chair, eyes fixated on my sleeping cat's rapid, subconscious ear movements. I wallow in the shiny newness of each morning.

My horoscope dictates that I have a tendency to overindulge. It warns me about gaining weight from gluttony. It assures me that I am stubborn, almost insists that I am lazy. I once looked to my aura for some better, alternative perspective. It was a baritone blue that oozed into a fringe of black. It silently screamed: *You are plagued by ambivalence.* What gives?

I'm twenty-seven and desperately trying to know myself. But how to know oneself? How to love oneself? I'd crawl down every pulpy cavern of my brain to find out. But I'm always too tired.

On the street I passed a man discussing vegan lasagna with his companion. As he passed I could not help but mutter the words: "Vegan lasagna! Vegan lasagna!"

I mocked a strange man for his vegan lasagna. I wonder if I will always be this cynical.

It occurs to me that I do not possess the "womanly" qualities that my seventeen-year-old self fancied I would. I still am bad at laundry. I still cannot walk in heels. And I still can pass for seventeen if I wear my hair a certain way.

I'm the type of person who will leave a near-empty bottle of Diet Coke in the fridge, not because I'm convinced that I will savor that last drop of flat, caramel-colored liquid, but because, hey, I'll just throw it out next time. I leave glossy catalogs and oversized envelopes to amass in my narrow, cramped mailbox. I let my plants die.

But my mother is a myth wrapped in an exquisite layer of flesh. She exudes femininity with celestial ease. At the beach, she drapes her skin in linen. She has a greaseless stovetop and dons red lipstick to the grocery store and she always smells sweet. The scent of my perfume never lasts past three o'clock. My lips are always chapped. I often feel unsexy.

Will I ever be like my mother? Will I be a mother? Will I get cancer? Am I going crazy?

I'll find out, I'm told, when Saturn returns.

JACQUELYN EKE

YEARS AS MENTEE: 2

GRADE: Senior

HIGH SCHOOL: The Bronx School for Law, Government and Justice

BORN: Bronx, NY

LIVES: Bronx, NY

PUBLICATIONS AND RECOGNITIONS: Scholastic Art & Writing Awards: Honorable Mention

MENTEE'S ANECDOTE: *I enjoyed working on my college essays in our pair sessions.*

JOCELYN CASEY-WHITEMAN

YEARS AS MENTOR: 2

OCCUPATION: Writing and Yoga Teacher

BORN: Annapolis, MD

LIVES: New York, NY

MENTOR'S ANECDOTE: *Jacquelyn is a strong, determined, and honest young writer. Her courage to write through challenging circumstances and her commitment to building a bright future for herself and her community inspires.*

The Letter

JACQUELYN EKE

This is a voice from my generation speaking to another generation.

Grandfather, Mom, and Grandma are going at it again.

The cement covering of your grave is still intact.
During the rainy season, it grows mold.
Sometimes we play on it; sometimes, Grandma strokes it,
    whispers.
Tears on her mahogany skin.

I'm sure she's telling you about her day. I'm not sure
you can hear.

They have cut the mango tree in the backyard. I don't know why.
The one in the front is still there. We eat from it during the
    dry season.

Your children speak your name with reverence,
but Grandfather, I'm afraid you'll be forgotten.
Your friends are dying, too.
Your siblings succumb one by one, children also.

Do you see them where you are?
Do you see my father or have his sins caught up to him?
Does he speak of me?
Does he love me?

Grandfather, things are the same, but so different.
The sun shines while it rains.
Our hearts are stitched but still broken.

Ceremony

JOCELYN CASEY-WHITEMAN

This poem considers resilience in our current moment.

Sun through cobalt glass pours a river
on hardwood floor. Lines contain grit

the broom could not. Outside, the weather
rearranges wheat until the field

fills with roman numerals brushed in gold.
Inside, nerves begin to soothe after a shock

that made the blood beat hot.
Clouds spread charcoal blue.

I try to count the field before night takes hold.
I don't know if life will ever be fair

but when it's quiet and without threat
I feel roots reach through earth,

and in my chest, a rhythm I remember.
Despite the wind, I keep the candles lit.

Maybe the world isn't ending.
Maybe it's a mirror that takes courage to see.

ABBY FISHER

YEARS AS MENTEE: 2

GRADE: Junior

HIGH SCHOOL: The Abraham Joshua Heschel School

BORN: Riverdale, NY

LIVES: Bronx, NY

PUBLICATIONS AND RECOGNITIONS: Scholastic Art & Writing Awards: Silver Key; "When Is the Me Too Movement Finally Going to Make it to My High School?" *The Huffington Post*

MENTEE'S ANECDOTE: *I was nervous when I met Aimee for the first time. Getting matched with a mentor is like going on a blind date. But this blind date went so well, we might as well be an ad for Match.com. Aimee gets me. She pushes me out of my comfort zone and our discussions are always interesting. In our meetings, I feel myself growing both as a writer and as person.*

AIMEE HERMAN-DURICA

YEARS AS MENTOR: 1

OCCUPATION: Teacher

BORN: Somerville, NJ

LIVES: Brooklyn, NY

PUBLICATIONS AND RECOGNITIONS: *My Body, My Words: A Collection of Bodies*

MENTOR'S ANECDOTE: *The first time Abby and I met, we unraveled our thoughts on feminism and our reactions to the state of the world. Our conversations have been deeply nourishing to me. She is so articulate in her self-expression. I've also been so impressed by Abby's drive and dedication not only as a writer, but as a positive and well-educated presence. I've enjoyed thinking up new prompts to bring to our sessions, and I find that she helps me to approach my own writing in new ways. I feel better about the future of this world knowing she's a part of it.*

Song of Myself

ABBY FISHER

My poem aims to turn the challenge myself and other girls of Generation F have to face into something worthy of celebration. It is a modern reimagining of Whitman's "Song of Myself."

I celebrate every letter in my name and every word in my body
Every comma of bone
Every exclamation point smile turned
    question-mark frown . . . and back again?
My semicolon waist . . .

Have you yet learned the grammar of your ligaments?
Have you yet become self-literate?
Do not erase your graphite smudges
    to become legible to others
Replace all your "but"s with "and"s . . . let yourself be plural
Live in the contradictions without . . . fear of being
    understood

I celebrate my allergies . . . the ways my body knows her limits
    there are some things she will not accept . . . I will not accept
Any cell in my body is a fighter . . .
    any self in my body is a fighter

The song of pen scratching paper . . . the sound of beautiful
    friction,
    Pulse, raw cuticles, the taste of metal, the school bell,

The world's conjugation and subjugation
The rhythm of sweat sliding at the pace of tears . . . My
    anxiety is worth boasting about
I am worth boasting about

The cacophony of my heart burning madly is not a disorder
How long have you believed the world . . . . you are the
    one in need of reorder?
I celebrate the lone eggshell in the sink
The recipe called for three . . . I cleared away two
Know I was here
Accept my un-apology for taking up space

I celebrate each superstition . . . religious as a holiday . . .
    spiritual as a bedtime story
I look away from the teapot so it can boil
I deliberate over eyelash wishes
I turn reality into ritual . . . I am not pretending

Study the language of yourself
Teach it to others and be patient
Remember that for so long you had dyslexia of the self . . . the
    world twisted you into an alphabet you did not recognize
Learn your letters, the words of your body
Start with your name

Dear Universe (A Manifesto)

AIMEE HERMAN-DURICA

I was walking my dog, singing prayers to the universe, thinking about all the ways wishes can be manifested through footsteps and howls. This poem fell out of me, followed me home, ate lunch with me, asked me why I call myself a feminist and all I could say was: Because the fight continues and I'm sharpening my tongue.

Dear Universe, I want a full-time teaching job and at least two closets in my apartment and a complete understanding of the difference between "effect" and "affect." That time I asked my students to stare at one another for sixty seconds (insert laughter, discomfort, and a continuous need to look away) and my student, who tried so hard to share his eyes with me, kept whispering how hard it is to look at someone who isn't speaking. And when we shared our experiences afterward, I asked him the color of my eyes; he said *silver.* Dear Universe, I want to see the shiny in me too.

Dear Universe, when did you tell me that none of this would end, that brains congeal and there is only so much a scalpel can remove?

I used to collect ants, scooped them up like cake crumbs and spelled out prayers with their slow-moving bodies. Dear Universe, can religion be that simple?

Dear Universe, I don't know how to hashtag, but it happened, keeps happening.

Dear Universe, when my ribs were the only cage I climbed into. Yes, can we go back to that?

One night when I ran out of things to hold, I gulped down enough street signs to make me feel like I understood what I was doing. Cut my tongue on their sharp edges and I still got lost. Dear Universe, my belly contains a GPS but it always brings me back to where I am afraid of going.

Dear Universe, there is a mouse living inside my oven, so I haven't cooked anything proper in months. I rolled up a poem and set it on fire hoping the ashes of words would lead it elsewhere. Like that time I read Vera Pavlova and she led me out of that mental hospital. Sometimes we just need an extra map to free ourselves from borrowed kilns or bone breaks.

I want a backyard to plant dandelions and hyaloclastite. Universe, can you give me some land to roam against?

Somehow my wrists slipped their way out of midnight and I am collecting sharps again. Like a brushfire. Like a tic-tac-toe board of blood and guts. Dear Universe, I don't need any more Band-Aids; it's surgery time.

Remember when guns sprayed water instead of organs? I left the country of my body because my passport expired and I lost the code to get in. Dear Universe, can you leave the back door open?

ZOE FISHER

YEARS AS MENTEE: 1

GRADE: Junior

HIGH SCHOOL: The Clinton School

BORN: New York, NY

LIVES: New York, NY

MENTEE'S ANECDOTE: *Meg is very kind and generous. On our first meeting outside of Girls Write Now, we both wrote a poem relating to a rainy day. I didn't know her for long when I was invited to see a play along with her family. She has challenged me to want to be a nicer and more caring person. Meg uses her computer a lot since most of her work involves one, but once you step into her house there are so many books and aesthetic-looking items. When I saw that, it made me realize I need to read more real books.*

MEG CASSIDY

YEARS AS MENTOR: 4

OCCUPATION: Book Publicist

BORN: Milwaukee, WI

LIVES: New York, NY

MENTOR'S ANECDOTE: *I so look forward to my Wednesday-evening sessions with Zoe; she always has funny stories to share from her school day, and it's the perfect break for my own work-day stressors. It's been amazing how often our thoughts and themes on the page overlap, despite what different worlds we come from. She's inspired me to be more bold in my own fiction writing, and I've been so impressed with how much of herself she has shared with me this year through her poetry writing. I feel honored to get to know her more each time we get together.*

REBIRTH

ZOE FISHER

Alexia lives in a future world where people choose their appearance, then get transmitted into a file to live in a technological world forever. In this piece, I try to address how social media affects women's views of themselves.

The electricity runs throughout my body, turning my veins neon blue. The feeling is exhilarating as it spreads everywhere. My hands explore my new-and-improved facial features. All of the liquid inside the syringe is injected in my veins. I waste no time pulling it out, but as I do, the same liquid shoots up from the bottom of the tank. I try to stop it, but I can't find the source. I start to panic as it reaches my ankles. I don't remember this happening in the transformation videos. I pound rapidly on the glass, but the robots just continue working. I try to yell at them to do something, but nothing changes. As the liquid fills half the tank the sirens go off. The bots only turn their attention to me now and finally begin to scramble for what I hope is a solution.

I don't want to be here. I've dreaded my eighteenth birthday for this very reason. The whole idea of becoming a part of technology has scared me. An idiot named Klaus decided that instead of everyone hating their appearances, what if we chose what we wanted to look like? Sounds great, right? No. It was fine when it was just plastic surgery and it was optional. But this guy, he wanted it to be enforced for *everyone*—to implant technology into every human vein. Just one problem, no two people can look the same. So the features and skin tone options always change, not to mention you can't choose your original features. However, people still didn't like the way they looked, so what happens? Pills. When you start feeling insecure you take a pill, when you feel sad you take a pill, when you feel depressed you take a pill, when you're feeling anything except euphoria, pop a pill. No one knows what's in these pills, but hey, they make people happy.

This whole problem goes way back to the twenty-first century. Social media gave people a chance to hide and be someone they weren't. They were able to see people from all over the world and envy them. But because they were hiding behind a screen they weren't actually being seen. No one could tell if they were ugly or pretty. That ideal inspired that stupid idiot to create this Design Yourself law for all of society. Klaus became worshipped like a god. It would've been wiser for him to try to help people understand beauty lies within, but it's too late for that now.

The liquid is almost at the top of the tank. Maybe this is what I get for hating this system so much. I take my last breath as I prepare myself to die. I've been raised like everyone else to love this day. The "Rebirth" is the official name. But I was fine with the way I looked. I didn't want to change, but I didn't have a choice. Maybe dying is freedom. I feel my lungs needing air, but there's nowhere to go to get it. A robot with a giant drill comes up to the glass. My body starts to shake and I close my eyes as the bot begins drilling into the glass.

I open my eyes, but they immediately shut from the bright light above my head. They open slowly adjusting to the light. The smell of rubbing alcohol fills my nostrils. I'm in a hospital. Someone holds my hand and I follow their arm until I see them.

"Mom?" I ask, dryly surprised to see her here.

"Hi Alexia sweetie. You look beautiful." She cups my cheek. I've only seen and heard my parents through an iPad. I've waited all my life for this moment. I hope she's here because I'm in heaven.

"I'm not dead?"

"Of course not, baby. You made it through Rebirth. You're in Technotopia." My heart breaks. I'm just a file in some department somewhere. My body is gone. I'm just digital makeup now. I look past her to see the window. My mouth drops as I see the tall buildings and hovering transportation. I can see the same blue electricity that ran through my veins in everything. I look at my mother and the room only to see that I can see it in her, too. The overexposure to the liquid has allowed me to see the currents running through everything here. "Sweetie, what is it?" My mother's calm voice brings my attention back to her.

"Nothing," I lie. "It's just Technotopia is better in person," I add to convince her.

"That's what everyone says." She smiles warmly. "Well, let's take you home." *Home.* My home is back out there. Back in the real world, but it's too late to go back there now, so I nod and sit up. She helps me to my feet as I accept my fate. I'm forever stuck in a mask of a false reality, far from understanding the truth of beauty.

Spring Green

MEG CASSIDY

I found it interesting that Zoe chose to write about a generation in the future, whereas mine is about a woman, and a town, very much stuck in the past. Springtime and adolescence have an obvious correlation, but in this story I wanted to explore how the "late spring" season in a young woman's life has expanded so dramatically over recent years, at least for some of us.

Thanks to the rarely washed windows at the front of the diner, I can see just enough of my reflection to pretend I'm still fifteen. When I started working here, my mind ran wild with thoughts of saving for one-way tickets to California, college tuition, a tiny apartment of my own in a big city. I counted every penny, letting the same men I went to church with pinch my ass as they ordered lunch. It all seemed worthwhile watching the measly tips add up. And my boyfriend joked that I'd amassed a small fortune—right before we drained it all on a modest wedding and baby furniture.

These days, I could run the place in my sleep, serving up rounds of corned-beef hash in a fugue state to the locals, who now treat me indifferently. The tips were slightly higher when I started, sure, before they got used to seeing me in the same uniform, sometimes stretched over a pregnant belly, but I prefer their apathy. No wagers over my virginity as I walk away from card games, no phone numbers written in threatening scrawls on bar tabs. We've settled into a dysfunctional family dynamic I'll probably be part of until this place implodes.

It's fine, I convince myself, whenever my girlhood daydreams reappear. It's easy to spend my days here. And what else would I do at the ripe old age of twenty-six?

My biggest worry is that Daisy, my teenage sister, won't get out of this town, either. As messed-up as it sounds, she's become my second chance. Weekends are a drag without her coming in after school once the lunch crowd clears and all the rusty Trump-stickered pickup trucks have driven away.

I was surprised the first time Daisy and her friends came strolling in like regulars. I'd hosted them for sleepovers, but standing there in my dull blue dress made me self-conscious. Still, I was tempted to pull up a chair and join them over Cokes and grilled cheese. Ron, the owner, often told me it was good business to have "pretty young things behind the counter," so I assumed he'd have no problem with them loitering on the other side.

I realize how pathetic it is that the promise of them coming in defines my days. Staring back at my muted reflection in the window, I tell myself, for the first time in years, that something has to change.

REGINA FONTANELLI

YEARS AS MENTEE: 2

GRADE: Senior

HIGH SCHOOL: Edward R. Murrow High School

BORN: Brooklyn, NY

LIVES: Brooklyn, NY

PUBLICATIONS AND RECOGNITIONS: Scholastic Art & Writing Awards: Gold Key and five Honorable Mentions; Posse Scholarship recipient

MENTEE'S ANECDOTE: *If there's one person who deserves credit for helping me develop my voice and confidence as a writer, it's Shannon Carlin. She's such a hard worker and a lil' competitive, but I am, too, so we fuel each other. She's my FAVE to talk about the Oscars with (though we disagree about* Lady Bird*), and other subjects in general. THE LADY KEEPS ME SANE, BRO. Seriously, I came to Shannon a sweaty mess, and while I'm still sweaty, I'm not a mess. Truly blessed to have this extremely talented, confident woman as my role model the last two years.*

SHANNON CARLIN

YEARS AS MENTOR: 3

OCCUPATION: Entertainment Journalist

BORN: Ronkonkoma, NY

LIVES: Brooklyn, NY

PUBLICATIONS AND RECOGNITIONS: *Bustle*, Refinery29, *Bust* magazine, and wrote a feature on Rupi Kaur for *Rolling Stone*

MENTOR'S ANECDOTE: *Regina spent this year writing about herself. First, with her college essay, which helped her get a full scholarship to Middlebury College. (I'll brag for her in case she doesn't.) Then her memoir, which is excerpted here. When we first met, Regina was a poet who wasn't ready to tell her own story. Now, a year later, she's putting her vulnerability on display with a confidence I wish I had. I can't wait to see what she writes next, long after Girls Write Now and our weekly meetings. But I hope she knows I'll always be here to give it a read.*

Swing Sets

REGINA FONTANELLI

This is an excerpt from my memoir, Swing Sets. *In the piece, I share many of my truths for the first time. In this particular section, I'm fourteen, struggling to accept myself and my situation.*

High school is a welcome change. Here, dressing like you're poor is cool and my long hair is beautifully feminine, though the reality is that I'm just too broke for a haircut. It's not long before someone notices my glow sophomore year, and it all goes downhill. He is long, like a string bean, and pale as a sheet of paper. His Adam's apple bobs awkwardly and his dark bangs contrast so greatly with his complexion that he looks ill. From the way he eyes me, I know he thinks I'm beautiful. Sexy. I sop up his attention like a sponge would water. Glance back at him, shy, the way I think I'm supposed to glance at him. It's only a number of days before we are dating. By dating, I mean hooking up in his apartment after he gets me high.

The joint and his mouth taste bitter. Blacken the inside of my lungs, but I don't care. My euphoria with freedom is becoming tiresome, and I wish I had a mother who didn't vomit first thing in the morning, and ate meals at regular hours of the day. His parents, an art dealer and a music producer, have three well-balanced meals a day *around a table.* Whenever I kiss him, I think about how charming I'd be if I were to meet them, how I'd pass a porcelain bowl of snap peas to his dad and heartily laugh at his mother's jokes. Like every ingénue on every show I've ever watched.

I take up drinking with him and his friends by the Gowanus and unknowingly tag along on trips to steal Triple C at Rite Aid. One boy with a triangle face and piercing blue eyes becomes a friend. I share with him how my boyfriend treats me, and he shares with me how my eyebrows are too dark. He tells me I'm fucking dumb, but only because he cares.

By March, I'm cutting myself with butter knives and razors. In my mind, I see myself going too deep, being too absorbed in the process, and slicing through my jugular veins, so tiny Bic blades and ribbed knives are all I use. Another cutter and I become friends, and we spend hours in her bed, counting scars and crossing each other's wounds. My journal at that time, a fifty-cent marble with pages loose at the binding, soon fills with poetry about her. This is when I realize there may be more to the jittery feeling I get around girls.

On Easter Sunday, my mom cannot cheer me up. There is a small, momentary reversal in the roles we share. She applies blush haughtily in our toothpaste-flecked bathroom mirror, while I stare expressionless at my reflection. I do not put on makeup. I do not speak. I do not change.

"What's wrong, Gina?" she asks. The holiday has rejuvenated her Catholic spirit and brought to life her favorite memories.

I say nothing. Pull down my pants to reveal where my thighs are marked and bleeding. The expression on her face falters, but her lips quickly resume their previous position. Her eyes take on a stony look.

"Go get dressed."

So I do, but the next day, I ask my friend for her therapist's number, because it's clear no one is there to take care of me but myself.

Rebecca is a holistic Wiccan. In her drawer, there are salves and serums and lemon-scented lotions she makes herself. She's on the skinny side, with a sunny face. In her office, I mourn the life I have always wanted. The one with the father who carries me on his shoulders and threatens to "take the bat out" on boys my age. The one who held my left hand while my mother held my right, and lifted me across the street. The one where my mother is an art dealer, or a kindergarten teacher, or a veterinarian who asks me how I'm doing every day after school, and always makes sure there's food in the house. The one where we all sit in the library talking about the books we've read and the grades I'm getting and how I'm liking the drama classes they've enrolled me in.

In her office, I've killed the dreams of being beautiful, owning stylish clothing. The dreams where boys fawn over me, lust over me. Where I own jeans that fit my heart-shaped bottom perfectly. Where I wear PINK sweaters and have perfectly straight hair, perfectly straight nails, and perfectly straight sexuality.

I've put flowers on the grave of being everything I'm not. Set up a lovely ceremony; hired a priest to bury my Catholic upbringing; and invited the pew of old, wrinkly leather-ladies who made me feel I wasn't light enough, skinny enough, *woman* enough to be beautiful. I've done my alms, burned my palms, got my last rites read, all under the concerned, squinting eyes of my kind, hippie therapist.

The Memories of My Mom, Hidden in Pierogi Dough

SHANNON CARLIN

At the Intergenerational Memoir workshop, I wrote about my mom and the power of food memories. It was mostly ramblings about pierogi, but after reading Regina's memoir I wanted to turn it into something real.

My mom picks and chooses how she remembers her family. That's the only luxury of them no longer being around. While my dad's family boasts all six of his younger siblings, their seventeen kids, five grandkids, and his over-eighty-year-old mother, my mom's family has been depleted by dementia and cancer. Worse may be those relatives who've just been lost to time, completely forgotten, to be remembered only through foggy hindsight once they're physically gone.

My mom jokes, like most people do, that her family is weird, but in actuality, they're gamblers, liars, and con artists. It's hard to imagine this is Jeanne Lamb's lineage. The woman who wouldn't let me cheat at Pretty Pretty Princess, concerned it would lead to bad habits. The woman who once drove an elderly stranger around my neighborhood until she remembered where she lived. If there's anything seedy in her past, she's hid it well, but that wouldn't surprise me. My mom's memories are hers and hers alone, locked away, possibly forever. I know only what she wants me to know.

My mom will talk about her mom, Lydia, who tap-danced

and played softball well into her seventies before Alzheimer's made her forget who she was. My mom never will, though. My nanny and poppy, James Philo—a Boston Bruins farm player, hotelier, and a chef—are in every recipe my mom has managed to salvage over fifty-nine years.

My mom makes pierogies every Christmas Eve and it's in the preparation of those delicious Polish dumplings that I begin to understand where she came from. The care she takes when mashing the potatoes with a hand-me-down medieval tool and grinding in her ruby-red KitchenAid the brisket that she scoured multiple stores to find. That agony of finding the perfect re-placement four-inch-diameter glass to cut the dough after the one my nanny used shattered. It's all to keep the best parts of her family alive.

My mom used the "wrong" flour one year. "It's always Gold Medal," she said, barely audible over everyone's chewing. But I understood, it didn't taste like her mom's, another sad reminder of how easily she could lose them all over again.

My mom keeps those memories hidden in that dough, tucked away so she doesn't have to say them out loud. For now, I will quietly eat them, pretending that is enough.

MARIA RITA FURTADO

YEARS AS MENTEE: 1

GRADE: Senior

HIGH SCHOOL: The Mary Louis Academy

BORN: Recife, Brazil

LIVES: Queens, NY

PUBLICATIONS AND RECOGNITIONS: Scholastic Art & Writing Awards: Honorable Mention

MENTEE'S ANECDOTE: *My mentor opened me up to new forms of poetry that are different from the classic schools of poetry I have learned in school or from my peers' poetry. I never knew poetry could be the way it was until Emily took me to my first poetry reading and exposed me to more radical and expressive forms of writing. I was also inspired by the writers I met who were pursuing their writing no matter what.*

EMILY PRESENT

YEARS AS MENTOR: 1

OCCUPATION: Administrative Assistant, Jefferies; Editor/Founder, *Glitter-MOB*

BORN: New York, NY

LIVES: Brooklyn, NY

PUBLICATIONS AND RECOGNITIONS: *Souvenir Lit, METATRON, Hobart Pulp, Cosmonauts Avenue*

MENTOR'S ANECDOTE: *My mentee has inspired and challenged me to think differently about how to share and express experimental work to a younger audience. I was so thrilled to take her to an art exhibit at MoMA and a poetry reading in an artist's studio. But above all else, she has constantly awed me with her creativity, her candor, and her courage.*

The Colors of You

MARIA RITA FURTADO

This poem represents Generation F because it is about fierce emotions and not being afraid to express them. I believe this is something that embodies my generation.

Evil comes in all different colors
Especially the green in your eyes
And the golden specks of amber

That gleam in the moonlight.

But also in the faded blue of your jeans,
The ones that fit my hand just right
When I slip it into your back pocket.

It comes in dark brown—
That scar you got
From the last homecoming football game.

It comes in polished wooden brown—
your hair
whenever you run your hands through it,
or when you don't run your hands through it.

I like it better like that anyways.

But mostly,
It comes in Fire Island orange.

Because I remember that as the last color I saw—
Before you turned off the lights
And everything went black.

Colored Death

EMILY PRESENT

My poem was inspired by my mentee's poem—a representation of Generation F. A fiery sense of self—an ability to look at the uncertain and scarier sides of life unabashedly and with grace.

There is death in every color
I proposed in a vitrine
It was faded purple and black
I proposed to, you
Do you remember?

There are little lies scattered in a death
Quiet and precise

My heart renders itself useless
and you accept

You put a tiny rose on my finger
and kiss it gently

I want you to bow to me and say
you'll Encase me in gold
When I return from my peril

But you don't and I'm quiet

Thinking my spaceship solitude

The rose has left a mark; a sketch of itself
And a few faint scars
Quiet, red

But you are a child's laughter in an office room

And I am learning to grow a new limb

I am learning to denounce my color
And learning rather, to live

MARIAH GALINDO

YEARS AS MENTEE: 2

GRADE: Junior

HIGH SCHOOL: Success Academy High School of the Liberal Arts

BORN: New York, NY

LIVES: New York, NY

MENTEE'S ANECDOTE: *During one of our sessions, Nikki set a timer for ten minutes and the both of us were to freewrite. Prior to the free write, our discussion fueled an angry fire in my soul. Nikki handed me a piece of paper. That one piece of paper turned into eight pages. Eight pages of my personal feelings toward being a minority and comparing myself to others more fortunate, diving deep into my insecurities and making myself aware of how self-conscious I am. As a result, I came out of that practice knowing much more of myself than I did before.*

NIKKI PALUMBO

YEARS AS MENTOR: 2

OCCUPATION: Comedy Writer

BORN: Union, NJ

LIVES: New York, NY

PUBLICATIONS AND RECOGNITIONS: Upright Citizens Brigade, *Funny or Die, Reductress*

MENTOR'S ANECDOTE: *This year, Mariah and I made vulnerability a priority both in our writing and in getting to know each other on a deeper, more honest level. Crazy idea, I know! But with every emotional roller coaster, there's a great reward. And I'm so proud of the topics we've been able to tackle that were previously very walled off—even to ourselves.*

Dejar Pasmado

MARIAH GALINDO

My writing piece is influenced by actual events that happened within my family. These events caused strained relationships and continue to affect the next generation with underlying judgment between siblings.

Flora woke up to the sound of yelling outside her bedroom door. Two voices clashing against each other, intertwined with the feeling of hatred and hostility. Aimed at each other. Flora stood still, listening to their shouting.

"You're not my father! You never were!"

Flora got up from her bed and quietly opened the door. She hadn't seen her sister in two days. Her sister was dressed in a tight black shirt, her hair flat-ironed. She wore a necklace laced with gold and a little diamond at the end. Her nails were acrylic and smelled new.

"Then why did you come back?"

Flora's father yelled back. His stance was crooked and faltering—back and forth. In his hand was an empty Corona bottle. The two continued to argue, voices rising. Until her father raised the empty bottle and brought it down with a smash over Flora's sister's head.

"Linda!" Flora yelled.

Linda couldn't hear as she got up and dug her nails deep into her father's face. He yelled in pain and the two continued to fight. Flora's eyes opened wide, not knowing what to do. Instead, she went back into her room and put on her clothes. It was a Monday and she did not want to be late for school.

Flora's room was tiny. She shared it with her mother, who slept on a mattress on the floor. Flora often felt guilty for having an actual bed but couldn't do anything about it because her father wouldn't buy a bunk bed. After she was dressed, she looked at the full-length mirror where she criticized herself, daily. It was part of her routine to judge what was reflected back in the cracked mirror whose wooden frame was chipped away. It was a gift from her father. He found it on the street with his friend Marco.

Flora took a long look at herself and hated it. She was large in the wrong places and hated wearing shirts that showed it. She pulled up her jeans, hoping it would tuck in her rolls. The least she could do was flat-iron her hair and put on hoop earrings that highlighted her above-average face. She couldn't see it now, but she would turn into a beautiful woman. But even so, she would always feel overshadowed by her sister, whose beauty was apparent and treasured.

She skipped breakfast, later gorging herself on dinner. As she walked to school she bumped into her friends along the way.

"Hola, Cuy!"

A short boy with long black hair greeted her.

"Hola, José," Flora responded.

On the inside Flora hated that nickname, Cuy, but would never say so. She instead looked behind and saw her sister stumbling out of the apartment building, clutching her hair. Flora turned around and walked away, leaving her sister to wander out in the morning alone.

Linda didn't know exactly what set off the fight, but she was sure that she needed to get out of the house. She slowly walked toward the end of the block, the wind blowing out her hair. She delicately examined the bump forming in the middle of her head, wincing at the pain. Her feet blistered in the heels she'd never worn before. She chastised herself for *needing* to have these shoes. But she was interrupted when she saw a man walking toward her.

"Linda, hurry up, we're late."

Linda quickly walked up to him, swaying back and forth as the shoe tag poked her heel.

"Why are you walking like that? It's weird."

Her face grew bright red as the man's arms pulled her close. He was wearing a black shirt that hugged his chest, showing the outline of his chiseled body. His brown skin glittered under the sun, the Virgin Mary permanently apparent on his arm.

He held Linda tight under his arm as if he was a boy holding on to his favorite pet, making sure no one else got a hold of it. As they were walking, Linda's back twisted in his tight grip and her courage mounted with every step, until she could free herself from his hold. When she did, he grunted and glared at her.

"*Lo siento, Giovanni,*" Linda apologized.

"*Está bien.*"

Linda suddenly felt unprotected now that she was free from Giovanni's grip. She ran her fingers through her hair, hissing when she touched the bruise her father gave her. Giovanni noticed this and stopped in his tracks.

"*¿Que pasó, niña?*" he asked.

Linda shrugged.

"Nothing."

"Don't fucking lie to me, *niña*," Giovanni hissed.

Linda jumped when Giovanni pinched her arm, grunting in pain.

"I had a fight with my father earlier, nothing important."

Giovanni's pupils dilated. Linda hung her head down in defeat. She didn't need a second fight to occur between her father and her lover. The deep disdain they had for each other had an evil stench to it whenever they were in the same room. A much more malicious rivalry than the one she had with her sister.

Moms: A Study

NIKKI PALUMBO

Inspired by Mariah's piece, in which she explored Generation F with familial relationships, I examined my own relationship with my mother, as it was passed down from her mother.

"Be the change you wish to see in the world." —Mom Gandhi

I come from a short line of strong women. My mother is patience incarnate. The mother before her—her own—is not. It's one of their many differences, all of which I've very unscientifically cataloged in a federally unfunded case study of nature vs. nurture.

It's my biased belief that you can make yourself into anyone. You observe, you choose, you become. A hypothesis based on nothing more than witnessing how my relationship with my mother (or, rather, hers with me) is diametrically opposed to my mother's relationship with her mother.

It seems to be the ebb and flow of "mimic the good and eradicate the bad." Assess, recalibrate, progress. My mother is the rock of our nuclear and extended family. She's every emergency's first responder and every celebration's first RSVP. It's the role she was ostensibly born to fill: nurturer, matriarch, glue. I didn't know there was another way for mothers to be, and for that reason, I rely too heavily on my mother, according to my cardiologist and most ex-girlfriends whose support in moments of panic has been eschewed for the preferred phone call to my mom. It's a relationship she set the boundaries for. My younger sister and

I were always welcomed to call, text, knock, barge in. Nothing was off-limits. Nothing *is* off-limits.

My mother's given me more than she's ever gotten. The gardener to a flower she was never herself. She takes care of my sister and I because she wasn't tended to. Her proactivity, a reaction. And it's frustrating to know that I have it so good *because* she was determined to not let us inherit feelings of tension and distrust in the person you should be most comfortable around. She willfully stopped the cycle and didn't pass along a strained relationship. She never once spoke derogatorily about my grandmother. Instead, my mother became the potting soil for the nurturing that was to come.

And I observe and choose to become her—completely. No calibration necessary.

KIMBERLEY GARCIA

YEARS AS MENTEE: 2

GRADE: Junior

HIGH SCHOOL: University Neighborhood High School

BORN: New York, NY

LIVES: Queens, NY

MENTEE'S ANECDOTE: *Being in Girls Write Now is amazing, as well as having my mentor, Rosie, with me. Rosie has always helped me reach my full potential, and she is great at giving advice. She helps me become a better writer by critiquing my work and reviewing my applications for jobs or internships. When we don't have deadlines, Rosie comes up with fun writing assignments or we just talk about books.*

ROSALIND BLACK

YEARS AS MENTOR: 2

OCCUPATION: Accounting Assistant, Writers House

BORN: Minneapolis, MN

LIVES: Brooklyn, NY

MENTOR'S ANECDOTE: *This year—our second year together—we have visited libraries, bookstores, and macaron cafés. We have discussed everything from math to manga. Kimberley even brought me a piece of her birthday cake when we met for our pair check-ins. She carried it with her all day, just to share it with me! If that doesn't warm your heart, I don't know what will. As if that's not enough, Kimberley has made strides in the skill and creativity of her work. It is truly astounding to witness, and I am honored to spend time with such a lovely, talented human.*

Goodbye, Father

KIMBERLEY GARCIA

This piece represents family, forgiveness, and fall. I wanted to write a story representative of Generation F. However, the letter "f" can stand for anything, and that is how these three words come into play.

The air is still and silent. Time almost seems frozen here. The trees are naked and showing their bare bark to the world. Such deep brown reminds me of mud or dirt that seems to complement the white snow. It's so blinding, it almost stings my eyes. Outside, I feel myself relax. I haven't slept properly since finishing finals. Normally going outside helps me clear my mind.

As I walk, I see a snow angel fading away. It reminds me of winter days with my family when I was little. I'm going back home in three days for the holidays. Then it's back to school to face adulthood.

"Adult." The term has followed me since my father died when I was thirteen. After his death, my mother and I tended to each other, trying to keep our heads above a sea of depression. I was worried about losing her, too.

My father was just supposed to go to the supermarket. I saw him leave the house and get into the car. That night, police knocked on our door to inform my mother and me that my father had died in a drunk-driving accident.

"Huh?"

An audible gasp escapes from me. I could swear I just saw a jersey jacket with the number 10 and the name "Shannon" emblazoned on the back. I rub my eyes but the jacket is still there.

"Dad?" I call out.

I look up and see the jacket beginning to fade away.

"Dad."

It's not real. This must be a trick. It has to be. I'm tired from all this studying, the crush of finals week. I take off my gloves and reach out to touch the snow. I want to feel the cold snow and wake up. I feel nothing.

Instead of a handful of snow, a yellow leaf sits in my hand.

I rub my eyes again. More snow becomes autumn leaves floating down around me. I'm getting scared now. I pinch myself to wake up. But when I drop to my knees to try to grab the snow, it is no longer there.

Instead, I see grass, light green as grapes, coating the ground. My fingers curl into a fist, picking up a pile of dirt in my hands. My hands begin to tremble when I feel mud squish through my fingers. *Boom-boom. Boom-boom.* My heart pounds against my chest. I lift my head and see the trees are covered in leaves of yellow, orange, green, and brown.

That's when I see somebody moving in the shadows. I stand up, heart pounding, and start chasing the shadow. I almost stumble when I see who it is.

"Dad."

My father, Elliot Shannon, is standing three feet from me. His tan skin makes him glow, his brown eyes twinkle with pride.

"It's good to see you, Robin."

I bite my lip in order to stop tears from forming. I stand straighter and face him.

"Robin, you have . . ." He pauses and looks at me. "You've grown up as I always thought you would."

My jaw clenches and water springs to my eyes. I feel my face heat up.

"Dad, I-I-I missed you."

"Robin . . ."

Beep-beep. *Dad grabs his keys and puts on his coat.*

"Dad, my friends are coming over today, buy some popcorn and chips," I say. "Okay, little Robin," he says. I walk outside with him and notice the autumn leaves piling up. I need to rake them soon. He gets into the car. Vroom-vroom. *"See you in ten," he says.*

"I'm sorry for taking your childhood away from you," Dad says, heavy.

I take a deep breath. "You didn't take my childhood away from me," I say.

"Shannon, don't lie to me." Father never called me by my last name unless it was serious. "I know—"

I can't help but scream, "You were supposed to come home, not get yourself killed." I raise my arm, exasperated, and feel tears streaming down my face.

Dad stands there saying nothing. I don't need him to, I can tell what he would say. Dad comes to me and wraps his arms around me, placing the jersey jacket on me. The strangest thing is, I actually feel the jacket: its weight and smell of soap and grass.

"Bye, Robin," he says with twinkling eyes and a half-smile.

"Goodbye, Father."

The wind blows around me. I close my eyes and raise my arm to protect my face. I open my eyes again to see a white light. It's shining brightly, yet I feel so cold. It's snow. I realize I'm lying on the ground. I try to get up but feel a heavy weight on me. As I move my arm, a sleeve falls—it is the jersey jacket. The one my father gave me.

"Are you okay?" says a concerned voice.

A shadow hovers over me. I can't tell who it is.

"Stay with me. I'll call 911."

My eyes begin to droop. I hear somebody in the distance saying, "Stay with me." I curl my body and close my eyes.

I Feel

ROSALIND BLACK

I propose Generation Feeling—I believe that, by increasing awareness of our feelings and what they mean for us, we learn about ourselves and others, and the path forward becomes easier. In this poem, I reflect on the sensations, sights, and feelings I associate with visiting the ocean.

In the sloshing liquid shine, glints glancing off
crests both angular and soft,
smooth and ragged, foamy and clear,
I feel.

I feel . . .
buoyed;
light;
shaken.

Swirls of silken water rush
around my shins, suck
on my heels with each step and slap my thighs—
a playful admonishment.
Me, a happy submission.

Molten green sings a siren
song. Murky deep, clouding my feet,
might suck me under.
The surface will forget me.

I feel . . .
afraid;
unknown;
abuzz.

Pierced from below, I seek my
assailant. There is none. There is nothing.
Nobody. Nowhere. Anywhere.
Everywhere. I drag air into my lungs. I laugh.

BERENIZE GARCIA NUEVA

YEARS AS MENTEE: 1

GRADE: Sophomore

HIGH SCHOOL: Uncommon Charter High School

BORN: Brooklyn, NY

LIVES: Brooklyn, NY

MENTEE'S ANECDOTE: *From sunny to snowy days, from ice creams to hot chocolates, from superheroes to feminists, from a small café to a world without limits, is how I describe my Thursday evenings with my mentor, Anna. She has inspired me to write and paint the female worlds that go unnoticed. She has inspired me to write poems that speak not only to me, but to all women. I really appreciate her patience and time she has invested in me to become a better writer; without her I wouldn't have discovered my passion for the genre of journalism. Thank you.*

ANNA FIXSEN

YEARS AS MENTOR: 1

OCCUPATION: Senior Web Editor, *Metropolis*

BORN: Le Sueur, MN

LIVES: Brooklyn, NY

MENTOR'S ANECDOTE: *When I met Berenize, we decided our internal theme would center on her favorite fictional character: Wonder Woman. But as our relationship developed, I began to realize the real Wonder Woman was sitting right next to me. I am consistently blown away by Berenize's intellect, and writerly range, from finely wrought poetry, to moving family memoirs, to incisive political commentary. It's been a pleasure to watch her grow, and to grow alongside her as a person and a writer. Though we live in a turbulent era, my time with this wonderful young woman gives me hope for a brighter future.*

The Undocumented Wonder Woman

BERENIZE GARCIA NUEVA

Undocumented mothers deserve more recognition. They are portrayed by the media as frightened kittens, hiding. But inside each of them there is a roaring lioness, a fierce she-warrior.

She was seduced by the brilliant red sun between the
    mountains,
By the Green Lady who lit the way with her fiery torch,
By the *unalienable* promise of Uncle Sam: *Life, Liberty, and
    the Pursuit of Happiness,*
the American Dream.

She dared to crawl the dry sea, under an unforgiving angry
    sun.
She used her bracelets to ride *La Bestia*, a monster known to
    kill, and remove human parts,
But also the only train ride to freedom and equality, away
    from even bigger monsters.
She reached *El Rio Grande*, its water fierce, strong, ready to
    drown anyone, ready to drag their dreams and hopes down
    its currents.
She used her lasso to tie herself to the Land of Dreams.

She survived.

But it was all a lie,

The dry sea, *La Bestia*, *El Rio Grande* were her true
   guardians.
They were fierce and intimidating, begging her to stay away
   from the true monsters.
No—demons.
The white men were no longer those warm smiling faces, they
   only smirked with cruelty, they used her dreams and
   twisted them into nightmares.
Suddenly the home she fled seemed better than the
   concentration camp she was in.
They clawed off her bracelets and stole her lasso and chained
   her to a crippling life,
Constantly running from the men in green suits, the men
   with the word ICE across their chests.

But she hasn't broken.

She sleeps in a small corner knowing her children go to sleep
   with full stomachs, and dream with their eyes open.
Her new refuge is God, surrounded by saints.
People outside envelop her, raise their fists and yell,
SHE IS NOT AN ALIEN SHE IS A HUMAN, A MOTHER!
She doesn't beg, *she demands.*
She isn't on her knees, but she stands with her head held high
   and, with the same fury she fought the monsters,
She will fight the demons outside.

A Hero Is a Heroine

ANNA FIXSEN

Berenize and I often discuss the importance of telling stories about women—stories that are overlooked all too often. This poem (my first in many years!) was inspired by recent Women's Marches and the countless Wonder Women that surround me.

A hero is a heroine
who doesn't have a name
Hoisting the heft of the world, its oceans
atop her fragile frame

Her forehead is lined with creases,
unironed from life's unfolds
Yet her spirit is steel and time-tempered
and Wisdom is her gold

A heroine is the dreamer
in Keds and simple garb
But a pen is her weapon, truth her shield
the words her lethal barb

She joins them in the pulsing streets
a rivulet in the azalea flood
Truth and justice live on her lips
and fire in her blood

Our protectors don't perch on hills

or hide behind Roman colonnades
No, true champions are our sisters,
ordinary renegades

A hero is a heroine
her song unlocks the shuttered doors
No nightmares, no limits, no gravity,
above the ground she soars

SENJUTI GAYEN

YEARS AS MENTEE: 1

GRADE: Junior

HIGH SCHOOL: Stuyvesant High School

BORN: Dhaka, Bangladesh

LIVES: Queens, NY

PUBLICATIONS AND RECOGNITIONS: Scholastic Art & Writing Awards: two Gold Keys, Honorable Mention

MENTEE'S ANECDOTE: *When I first signed up for Girls Write Now, I did not anticipate how much it would mean to me. I did not anticipate how much bubble tea my mentor and I would drink together—tea I would never have been able to find if my navigation-challenged self had not met Alikay. I did not anticipate thinking of my mentor as an amazing close friend, while also being a trusted adult in my life. The one thing I was sure of was that Girls Write Now would be one of the best things that ever happened to me. And it is.*

ALIKAY WOOD

YEARS AS MENTOR: 1

OCCUPATION: Editor, *Guideposts*

BORN: Sacramento, CA

LIVES: Queens, NY

MENTOR'S ANECDOTE: *Senjuti and I clicked from the moment we learned we were both Slytherins. I felt like we connected on an even deeper level on our walk to the train after our mid-year check-in. We'd been discussing her writing and our goals and she turned to me and said, "Before joining Girls Write Now, I didn't feel like a real writer. And now I do." Her confidence in her right to call herself a writer has inspired me to take more ownership of my work. It's been a wonderful year of growth for both of us—as writers and as women.*

(Im)Perfect Rose

SENJUTI GAYEN

I chose to write this sestina because it was the most difficult form of poetry we discussed at the Girls Write Now Poetry workshop. I tapped into my desire for perfection. I realized through the writing process that perfection is impossible—but it is possible to love yourself.

Every day and every night, I wonder: I question everything.
I look deep within and I ask myself: am I perfect
in every way, shape, and form? Or, am I an imperfect
vision of what should not be, of cracked glass?
It's like walking on a stony path, in a garden
full of dark velvet-petaled roses.

Have you ever held a creation so *perfect*, so unlike you? Roses
I once held in my small hands, and yet I felt like I had
    everything.
I felt no need to search, to wander through a garden
of other exotic flowers. For the small red roses I held in my
    small brown hands were perfect,
perfect like a broken mosaic put back together, like a sculpture
    of glass.
It may shatter one day, as all things do, but it will never be
    imperfect.

The bump in my nose is a hill that leads to the ravine full of
    breath: my lips, small and imperfect.

The shake in my hands, in my bones comes from the anxiety
    bubbling in my belly like an unfurling rose.
My eyes, framed with dark lashes, black like a shadow, reflect
    like glass
my restless and eternal soul. Within it are visions of my past
    lives, prophecies of my future lives—they are my wrongs,
    my rights, my everything.
If I look within, ignore the hurricane of thoughts, the drum
    beat of my heart, will I see a perfect
being? Will I feel as if I am an intricately beautiful painting in
    a museum, a rose in a garden?

I wish I could find within myself confidence and sureness, like
    a garden
growing with every tick of the clock, not a desolate tract of
    uncultivated land filled with imperfect
creations, of crumbling rocks. I do not want rocks—I want
    perfect.
I want a bouquet of blossoms, of fulfillment, of a warm feeling
    on a cold day, of roses
with petals soft like silk and an aroma like rain. Everything
disappoints me, makes me feel as if I have become melted glass

which gleams with treacherous truth, which hides shadows
    and reflects light—a glass
mask, thrown on in haste: an effort to show the world the
    garden
I have not yet grown. I am working hard to plant seeds, to
    plant small pieces of myself, of everything
good, of everything that is an imperfect
reflection, of scattered and sharp thorns like swords on the
    body of a rose.

What I am is flawed, yes, and what I am not is *perfect*.

If I were to look at myself, if I were to see a carefully
    constructed human like a house, perfect
in the slope of the roof, the curve of the door—I would be
    alive but trapped behind delicate glass.
I do not want the fragile idea of perfect painted on my body
    like a tattoo of an incomplete rose.
I want the expansiveness of a library to define me, the
    powerful knowledge of words on a page like flowers in the
    garden
of my mind, nourishing my network of neurons. You see, I am
    not imperfect,
the same way I am not perfect. I am, I am, I am: a cryptic
    collision of everything.

Yes, perfect I am not, but everything
else, I am. I am human and thus I am fragile and I am glass.
I am human and as I am full of life, I am imperfect.
And while I may not be a rose, I am a dandelion, a wishful
    vision of hope in a garden.

The Proper Way to Shatter a Girl

ALIKAY WOOD

One of the topics Senjuti and I explored this year was perfection and its illusory qualities. I used some of the ending words Senjuti chose for her sestina to create a fictional piece that explores how abandoning false ideals of perfection can be liberating.

There was a girl who was made of glass. She was perfect, and she lived in the garden.

The garden was small and tidy. The girl kept it so, though being a perfect glass specimen required a certain level of caution.

Every day the girl filled a pail with water and sloshed it over the peonies and daisies. She plucked weeds, pruned branches, and turned the sunflowers toward the sun when they got confused.

Time passed. The plants grew. The girl grew restless beneath the glass. She pricked her finger on a thorn just to see what would happen. She let the vines grow high. She stopped helping the sunflowers find the sun.

There was no inciting incident. There was no hero's call or villain in the village. Nothing changed at all except the girl let herself feel hungry.

So she grabbed a vine and she was not gentle. She clamped one hand over the other and shimmied up. The plants wailed and thirsted beneath her. What would they do without her?

The girl did not relent. She climbed until the greenery thinned and she could see that there was light and clouds and blue, but between her and all that wide freedom was a wall. This was not a garden at all but a cage.

She climbed until her hair grew wild and her muscles thick. Until her head bumped the ceiling. She reached up a fist and knocked, pounded, raged. She punched until the crack widened and the cage shattered around her and she fell and fell and braced herself for the inevitable fracturing the ground would bring.

Only—and this is where things get interesting—when she fell she was damaged, yes, less beautiful than before, of course, and hurt beyond imagining. But the world was before her. And she did not land on her feet, but she didn't shatter, either.

She lived.

ANALISE GUERRERO

YEARS AS MENTEE: 2

GRADE: Senior

HIGH SCHOOL: Middle College High School

BORN: Queens, NY

LIVES: Queens, NY

MENTEE'S ANECDOTE: *Girls Write Now is an amazing and supportive group. I felt challenged various times because I felt that I wasn't a good enough writer. I felt so proud of the progress that others made, but I also looked down on myself as a writer because I felt like other girls were growing in their writing careers and I wasn't catching up with them. My mentor, Catherine, showed me that everyone goes at their own pace. She most definitely has kept a smile on my face and encouraged me to keep writing!*

CATHERINE LECLAIR

YEARS AS MENTOR: 4

OCCUPATION: Associate Creative Director, Gizmodo Media Group

BORN: Bangor, ME

LIVES: Brooklyn, NY

PUBLICATIONS AND RECOGNITIONS: My features have been published in *Jezebel, Deadspin, Racked,* and more this year.

MENTOR'S ANECDOTE: *This year, it has been amazing to witness Analise grapple with the writing process, from pushing through self-doubt to working on revising and critiquing her own words. Her excitement for and true appreciation of the beauty of the world around us (she even likes pigeons!) has inspired me to find more moments of joy in everyday life, and her ability to be her vibrant self in a room full of people makes me want to be more genuine and present always.*

Identical

ANALISE GUERRERO

I wrote this piece to show that it is ridiculous for others to judge based on a choice that doesn't affect them. This relates to Generation F because we as a generation represent a future that should be free of judgment.

We as a human species are beautiful
All full of life and color
Handcrafted with the most precise decorations
It's wonderful to be a part of something so great
So intelligent
And yet
When two men are seen holding hands
It is *looked down* upon
When two women show affection to each other
It is *'disgusting'*
It's shameful to witness people today act so foolish
When we die
We become nothing but bones
Or ashes
We cannot look into a dead corpse
Or in a jar of ashes
And know whether that being was an alcoholic
Mother
Doctor
Gay
Transgender

What does it matter what someone else's passion is?

A gay man
Would not be able to serve his country
Until 2011
A transgender man
would face the same problem
Until this year, 2018.*

Why is it a punishment to love someone because others do not
    find it normal?

We are such a unique species
Developed from nothing
And will go back to nothing

We are not robots designed to follow a code and perform what
    we are told

We are our own creatures who have a mind to pick
And choose

---

*This story was written before the transgender military ban was announced.

Blender Night

CATHERINE LECLAIR

The following is an excerpt from a longer essay about my relationship with the generations of women in my family who precede me, as told through the story of the night my aunts discovered frozen alcoholic beverages. Generation F inspired me to consider my own relationships with past generations of women as I also witness the future generation of women through Girls Write Now.

I come from a family of mothers. There is a fierce, packlike protectiveness that binds us all together, no matter that we consist of many nuclear families, each with their own matriarch, sets of rules and expectations. As a toddler, I was grabbed out of the sun and slathered with sunscreen by each of my aunts as if I was their own child. I've been fed squishy PB&J sandwiches on pillowy white bread that were made by the dozen and handed out to our grubby herd without any designation as to whose kid was whose. Those delineations mattered less here. Now, as an adult, I can feel the love with which my aunts dutifully fed us and protected us during our childhood years translated into genuine interest in our adult-sized lives.

As the night continues on, the blender drinks get stronger and stronger. You see, my family drinks in spite of its alcoholism. In the '70s, in the span of one year, my grandmother and her sister both divorced their first husbands, who turned out to be violent, dangerous alcoholics. Their ex-husbands' tumultuous relationship with alcohol is how they both found themselves single mothers, my grandmother raising three daughters and my great-aunt five daughters and one son. So they moved in to-gether, their two nuclear families splitting open and sewing themselves back together into one big family, with two sisters as the heads of the house. They even shared the master bedroom. Their tiny, overstuffed home was far from ruled with an iron fist, and as my mother puts it, "They had lost control of us by the time we were fifteen." They have stories of skipping prom, crashing cars before they had their licenses, and plenty of un-derage drinking. They were sisters and cousins, each other's best friends and partners in crime. And if it sounds like a weird cult mixed with *Full House*, that's because it was.

Every booze-fueled night of hijinks is a way for us to chal-lenge our family's history of addiction and say, "You haven't made us victims yet!" But it's also temptation of fate. It is some-where in the murky hours well beyond the third or fourth round of daiquiris that my aunts decide that the time has come for all of us women to burn our bras. Now, before you begin to paint a picture in your head of the women in my family as renegade women's-rights activists, the kind who quote Gloria Steinem or have opinions on Lena Dunham, let me continue. Because the burning of the bras is not limited to the women at the fire. Oh no, the men are told to burn their underwear, too. And while this perhaps undoes any possible feminist symbolism you could have read into this, it does feel a bit more inclusive, doesn't it?

GIANNY GUZMAN

YEARS AS MENTEE: 2

GRADE: Sophomore

HIGH SCHOOL: Academy of American Studies

BORN: Long Island City, NY

LIVES: Queens, NY

PUBLICATIONS AND RECOGNITIONS: Scholastic Art & Writing Awards: Honorable Mention

MENTEE'S ANECDOTE: *This year I had my first performance outside of Girls Write Now. When I went up to that stage I was confident and as I walked off I was proud of myself. Before I met Hermione I was too intimidated by crowds and had anxiety about sharing my work with strangers. I used to be ashamed if I was proud of myself because I never wanted it to make me look conceited or obnoxious. Hermione taught me how to be proud of my work and share it with confidence. I will forever be thankful for that.*

HERMIONE HOBY

YEARS AS MENTOR: 2

OCCUPATION: Professor, Columbia University; Journalist, *The Guardian, The New York Times,* and Novelist

BORN: London, England

LIVES: Brooklyn, NY

PUBLICATIONS AND RECOGNITIONS: *Neon in Daylight* (Catapult, 2018)

MENTOR'S ANECDOTE: *This year Gianny was invited to participate in a public poetry reading in Manhattan. As she took to the stage with confidence and read her work with conviction and passion (to much applause) I was reminded of her telling me only a year or so earlier that she didn't feel she could ever write a poem. It continues to be amazing to watch her challenge herself and push past a sense of limitation. I'm so proud of her.*

Darkness and Dolls

GIANNY GUZMAN

In this coming-of-age fairy tale, I tried to illustrate the best way I could how a girl transitions to a woman instantly and sometimes even if she doesn't want to; how there is so much we are kept in the dark about, then forced to know all at once.

The little girl sat in the middle of a wide room playing dolls with the darkness. She has never seen the light and craved seeing it. She could not tell the expressions of people in the dark. She could not see what someone was doing a few feet away in the dark. She was oblivious to it all in the dark.

She knew she had a huge window overlooking the world, but she was content with playing with her dolls.

From one day to the other the darkness did not want her to play anymore.

It held the girl's arm tightly and her yells were too soft to be heard. It dragged her to the window and dragged the curtains open.

Light spilled in and for a split second she was blinded and then she could see.

She saw her own reflection. She saw the facial expressions on everyone passing by and she saw what everyone was doing.

The girl never thought about how her eyes were too small for her face or how her lips were too thin or how no matter how far she pulled her head forward there was still a flap of fat underneath her face. She was scared because she didn't want to be the girl in the reflection, but just moments ago she was fine with who she was.

The girl never saw how behind everyone's eyes was desperation and sadness because no one can ever get everything they wanted. Some even less than others. But they continue to move through life even with the scraps of dreams they once mapped out.

She pulled away, scared with what she saw, and tried to escape the light. The curtains wouldn't close and even if she shielded herself from the light, she saw it all behind her eyes, playing like a broken record.

She glanced around her room. She looked at her doll discarded in the middle of the room and walked toward it. Her mind thought it knew what to do, but her body shivered in anticipation. The doll was gently placed in the back of her closet, with the doors closed and the darkness, alone.

The girl remained alone in the middle of her room, nowhere to hide in the light. She walked out the room, leaving her doll behind; and the darkness that concealed the world from her and her from the world was left behind, too.

Excerpt from book in progress

HERMIONE HOBY

This is taken from a novel in progress, whose narrator reflects on the upheavals of 2017 from his deathbed in 2064.

There can be a kind of gratification to a really bad birthday. Toward the dull and lurid end of 2016, the year all our idols died, I turned twenty-two alone. I spent the evening failing to read a book in the eggy lowlight of a deserted Chinatown bar and I deemed this non-event, in its solitude and misery, so much more preferable than, say, drinks with a few people mustering anemic cries of "Happy birthday!" or, god forbid, trying to sing it, a song that was always too slow, maddeningly so, always went on longer than you thought possible, groaning toward that final, protracted lift on the "birth" of the penultimate "birthday" with wincing strain, all while I stared at a lone candle shoved in a cupcake and waited it out. I'd hoped that being alone might feel sort of heroic. Or at least dignified. Or, at least, grown-up.

An overweight barmaid had cajoled me into ordering the house cocktail, which arrived in a small coupe glass, an embarrassingly fruity shade of puce, a mocking strawberry spliced and listing down the side. I'd grinned, sipped it, suppressed a shudder as I felt it sheath my teeth with sugar while I wondered where glory had gone.

It was November, a nothing month, the weekend after Thanksgiving, and I remember rain, a vague but unremitting overlay of pathetic fallacy as the nation failed to accept the reality of what it had done. The sky had a sort of passive-aggressive quality: bruised clouds, withholding their light while telling you they were fine not to worry about them you didn't care about them anyway. Ahead lay the grotesquerie of the reality-TV boor who would soon be in the White House, eating McDonald's and watching TV in his bathrobe. A bad joke. The worst possible joke that was now the forty-fifth president, executive producer of The America Show as it barreled ever faster, with more and more improbable drama, to its season finale. The ratings were great. Later, Zara would say, in that flattened-dead way that made the notion of "joke" quail, that they'd all peaced out because they knew what was coming. They'd ducked out before the shit hit the fan. Prince, Bowie, Muhammad Ali.

In November, though, I was newly arrived in New York, with few friends, or, at least, nobody with whom I'd wish to eat pie and turkey or celebrate a birthday. After Dartmouth, least impressive of the Ivies, I'd been eager to delay adulthood a little longer, and had spent a year at Oxford, during which my impressionable speech became infected with the rounded vowels of rich English youth. English youth who fetishized me, ribbed me, paid me attention, ultimately, for being "a bloody Yank." In those first months in Manhattan, then, I was mistaken, frequently, for an expat. Often, I went along with this, murmuring the lie of "London" with a diffident smile when a cashier or barista asked where I was from. In truth, I was from Ohio, an only child, a former fat kid, an English lit, major, son of a physiotherapist named Marjory—a woman whose life had been a slow cavalcade of disappointments, a landslide, chief among them my father's departure ten years ago, closely followed by my own callous and total refusal to remain in Toledo and lend a little succor to her sadness. She'd christened me Luke. The day I arrived in Oxford, I became Luca.

They knew me, then, Paula and Jason did, as Luca.

NYLAH HARRIS

YEARS AS MENTEE: 1

GRADE: Sophomore

HIGH SCHOOL: Medgar Evers College Preparatory School

BORN: Jamaica, NY

LIVES: Brooklyn, NY

MENTEE'S ANECDOTE: *In our pair sessions, Kathleen and I give each other prompts, but with one in particular, I thought it would be a good idea to start off a story and then switch after ten minutes and continue each other's ideas. That's the most creatively challenged I've been, and I loved every minute of it. We bonded over the fact that even though we started our stories one way, we loved how we each steered into a different direction just as exciting. It's one of the many great pair sessions we had but also a turning point for later ones.*

KATHLEEN SCHEINER

YEARS AS MENTOR: 7

OCCUPATION: Freelance Writer and Editor

BORN: Biloxi, MS

LIVES: Brooklyn, NY

MENTOR'S ANECDOTE: *Nylah and I both share a love of true crime, and the stories we write together tend to be pretty dark. But I remember being knocked out during one of our first exercises, where the prompt was to rewrite a story we've read from the male point into one told by a female. Nylah had a hard time with this exercise, telling me, "I only read stories about females." This was such a refreshing problem to have, and one of many surprises Nylah's had for me being part of Generation F.*

Hear My Voice

NYLAH HARRIS

*I wanted to write a piece about society's expectations and standards.
It took me some time, but I feel it discusses some of the hardships that
people fail to realize I experience as a young girl, part of Generation F.*

I am a girl
Living in the roar of society.
Can you hear me?
I am submerged in the lights of the man.
They drown me with their controversies and outlooks.
I am beautiful.
No, you are cocky and arrogant.
I am ugly.
No, you are my damsel and I will rescue you.

I am expected to blow, suck, and swallow what society brings
    to me.
But I didn't ask for that.
Why didn't I get a second to figure out what I want?
Fear has change by the throat and man won't lift a finger.

I am a girl
Learning to be a woman.
Do you see me?

Why won't you see me?
Drowning in the future society wants for me.
Black is the solitude in which I choose to shame the cruelties.

The Quarry

KATHLEEN SCHEINER

This is part of a work in progress, in which my protagonist has an accident that coincides with the beginning of her psychic talent. She's part of Generation F, brave, and refusing to abandon her friend.

She couldn't leave her friend down there alone. Though everything in her head said no, Cassidy took off her top and unbuckled her belt. She stepped out of her shoes and made a neat pile of her clothes, then stopped when she noticed somebody standing off in the tree line. It was Travis, propped up against a tree trunk like he might faint, pushing his thick glasses up his sweaty nose. "You shouldn't be swimming in the quarry," he said in a prissy voice. "It's dangerous. There's junked cars down there, and slate at the edges so sharp it could cut you."

"I have to," Cassidy said. "My friend's down there. But do me a favor? Would you call somebody? I think something bad's going to happen."

He stared at her, then turned his back and went into the woods.

She walked up to the cliff edge and heard Jacey frantically call, "Come down, Cassidy. It's really nice." Cassidy shielded her eyes from the sun and could see how worried Jacey was.

Cassidy closed her eyes and willed her flip-flopping stomach to stop. *One, two, three,* she counted off in her head, then added, *Help me, God,* before jumping off the cliff, feeling the hair lift off the back of her neck as she plummeted into the water.

She went down deep, the water getting colder as she descended. Then Cassidy felt something grasp her ankle, keeping her rooted to the depths. She was scared to look, but when she opened her eyes, she saw that her foot was lodged between an old mossy window and a rusted car door. She looked up and could see wavering sunlight at the surface of the water, along with the churning legs of Jacey and the boys as they treaded water. Then she felt something else touch her leg.

Cassidy thought maybe her contacts had slipped out in the water because she couldn't believe what she was seeing—a hand snaked out from the open window of the car with green mold or algae on it. The thumb grazed her shin and that digit felt colder than the water, causing all the air to bubble out of her lungs as she silently screamed. She took in a lungful of brackish water and her vision was starting to go dark when she saw a face she recognized—Chuck.

STEPHANIE HASKELL

YEARS AS MENTEE: 1

GRADE: Senior

HIGH SCHOOL: Curtis High School

BORN: Staten Island, NY

LIVES: Staten Island, NY

MENTEE'S ANECDOTE: *I liked doing a "show vs. tell" exercise using elements and characters from the novel I am working on. It helps me do more with my writing and bring the characters alive. In general, Emily has been supportive by encouraging me with what I'm good at but also pushing me to grow with constructive criticism. It makes me more confident in my writing and I've learned a lot about myself and how/what I like to write in the process.*

EMILY MORRIS

YEARS AS MENTOR: 1

OCCUPATION: Planner, Zeno Group

BORN: Stamford, CT

LIVES: Brooklyn, NY

MENTOR'S ANECDOTE: *I am so inspired by Stephanie's pure love of writing and it reminds me of what I love about the form—that all you need is dedication and keys to type on to be able to call yourself a writer. Recently I've been joining her while she does writing prompts during our sessions, and effectively making myself more disciplined in the process. It's been so fun to exchange our ideas and to see how those short, informal bouts of writing open both of us up to new and unexpected possibilities.*

Abnorminials

STEPHANIE HASKELL

This is an excerpt of a bigger story about a kid named Robert who is misunderstood in the world he lives in, even if that world involves people with special abilities.

Outside held a gloomy fate. It was pouring outside, and I heard police sirens blare in the background. The buildings by me were run-down and grotesque, paint peeling from worn brick walls. In the corner of an alleyway I saw a lumpy form on the ground that oddly resembled a body.

The fluorescent lights flickered as I climbed the stairs. I stopped at door 207, turned the key in the keyhole, and went inside.

This house was not as good as my last one, but it's the one my aunt Lucy owned when she took me in, and I love her deeply for that. The place was dark as I creaked open the door. It was pretty late, so Lucy must have been asleep. I placed my bag down, took off my jacket, and placed it down as delicately as I could. All of a sudden the lights flickered to life, dousing me in brightness.

Aunt Lucy glared at me with her dark eyes. It turned out she hadn't been sleeping at all, because she still had a neatly tied bun in the back of her head from work.

"I've been waiting for you to come," she confirmed.

"Well, honey, I'm home!" I answered, which automatically got me a pillow chucked at my face.

"You've been drinking again." Sheer disappointment anointed

her face. "You're sixteen years old! Why don't you do normal sixteen-year-old things?"

"Because I'm not normal!" I snapped back.

This marking on my upper arm was nothing more than a symbol of a curse. I was just nine years old when this weird marking changed my life forever. It resembled a DNA strand, but closed into a circle, like something you would see in a kid's science experiment. I didn't have a clue why this symbol appeared and gave certain people abilities as a child, or why this even had to be the symbol to represent all of us abnorminials in the first place. Mine happened to be a light blue, which was unbearably fitting for my ability.

If I were normal I wouldn't be living here now.

Aunt Lucy looked me directly in the eyes, her brown irises softening for a moment. She took my hand as I resisted the urge to squirm away.

"You're right, you're not. But that doesn't have to be a bad thing."

She didn't have the mark of an abnorminial, she didn't know the heartache it brings. But other abnorminials felt pride from their abilities, so I guess it was just me. There are some of us who use them all the time. Once I happened to pass by a construction site. They were going about their job and this abnorminial man used his power of super-strength to lift up a massive iron bar over to where he wanted. He treated the compacted metal as if it were a small twig he'd picked up off the ground.

There are other cases where people use it for fame. Kohl Nickelson thought he was a big shot because he happened to use his powers—laser eyes and teleportation—at the right place at the right time. Just another basic middle-schooler until one day we were on a school trip walking across the Brooklyn Bridge. We all stopped in our tracks when a helicopter hurtled toward us. One of the propellers was bent at an odd angle and losing altitude pretty rapidly. Most of us kids were screaming, but Kohl stood completely still. I watched as his eyes glowed red, slicing the copter in half. A handful of people fell out, but before they could plummet into the water they all appeared in front of us, safe from harm. One of the passengers rushed over to him, thanking him profusely for saving their lives. She turned out to be a reporter, and asked Kohl to tell his story on camera. Ever since then he has claimed himself a hero.

Power changes people. Funny thing is it seems to always be a negative.

But Aunt Lucy wouldn't be able to comprehend my full resentment. My shoulders loosened up and I gave her the answer she wanted.

"No, I suppose not."

That strict sneer turned into a loving smile, and she embraced me in a warm hug. She tensed and tilted her head to the side.

"Ugh, you smell like martinis, go to bed!"

She shoved me off and tossed another pillow my way. It missed me by a foot but I got the message. I picked the pillow up gently and placed it back on the couch.

In my room I left the lights turned off. *When are you going to stop this?* a voice called to me in my mind. I heaved out a sigh, running a hand through my hair. *Is that even an option for me?* I looked back at the door longingly. I was tempted to open it and at least wish my aunt a good night. But instead I threw myself in bed, and looked up at the ceiling until I finally dozed off.

Girls' Trip Sestina

EMILY MORRIS

Written during our Poetry workshop. I don't normally write poetry, but I like puzzles, and sestinas are like a puzzle. Generation F *is about the power of femininity and its untapped potential that has yet to be expressed in its full range of possibility. With that in mind, I aimed to capture a few feelings: the tune of the ocean, the malleability of time, and the pleasure of female friendship.*

Traveling a winding road in the company of women
Will always lead to a wistful surf
We disrobe in the middle of the night
Together, unself-conscious in the tradition of girls.
Even in winter we will find a way to swim,
Warmed by spirits and the spontaneous drive

That spurred us on in the first place to get in the car and
    drive,
Our bags packed with comforts because we are women
It is always necessary to bring a suit for swim
As necessary as the lapping surf
That awaits us friends, us girls
Who have uttered secrets in every season at night

It is easier to speak straight, forward into the night
Whether looking out upon waves or still on the drive
Illuminated by traffic lights in the backseat as if girls,

Speaking officiously to their families, practicing to become
women.
We screech and shout, our voices dissipating into the frothing
surf—
It receives us as we dunk our heads and decide to swim.

Every time I've felt God has been during a swim
Or after, at dusk, as golden hour seeps into night
The black-haired girls drag silently from the sea toward the
surf
And try not to think of when we'll need to drive
Home, soon, away from this respite of women
A steady moving stream of sex and death and birth. Girls,

All the concerns of girls
Contemplating them with closed eyes as we swim
And float, we contemplate if we are yet women
Or if when we are them we'll still tell the truth at night
Will we be resculpted by a different route or drive
Will we still dare in the cold to run directly to the surf

Or will we no longer hear the surf's metronome
Will we have no time to remind ourselves that we are girls
Untouched by the idea of hustle, obligation, or drive
Dedicating our bodies to the virtue of swim
And the places we go together at night
And the divinity of women buoyed by women

Girls become women like the slap of a dive
Blue swims remind us of what we are at night

LILY HE

YEARS AS MENTEE: 1

GRADE: Senior

HIGH SCHOOL: Millennium Brooklyn High School

BORN: Brooklyn, NY

LIVES: Brooklyn, NY

MENTEE'S ANECDOTE: *No words can describe the moments of reflection, exploration, fun and jokes, and understanding that I've had with Lenna this year. When Girls Write Now started, I told Lenna that I wanted to try to write more memoirs this year, and although physically I haven't written down much, emotionally I have shared so many stories of my life with her that I haven't shared with anyone else. By talking to her, I am continuously learning and realizing new things about myself. She distracted me from the flaws of my story and instead taught me to focus on the strengths.*

LENNA STITES

YEARS AS MENTOR: 1

OCCUPATION: Subsidiary Rights Coordinator, Taylor and Francis

BORN: Torrance, CA

LIVES: Brooklyn, NY

MENTOR'S ANECDOTE: *It was inspiring to see how quickly Lily was willing to open up and share her writing with me. She really hasn't shied away from letting me get to know her, which in turn paved a path for us to figure out more about ourselves, and the city we live in. I think Girls Write Now is the type of program that I needed growing up but would have been too timid for, as it really forces you to come out of your shell. I hope Lily continues to be fearless as she goes on into college and beyond.*

What Happened to a Little Chinese Girl One Morning

LILY HE

Inspired by the hardships of everyday life, but also by the limitless fun that our generation today has, I wanted to bring out a small story that is easily looked past, and bring out the beauty and giggles behind it.

Beep beep beep beep beep.

I felt around my pillow for my phone and tapped the screen to snooze the alarm. I groaned in relief when the annoying sound finally ceased. Wait—no, I didn't have a phone back then. Then what was it that woke me up in the morning?

"Lily! Get up, you'll be late for school!" my mom called from the kitchen. I blinked my eyes open. *Oh yeah, adults.* They sure were useful back then. They are probably boiling mad now because cell phones took one of their main jobs away: waking their children.

I pulled myself up from my fluffy bed with all of my willpower and motivation for the day. To an outsider, I probably just look like I'm in bed, constipated. I looked at the clock on the wall, it was still a whole hour before school would start, since my school was just a five-minute walk away. *Mom, you call that late? Ugh, adults are such liars.*

I rubbed my eyes sleepily as I drunk-walked my way to the bathroom. Drunk from the rice wine that my parents cooked with for dinner, of course. I closed the bathroom door and turned on the faucet. I grabbed my toothbrush from my cup and placed it under the running sink for thirty seconds before plopping it right back into the cup. I stood in the bathroom, stared at the white tiled walls, and counted the seconds in my head. If I was going to fake it, I was going to do it right. I walked out of the bathroom like a champion because for the fifth day in a row, I escaped the whole "brushing my teeth" ordeal without my mom catching me.

But wait.

I tilted my face up so that my nose was aimed at the ceiling and I took in a deep breath. *Fried eggs and soy sauce!* I ran to the kitchen, which was three steps from the bathroom, and snatched a fried egg from the plate in the center and grabbed the huge bottle of soy sauce. I drizzled half a bottle of soy sauce on my egg and then proceeded to shove the whole piece in my mouth.

"Eat slower or you're going to cho—" my sister-in-law started to say before I broke out into a cough. Then another. And all the coughs in the world suddenly came at me.

"What did I say," she grumbled, as she patted my back to pull me from the brink of dying. Close call. The headlines for the newspaper almost read: EIGHT-YEAR-OLD GIRL DIES FROM EGGS AND SOY SAUCE.

"Thanks," I mumbled bashfully and gulped down a cup of water.

Evading death, I made my way to my room to get ready for school. I pulled on a pair of jeans that flare out wide on the bottom and a mustard-yellow sweater with a bear sewn on the front. I once got a compliment from my teacher about that sweater, and since then have worn it one too many times. The way that I dressed was so bad that I told others my mom dressed me just so that I could put the blame on her. What she didn't know wouldn't hurt her.

I finished getting ready and still had a half an hour before school started. It's all my mom's fault for waking me up so early.

I grumbled in frustration and plopped myself down on my favorite lime-colored chair and cupped my cheeks with my hands. I glared at the clock on the wall and watched the second hand tick slowly.

When the time was finally five minutes before school, I sprung up from my chair. I grabbed my backpack from the floor and swung it over my shoulder. In slow motion, that would've looked so cool. But in reality, it ended up slamming into my back and I had to bite back a tear. *T'was painful.*

"Mom, I'm leaving!" I called out before I slammed the door behind me. I winced from the accidental loud sound and prayed in my head that my mom wouldn't come out to scold me. I waited half a minute, and when that didn't happen, I sighed in relief.

I strolled up the street toward the school but I kept hearing a *thwack, thwack, thwack* behind me. It sounded as if someone was following me because with every step that I took, the sound appeared. I quickened up my pace before I walked in front of the old bank near my house that was all windows.

Usually, I stare at myself as I walk by, so I did the same. What I saw made me freeze in front of the glass window.

I was wearing my bright red flip-flops from home instead of sneakers.

Uses for Chewing Gum

LENNA STITES

I've written a very short story inspired by my mentee Lily's piece. Built around an anecdotal flashback, I wanted to reflect on the time we've taken to get to know ourselves a bit better, while having fun.

I was called in to my biggest operation when I was just a child. I was part of a team of three and it took creativity, time, and a few pieces of chewing gum. We were fairly resourceful for this age, the age of Barbie dolls and dress-up.

Ariel was the new doll to the room and one day she had an unfortunate accident. Two of my friends had come over for the weekend so we all saw it happen. She was swimming around before getting her legs, like usual, but this time, as she leapt into her first splits in the air, her right leg completely dislocated from her hip. All three of us, stunned such a thing could even happen, decided to test out her left leg. Well, we deduced that it, too, was plastic and could pop off. Ariel laid there, mostly torso and still smiling. Simply trying to snap the legs back into place wasn't working. This called for us to get creative.

Taking stock of what was available, the three of us, palms out, had some gum and a ponytail hair tie. I decided to chew a piece while we thought of a plan when my friend said, "Give me that gum." I spit it into her palm and she mashed it into Ariel's hip, attaching the right leg back into place. "Ooh! I'll do the other one." I said, my mouth already full with another stick of gum. Our third girl kept an eye on the blob and, once it looked passable as adhesive, I glued the left leg. "Christie, here. Keep her in place like this."

My palms were pressed to either side of Ariel's hips in demonstration. With the hair tie securely fastened around the waist, the gum took its time to harden. All we could do now was sit and wait.

If you were to stand her up today, Ariel would have the same doll face and the same split life between human and mermaid, but the scars of her accident remain. For now when she stands, she stands tall with each foot firmly planted facing the backward direction.

RUBIT HERNANDEZ

YEARS AS MENTEE: 1

GRADE: Sophomore

HIGH SCHOOL: Hyde Leadership Charter School

LIVES: Bronx, NY

MENTEE'S ANECDOTE: *Going to the coffee shop is one thing I look forward to every week. I always enjoy having conversations with Nicole because she's someone who I can trust and count on. She has really become an inspiration because she is an excellent writer with interesting points of view, styles of writing, and amazing thoughts to let free on paper. She comes up with new writing exercises to inspire our writing. Our relationship has grown over time, and I appreciate Nicole very much for being herself and for being an amazing mentor!*

NICOLE CHU

YEARS AS MENTOR: 1

OCCUPATION: Writer, New York City Public School Teacher

BORN: San Jose, CA

LIVES: New York, NY

MENTOR'S ANECDOTE: *I have many favorite memories with Rubit: taking selfies in Central Park at dusk, eating "Pac-Man" dumplings before winter break, and journaling side by side at UGC Eats (our spot in East Harlem!). While sitting in bright orange chairs and devouring almond croissants, Rubit shared her goals of expressing herself and trying new things. Since then, she has challenged herself to experiment with new genres, study the works of powerful female poets, and trek to new neighborhoods. Being with Rubit reminds me that an adventurous spirit can take us to unimaginable places in our writing and in our everyday lives.*

Silent Chaos

RUBIT HERNANDEZ

Nicole and I had a mutual goal to further explore poetry. We analyzed a few poems in which different situations and feelings were expressed. I used many of those poems as inspiration.

I stare blankly at the ground
while my eyes struggle to stay open
and my thoughts battle
to not create much of a burden,
thinking about a mistake I made months ago,
thinking about life itself,
my thoughts are the planets revolving around my head,
the sun,
the closer the planets are,
the hotter they become
the more my thoughts are buried into my head,
the more I become concerned

my thoughts are
dancing at a party
with all the lights moving around,
loud music playing,
lots of people dancing,

my thoughts are multifarious:
one moment, a bouquet of roses
the next,

a walk in a dark, haunted forest
these thoughts seem to wrap my head in this mess
and there's no way out
it's a dark cave in which I fall
with no exit

like a scared baby's heartbeat,
my legs quake
not because I'm worried,
simply because it's a habit
just like biting my lips,
or biting my nails
I overthink way too much
to the point where
the rest of my body has adapted

I apprehensively think about my future:
will life continue being a hardcore obstacle course
or will it become easier the more I succeed
and create a freshly paved road?

blinking rapidly,
I return to my reality,
watching people walk ignorantly through the streets,
nothing but streetlights to brighten the vibe
I plug my headphones in my ears
turn my music all the way up
concealing the silent chaos

Metamorphosis

NICOLE CHU

In one of our stream-of-consciousness writing exercises, Rubit wrote: "a dark night only brightened by the streetlights." I copied her poetic line in my notebook and let my mentee's words inspire my own poem.

> "What would happen if one woman told the truth about her life?
> The world would split open"   —Muriel Rukeyser

I saw her jump not with my own eyes
as if experiencing a dream without blood or sound

two orange cones and a strip of yellow police tape
did little to deter a growing crowd
that kept staring
up at the ledge of the hotel

a tourist's camera phone focused on
a single white sheet poorly
cocooning a body
melting onto the concrete

before that,
a blue-and-white sneaker
plummeted through the air,
somehow escaping its owner's flailing feet,
in seconds, it
flipped over on the sidewalk

open mouths like tiny wounds
gasped,
unable to fathom any explanation

I tried to tell myself in a poem:
she imagined herself
splitting open the world,
leaving behind
a dark night only brightened by the streetlights

but words are only words
you don't use them in mid-air
you don't use them with hands reaching
you don't use them to break tongue and bone

I tried anyway to
spin her into a silky poem
where she could
molt, harden, reassemble,
force dead cells to self-destruct,
digest and disintegrate spare parts,
stun this small world when she decides
once again
to release into the air,
hungry and unforgiving

WAEZA JAGIRDAR

YEARS AS MENTEE: 1

GRADE: Junior

HIGH SCHOOL: Jacqueline Kennedy Onassis High School

BORN: New York, NY

LIVES: Bronx, NY

MENTEE'S ANECDOTE: *Girls Write Now has been so empowering and inspirational. It is not just the writing that keeps you going, but the love and support that I have gotten as a mentee. Ashley has been a great mentor. I love that she listens to my rants and supports my decisions.*

ASHLEY SCHNEIDER

YEARS AS MENTOR: 2

OCCUPATION: Associate Teacher, Saint Ann's School

BORN: Phoenixville, PA

LIVES: New York, NY

PUBLICATIONS AND RECOGNITIONS: *Gravel, Vogue*

MENTOR'S ANECDOTE: *When I met Waeza in September, she was interested in writing but did not quite identify as a writer. As we began to meet in our spot, we explored different forms. Waeza wrote fiction and poetry, and journaled more regularly in her notebook. While we write often, we also share a lot from our week, noting that observations are important as a writer. On one such occasion, we were talking about how we notice tiny details about people, and Waeza said, "It's probably why we're writers." It has been such a privilege to be part of Waeza's journey in becoming a writer!*

Equality Begins with Changing Education

WAEZA JAGIRDAR

This piece was inspired by the lack of motivation in my school. As one person of many in my generation who feels this way, I wanted to talk about it because this needs to be heard.

Sometimes it seems that education isn't about learning anymore. It has become another business to this capitalist world. We, as a society, are more concerned about passing standardized tests than taking true wisdom with us for the rest of our life. It is unnerving that students at the age of five start school and feel they aren't "smart enough." Making children feel this way creates a generation that doesn't have enough motivation to continue education. The "common core" is not doing much justice to help children learn.

The mind-set that high school sets up for the next generation is that everyone should attend college. The message is that many will have better jobs if they get a degree. This changes the perspective of education and other forms of growing as a person. Maybe the setup of the school, where if a student doesn't pass Regents, that student can't graduate, creates this mentality. Although this may seem like an ideal way to see how far students have progressed, it puts too much pressure on them. They already have to worry about college and the SAT. Without adding these tests, there is enough pressuring them that can lead to failure.

When I hear people wondering about students failing in

the United States, I think of my honors class. I see the honors classes getting more privileges and resources than the average classes. That's a problem. It creates a status and a label that tells the average students they are not good enough to have this support. If schools keep providing to honors classes unequally, it sends a message to other students that their efforts are meaningless. Students should feel proud to be part of an honors class; this achievement should make honors students feel like leaders for their peers. However, honors classes should not make an average student feel belittled.

In the future, I hope schools will support an average student just like they support an honors student. I hope they will keep students motivated and focus on their growth over their test results. In a world where political issues like race and immigration can make students feel like they are already worth less than other people, I hope for school to be a place of empowerment. Everyone should feel like they are worth an equal opportunity to succeed and grow. Education can be that place.

From Kindergarten to *Generation F*

ASHLEY SCHNEIDER

Waeza and I often talk about school, her from the perspective of student and me as kindergarten teacher. We both drew from this experience in our pieces, thinking of the change that can come with Generation F.

Anger is powerful, I thought. Two minutes ago, a child in my class shrieked at the thought of changing activities. Deeply immersed in her play, she had no intention of resurfacing in order to do math. Rather than express the vulnerable emotions that lurked at her core—disappointment, frustration, and, ultimately, sadness—she took control. She yelled. She stomped her feet. She crossed her arms with a large gesture, just like a six-year-old would when she means to say *I am not going anywhere, and you can't make me.*

It is my job to get her to stop. But there are days when I leave work, and I want to scream, too. I want to dig my heels in and refuse the unfair change enforced by authority figures. The climate changes, human rights deteriorate, basic justice seems to hide in the dark depths of some faraway cave. Why should I move on to the next thing if it only seems to be worse? "You can be mad, you can be sad, but you may not be disruptive," I say to the little girl in my classroom. Why not? Sometimes disruption feels exactly right.

Of course, in the classroom, disruption of the screaming kind inhibits the ability to learn. To disrupt with a tantrum does not harness the exceptional power this little girl possesses in intellect and resolve. It is one thing to physically express anger and attempt to control what you cannot. It is another to use the power that anger generates to effect change. I have faith that this little girl will one day learn to channel her power into the fierce ability to advocate for her beliefs. And as she joins the fearless women of *Generation F*, I believe our voices will grow louder. We are and will be more powerful than anger. We will effect change.

SARANE JAMES

YEARS AS MENTEE: 3

GRADE: Junior

HIGH SCHOOL: Bronx High School of Science

BORN: Bronx, NY

LIVES: Bronx, NY

MENTEE'S ANECDOTE: *This year, Margo and I spent a lot of time reading work by other authors—women like Helen Ellis and Morgan Parker, whose command over words left us feeling awestruck. Inspired by them, we decided to go outside of our comfort zones and write from another author's perspective. One of the stories from* American Housewife *inspired an amazing fictional email chain packed with snark and passive-aggressiveness. While it was hilarious to look back at all the veiled insults we had written, it was also impressive that we managed to capture the voice of another writer—something I wouldn't have tried alone.*

MARGO SHICKMANTER

YEARS AS MENTOR: 3

OCCUPATION: Associate Editor, Doubleday Books

BORN: Lenox, MA

LIVES: New York, NY

MENTOR'S ANECDOTE: *Seeing* Black Panther *together on opening weekend was a golden moment for us this year. In the week leading up to it we kept texting about how excited we were. Even sitting together in the theater was more fun than usual—it felt like we were part of a cultural moment. Afterward, I was so happy that this movie existed, in general, and for Sarane. We could not stop laughing when we both said at the same time that if she was any character from the movie she would obviously be Shuri, the princess who is also a tech genius.*

Generation Futureproof

SARANE JAMES

When I started to write about Generation F, I soon realized that the people it covers are too varied for a simple word or phrase. This poem is an attempt to give this term a shape, while staying true to its diversity.

We are *Generation F.*
A generation that spans many ages, many people.
We're anyone from Joan of Arc
to Hillary Clinton to Marley Dias.

We're out here making fearlessness feminine.
We're firefighters, snowboarders and activists,
police officers, writers and politicians
who are pushing the boundaries every day.

Fighting for equality is our forte,
and feminism is just one of our many causes.
We fight for civil rights and women's rights
and immigrants' rights. We fight for human rights.

Our diversity is our strength.
We wear our hair down and under hijabs
and in dreads and sometimes no hair at all,
sneakers and boots and heels and flats,
dresses and skirts and sweats and suits.

We adapt to our changing world with impressive flexibility,
but have the fortitude to stand up to unfit politicians
and have fun doing it.
We write, we march, we organize.
We make them nervous. They tell us to stop.
We persist.

As females we teach ourselves to fly,
yet find that there's always someone there
to catch us if we fall.
We cherish the women who always have our backs:
mothers, grandmothers, aunts, mentors,
neighbors, preachers, teachers, muses.
The list goes on and on.

We've faced a flood of negative feedback,
but it's all just noise to us frontierswomen.
It's not our fate to be held back by the fainthearted,
and we don't need to be famous to follow our guts.

We know what this world needs:
people to destroy the idea that
money is more important than our right to life.
It's the same thing this world doesn't want,
but we provide it anyway,
at Marjory Stoneman Douglas and beyond.

We are fast-growing, fearless, and futureproof.
We are *Generation F.*

Orbit

MARGO SHICKMANTER

I wrote this poem in response to the many brave women who have shared their stories about domestic violence as part of the #MeToo moment. Because of them, I hope the next generation has fewer such stories to tell.

A blue red planet
eclipsing the orbital socket,
each shattered insurrection
caught bone. He tells you,
you are the fact of your stature,
but you have never been more
than how angry you make him.
The honeymoon: A tropical bird
flared on your rib cage.
At night, you pet its feathers,
so each one knows it is not alone.
When he saw it, he bucked,
hands trying to wring the fever
from his skull, gathering more
instead. Is it a trick of the eye or
did the bird shrink from him, too?
He is the pestle to your mortar.
Were you supposed to be harder
stone and no one told you?
No one told you, but
you are not alone.

BIANCA JEFFREY

YEARS AS MENTEE: 2

GRADE: Junior

HIGH SCHOOL: The High
School of Fashion Industries

BORN: New York, NY

LIVES: New York, NY

MENTEE'S ANECDOTE: *I am very proud to say that I am a second-year mentee. These past two years with my talented mentor, Jennifer, have revealed to me the true power of teamwork. This year we have both shared important experiences that have been reflected in our writing. This journey so far has been very exciting and I can't wait for another year with Girls Write Now!*

JENNIFER ROWE

YEARS AS MENTOR: 3

OCCUPATION: Writer

BORN: Miami, FL

LIVES: New York, NY

MENTOR'S ANECDOTE: *Working with Bianca is always a pleasure! She is so smart, humble, and hardworking. She continues to amaze me with her willingness to take on challenges, even when they don't totally suit her writing style. Her ambition is very admirable, and I see only greatness in her future. I am lucky to work with such a great mentee who supports me as much as I support her.*

We Want You!

BIANCA JEFFREY

When I started thinking about Generation F, I automatically thought of a generation of fearless females breaking down all barriers. I am proud to live in a society where young women are encouraged to express their feelings about the misogyny of the time we live in.

Let's fight for your rights
Come join an army of women
We'll take you in

Help silence the cries of those oppressed
The power of your voice will blow your mind
Your words are the sword for equality
They come from within

Don't feel discouraged
You can be the woman you dream to be
The myths of your inabilities will be put to rest
The job you want is yours

Don't let them restrict you
Walk with all the confidence in the world
And you won't be silenced
We'll make changes

With your strength, this revolution will end soon
We are a generation of feminine activists who will stand up

For the ones who were told to settle down
You will help us knock down the wall of misogyny

We are the force of females
Fighting this corrupt institution
They may not see the problem, but join us to give the solution

For that girl

JENNIFER ROWE

The theme Generation F *spoke to my younger self. I wanted to create an empowering piece that spoke to all generations of women. Sometimes we just need a friendly reminder to love ourselves, believe in ourselves, and trust our instincts.*

It's *your* turn to be first girl
be the one who changes the world
keep your head higher than the birds in the trees
and keep your desires on fire for all the world to see

you *are* that girl who can speak her mind as she pleases—
don't be afraid to say what you're thinking! be fearless!
be fierce, be free, be flawlessly true
remember the world needs a girl like you

the strength of a woman is measured in her spirit—
listen to your voice and learn to endear it
be powerful, believe and always remain wise
embrace all your beauty and be sure to never hide
give love when needed and love yourself too
be *that girl*, because it all begins with you

ZARIAH JENKINS

YEARS AS MENTEE: 3

GRADE: Senior

HIGH SCHOOL: Midwood High School

BORN: Brooklyn, NY

LIVES: Brooklyn, NY

MENTEE'S ANECDOTE: *This year Alexis and I became much closer. Our relationship is not only strictly about writing, but we talk about other things such as our day, our likes and interests, our problems, even politics. Alexis has taught me to be unafraid to express myself in my writing. There would be times that I was stuck on a piece and she would always be there to help me get through it. We're always learning about new things together when it comes to writing. I honestly could not ask for a better mentor, because together we make a great team!*

ALEXIS CHEUNG

YEARS AS MENTOR: 2

OCCUPATION: Content Writer, Derris & Co.

BORN: Kailua, HI

LIVES: Brooklyn, NY

PUBLICATIONS AND RECOGNITIONS: *The Believer, Catapult, T Magazine*

MENTOR'S ANECDOTE: *For the last two years, Zariah and I have met in the Connecticut Muffin bordering Prospect Park. Early in the mornings, while cycling groups sip coffee and chew toasted bagels, we sit and write and review what she has written. Very recently, we spoke candidly about her personal life instead: about school and friends, boys and dating, college and anxiety. I was struck by her calm conviction and clarity of vision. It is our final year together, and I am so grateful for those Sunday mornings, where she has shown me that the next generation is prepared to lead us all.*

My Female Superheroes

ZARIAH JENKINS

This piece is dedicated to the two women who have impacted my life. Without them, I would not be the strong and confident person I am today.

According to a random study I found online, the average person meets about 80,000 people in his or her lifetime. Still I can guarantee you that no one has ever met *anyone* like the women in my life.

My grandmother is about five feet three inches tall. She's small but mighty, and always keeps busy, whether she's working, testing new recipes, or hitting the gym. She's kind-hearted, sweet, and doesn't care what anybody has to say, especially when she's on the dance floor. At just ten years old, my grandmother and her family moved out of her home in Greenwood, Mississippi, to live in the "Big Apple." Not only was the transition hard for her, but she was bullied at school because of her small frame and thick southern accent. My great-grandmother would often tell her, "Not everyone will like you, but as long as you like yourself you are doing good. Never give up on yourself!" My grandmother was an honor student throughout elementary, junior high, and high school. Even after losing her mother at a young age and becoming a mother at a young age, she continued to become the strong independent woman she is today. My grandmother wanted the best for her children. So she provided them with everything that they needed for a happy and healthy life, just like my mother did for me.

I've always believed my mom is a superhero. She's five foot seven, has brown eyes and a smile that's contagious. She's fearless, and knows how to handle any obstacle. To this day, I admire her strength. My mother never lets anybody talk her down. She always stands up for herself, no matter what. She is confident, smart; she knows her capabilities. She's a go-getter, and she works hard for what she wants. Not only that, but she's funny; she always finds ways to make me laugh, even when I'm in a bad mood. My mother has always been there for me. When I used to come home crying because kids at school would comment on how small I was, she would tell me that I am beautiful just the way I am and that I don't need to change myself for anybody. Even when I felt like there was no one I could talk to about things that bothered me, she always made sure that I knew I could come to her for anything. I could rant to her for days about the same thing, and she would listen every single time. Over the years, she has shown me the importance of trying my best and always believing in myself. She has taught me to love myself and to never let anybody treat me as any less than I am. My mother always goes out of her way to make me happy, even when I do wrong. I'm extremely thankful for the sacrifices she continues to make for me, making sure I am getting everything I want and need, just like her mother did for her.

My mother and grandmother have both influenced me and helped me grow over the years. Because of them, I know my worth. I am a work in progress and I should never allow people to make me feel ashamed for how God made me. My lithe frame doesn't define who I am; neither do my mistakes. It's about my personality and drive. The mark I leave on the world. They have taught me to work hard and never do less than my best. They also taught me that life is too short to be sad all the time. I should continue to smile and do the things that make me happy because surrounding myself with negativity won't do anything but hurt me. I am extremely grateful for these women, and I hope to one day inspire people like they inspired me.

Although I don't express it enough, I'm very thankful for the women in my life. Even though I'm a couple inches taller (five foot nine), I look up to both my mother and my grandmother. If I grow up to be anything like these two amazing women, I know I am doing something right.

Ring Around Iceland's Ring Road

ALEXIS CHEUNG

This piece is for my Generation F: my two fun, fearless female friends who turn navigating this world (Iceland, in this instance) into a story worth sharing.

I flew to Iceland out of privileged pity for my best friend. "I don't want to go alone!" Hannah lamented. Because I free-lanced, I obliged. Then our other best friend, Marcela, joined the trip; our duo turned into three.

Together, we'd drive Iceland's Ring Road: an 827.7-mile looping journey along the coast.

After an evening of heavy drinking in Reykjavik, we stranded Hannah (who arrived one day after Marcela and myself) at the airport the next morning. Hours behind schedule, we began driving almost halfway across the country. The landscape changed from grassy and expansive, oceanic and peaceful, volcanic and otherworldly. I begged them to pull over so I could throw up, marring the breathtaking beauty.

We drove to one waterfall, then another. We lay in the grass, our clothes damp and clinging to our bodies. Then we peeled away our soaked layers, like soggy labels from beer bottles. Marcela drove; Hannah made cheese sandwiches; I tinkered with my phone. For hours we subsisted on gas-station snacks.

Female friendships, Elena Ferrante wrote, "are a terra incognita, chiefly to ourselves, a land without fixed rules." When both women declared me their best friend, I remembered my surprise and pride—the feeling of belonging, knowing we could navigate our friendship according to our own code.

Like romantic love, deep friendships dispel long-endured loneliness and pain. Shortly before I met Hannah, I left my boyfriend of four years. A few months later, Marcela lost her mom. Right before our trip, Hannah had lost someone like a sister. Packed together inside that tiny, rented car, as Iceland's lunar landscape rushed past our windows, our friendship became the balm soothing every unhealed hurt.

Curving along Iceland's coast, I watched lava burn into the sea. In the backseat Marcela and Hannah were jostled awake when I steered us onto a suddenly unpaved road. By now we had driven for ten hours straight. We were lost, we were tired, we were hungry: an unholy trinity that devours some friendships forever.

Yet no one yelled. No one screamed. No one hurled blame. Instead, we laughed. Marcela, always compassionate, spoke soothing words. Hannah, so solution-oriented, assumed her co-pilot position.

"It's shit on the right," Hannah warned.

"It's shit on the left," she confirmed.

"It's shit on both sides!" she said. And we barreled along in the darkness, together.

FAIZA KHANOM

YEARS AS MENTEE: 1

GRADE: Junior

HIGH SCHOOL: Baccalaureate School for Global Education

BORN: Dhakha, Bangladesh

LIVES: Queens, NY

MENTEE'S ANECDOTE: *Girls Write Now has introduced me to an amazing person this year. With the help of my mentor, Nandita, I was able to improve my writing skills, specifically in creative writing. We juggled through junior year, with our half-hour conversations about everything from how our moms bargain in Indian clothing stores to college advising. I was able to get one-on-one attention in my writing and learned so many more insane English grammar rules. Nandita has made me realize that writing can be fun and even the little stories in your life matter.*

NANDITA RAGHURAM

YEARS AS MENTOR: 2

OCCUPATION: Writer, Gizmodo Media Group

BORN: Chicago, IL

LIVES: Brooklyn, NY

PUBLICATIONS AND RECOGNITIONS: *Vice*, Refinery29, *Bustle, Chicago Reader, Racked*, and more

MENTOR'S ANECDOTE: *I always knew Faiza and I had a lot in common on the surface. We were both from Southeast Asia and our parents were immigrants. But it was not until I read her Anthology piece that I really understood just how similar we were. That pair session, reading about her grandmother, I realized we connected on a deeper level: We navigated the world in the same way. Seeing this piece develop over our weeks together has been truly special, and I am so proud of how far Faiza has come as a writer and as a young woman.*

My Nani

FAIZA KHANOM

This is a piece about my grandma. She died on September 21, 2007. My grandma made an impact on my life because she encouraged me to try new things and we went through many adventures together.

It was September 18, two nights before my sixth birthday. The smell of fresh, ripe mangoes filled the air of Sreemangal. I lay on the soft bed. Patterns swirled on the headboard. There was a flower in the middle, with lines carved into the petals. I stared at the fan. Netting surrounded the bed, protecting us from mosquitoes. My arm itched on my shoulder. The moist air melted on my skin. Rain banged on the steel roof above me.

Nani came in the room. She wore an orange cotton saree and had a glass of milk in her hand. Her hand was shaking as she approached me. The glass of white milk was glowing in the dark. The diamonds on her bangles shone.

I gulped down the milk, holding my nose with my fingers. I hated milk as a child. My grandpa's farm was filled with cows that had horns the size of my arm. Their horns would stab the air, scaring me. Huge globs of cow poop filled the cow house. Every time I saw milk, I would smell that stench: garbage mixed with soil. But if I refused to drink the milk, Nani would say, "Don't you want to grow?"

She sang her old bedtime lullabies in Bangla, her voice soft and crackly like an old radio. As she paused, I would hear the crickets chirp. We drifted to sleep. Nani's arm hung around me and felt warm and protective. The ceiling fan turned, but my hot skin still felt sticky. But that did not matter to anyone because we had each other's company.

I woke up the next morning to the smell of fried eggs. I loved mornings in Bangladesh because they were busy. I would wake up to the smells of eggs, tea, *kichuri*, and *parathas*. I would always lie in bed for a long time, enjoying the smells.

As I walked down the long hallway to the kitchen, I noticed my *jam* plant. A few weeks ago we had eaten fruit from my grandpa's farm. It was divided into sections for bananas, coconuts, mango, tea, *jam* fruit, and more. Hundreds of tea bushes on hills stood in green, curved rows. Women with barrels on their backs would pick up tea leaves.

Jam was sweet and purple. As I bit into it the purple juice filled my mouth and dripped all over my dress. I couldn't believe that food could grow from a seed, but Nani encouraged me, saying, "Just try, we'll see what happens." So I planted it. And that morning before my birthday, the plant had sprouted. Because of Nani's encouragement, I was able to accomplish something I had never done before.

As I walked to the cavernous dining room everyone had already finished their morning tea and biscuits. Uncle had already left for work, and Mom had left my fried eggs on the table. One of my pet peeves was uncovered food, and a fly was already making circles around my plate like a magnet. I lost my appetite.

Since my birthday was tomorrow, Mom and Aunt flipped through their phone books and started calling relatives.

"What kind of cake do you want?" Mom asked.

"I want Aunt to make the cake, the cake that she made for Tuha's birthday was so pretty," I replied.

Aunt would decorate the cake beautifully with different colored icing. There was no oven, so Aunt and Mom had to bake it on the stove. It would take five or six hours, so they started that day.

On the evening of my birthday, my favorite dishes filled the table. There were sandwiches cut in half with toothpicks from the shop around the corner. The cake that Aunt had prepared had pink and yellow flowers swirled around. Perfectly triangular samosas lay on a plate.

After we ate, we played a game of charades with my cousins, aunts, and uncles. All of a sudden we heard screams and everyone rushed over to the living room, Nani had started to throw up. It was weird seeing her in this condition because Nani was so active, walking one mile every morning. Uncle called the doctor to the house. All the offices were closed since it was eleven.

That night, Mom and I slept in Nani's room. The blankets moved and the bed creaked as Nani fidgeted. She complained about the heat, so Mom turned on the fan. I shivered that night, and my legs tightened.

The next morning, Nani's condition had worsened. Her dark eyes drooped. She was rushed to the hospital in Dhaka, a three-hour drive away. Uncle, Aunt, and Nani left before dawn. She wasn't able to walk, so Uncle carried her to the car.

We prayed for Nani. Mom cooked since Aunt wasn't here. A crash came from the kitchen, and I rushed in. A broken plate was scattered all over the floor. Mom frantically ran around the kitchen.

At noon, the Zuhr Adhan—the signal for prayer—boomed through the city. As soon as the Adhan finished the phone rang. Mom started crying. Nani had died.

Foreigner's Tax

NANDITA RAGHURAM

Inspired by my mentee's submission, I also wrote a piece about my grandmother and visiting her in India as a young woman and speaking up for myself. It is one part of a larger story about the trip.

When I was nineteen, I lived alone with my paternal grandmother in Bangalore. At eighty-six, she couldn't cook because her gnarled fingers couldn't curl around pot handles or the oven door. She would forget to wear her dentures; they would sit leering in a glass of water. But at twenty-two, she got her master's degree in physics and marched with Gandhi.

My mother had to convince me to go there. "She's getting old," my mother said. "It would mean a lot to her."

"But I hate India. There's nothing to do."

"Grow up, Nandita."

My grandmother woke up at six every morning and would walk to the corner store to get steaming plastic cups of *sambar*, tripping over the cracked stone sidewalk. She would stick her balding head into my room. I would pull the wool blanket over my head and sleep until noon.

During breakfast, she would stare at me from across the table. She would hand me the only fork and plate in the house, then scoop mounds of rice and *rasam* with her hands into her mouth from a banana leaf. I would crouch behind a newspaper.

The milk there was warm and lumpy. The cereal tasted of plastic. Once I tried to cook scrambled eggs. When my grandmother came home, she retched and made me pray for three hours.

In the kitchen, a brown photograph of my grandfather hung above the table. I never met him, but I inherited his last name, a nose that's squat like a mound of mud, and big, brown eyes.

There were only two other photographs in her house. One shows my brother and I in 1992. My brother's hands rest on my shoulders, and tight black curls stick out of my head. In another, my mother is twenty-two, shy on her wedding day, staring at the ground, marigolds in her hair and red *kumkum* powder streaking her forehead like blood. My father cradles the back of my mother's neck.

My grandmother never liked my mother. She was beautiful, brushing her hair 100 times before bed. She lived a five-hour train ride away, down broken roads and through sugarcane fields.

Twenty-five years after my parents' wedding, my grandmother told me, "That mother of yours, she's silly. It's good you didn't inherit that airy little head of hers."

I stared at my food, wishing I knew enough Kannada to yell. Instead, I nodded.

WINNIE KONG

YEARS AS MENTEE: 1

GRADE: Senior

HIGH SCHOOL: Stuyvesant High School

BORN: Guangdong, China

LIVES: Brooklyn, NY

PUBLICATIONS AND RECOGNITIONS: 2018 Scholastic Art & Writing Awards: Silver Key; *YCteen* (September/October 2017); early acceptance to NYU

MENTEE'S ANECDOTE: *I have always been a person with too many words, and Sarah helped me bring these words onto paper. She helped me explore my creativity in terms of writing, creating a safe space that would allow me to be okay with sharing my vulnerability.*

SARAH CUSTEN

YEARS AS MENTOR: 1

OCCUPATION: ESL Lecturer, Long Island University–Brooklyn

BORN: Ogden, UT

LIVES: Brooklyn, NY

PUBLICATIONS AND RECOGNITIONS: "Zoom-in Freewrite," *New Ways in Teaching Creative Writing for the ELL Community*, TESOL Press

MENTOR'S ANECDOTE: *When we went to see* Sheila *together, as we were waiting for the other mentor–mentee pairs to arrive, one of the cast members mistook me for a mentee. I was flattered—obviously—but I also find it apt: Winnie and I are both first-timers, learning the ropes, together. We are equally learners, writers, and teachers. She has taught me so much, like how to use slang, and the concept of the Model Minority. We have grown as individuals, and as a pair, in coffee shops all over Brooklyn. We are, as Winnie put it, "an iconic duo" ("but never on time").*

Dissolving the Spectrum

WINNIE KONG

With this piece, I wanted to convey the feminine/masculine culture through a subtle yet compelling story. It was important for me to tell a universally relatable story, so I started by reminiscing about childhood.

She has always been pink. I have never given her the chance she deserved. Even when I denied her the right to be pink, she was still pink. Just like how I am pink and choose to be pink, she was blue and chose to be pink. I am sorry.

Pink. That was the color I chose every time. Light-up sneakers, Tamagotchis, fluffy dresses, nail lacquer polishes, scrunchies. It was my color, I was *cute* in pink.

I fell in love with it the first time my mother bought me cotton candy. Going to the Asian supermarket, crying and stomping my feet: That was my ritual. That day, one hand held on to a bag of seaweed and the other clutched this strange bag with English letters. I had to choose one. "Money doesn't fall from trees," she would say, as if I didn't understand that from all the previous times. I was puzzled by the peculiar plastic bag and consumed by curiosity. The bag of seaweed seemed like a promise of crispy goodness, but at that moment I was infatuated with the pink bag.

I ripped open the plastic bag, and a mixture of baby-blue and pink clouds melted in my mouth. My hands quickly became sticky, my tongue obsessed with the sugary foreignness. It was like a game of tag where pink was my sanctuary, and touching blue was dangerous.

Blue. He is blue. Actually, he is *supposed* to be blue. Yet he was wearing a pink shirt. He messed up the pattern I created in my head. Why was he wearing a color that wasn't meant for him? Boy and girl, blue and pink—we were supposed to separate into two different ends of the spectrum.

The next day at recess I saw him holding a Barbie doll. It was the one my mother refused to buy me. I was mad. He is blue, this is not fair. My face reddened and before I knew it, pink took the initiative to snatch the doll away from him. His childish smile metamorphosed into something tigerish, and soon he was blue, exactly how it was meant to be. I was proud of myself, I changed him back.

But sitting in class with him the following week, I saw that he had on pink nail polish. So did I, and there it was—this connection between us. I touched his hand, slowly moving toward the baby-pink tinted nails. I could taste the cotton candy in my mouth. He placed his other hand on mine, pointing at my pink-colored nails. Could he be pink, even if he is blue?

The older we grew, the more he was pink than blue. We used our eyelids like blank canvases, coating them with colors of the rainbow from red to purple, with orange, yellow, green, and blue in between. We felt as if we were above anything.

Leopard, polka dots, paisley, gingham, tartan. Exploring patterns in the women's section became our favorite pastime. We adored the queerness it brought our outfits. We laughed at the looks our parents gave when they saw us.

It was his touch on my thick black wavy hair that gave me this feeling that I had never felt before. First, I felt warm, then electric. It came like second nature. As I ran my hands through his shiny blond curly hair, he became more gentle, docile, considerate, and *nice*, and I liked that he was more pink with me, but blue with others.

And then, one day: "I want to be a girl." *What? No. You are blue. You are blue. No. I am pink. You cannot be pink. No. You can act pink, but you will never truly be pink.* I didn't understand, this wasn't *right*.

He wanted me to call him "she." It was as if "she" became a brand-new person. I no longer felt the sweetness of cotton candy with "her" anymore. Nothing was the same; it was as if "she" used me to be more pink. All those times, I thought we were friends who just liked the same things. I wanted him to appreciate pinkness, not allow it to overpower him.

Pink. "She" told me "her" life as if I understood the concept of being blue but declaring myself to be pink. I told her, "You cannot choose to be pink. You are blue." I took the pink cotton candy from her hands. She wasn't pink, she didn't deserve it. And then she told me, "I am just as much a female as you." *Huh?* You couldn't be pink just because you decided you're more comfortable with an option that wasn't selected for you. Just like how you couldn't open a bag of cotton candy and later choose the color of it.

The day you told me that you wanted to be pink blurred my vision. I could not be in love with pink when I am pink. I wanted you to stay blue but I realize now that I fell in love with your pink.

Poor Virginia

SARAH CUSTEN

Winnie and I drew inspiration from Judy Chicago's The Dinner Party *(at the Brooklyn Museum); the creative process used by The Associates, whose play,* Sheila, *we saw together (courtesy of Girls Write Now); and—of course—each other.*

Whose idea were the white lace curtains? My sisters', probably, but they make the room look garish, encased as they are by coal-black wooden walls in an aching, old house. Ditto the faded, flowered bedspreads, the threadbare cotton sheets like girls' dresses in summer.

Marcella and Sophia, away now at college, their bedroom frozen like a single slide of film, caught between frames, just before the light shines through. My room lies at the end of the hall. No lace or flowers, just pages ripped from books, from magazines, tacked into the supple walls and waving their words, like flags, in the wind.

All of us female by birth, double X, though Sophia and Marcella more typically so. They are Mom's blood-daughters, betrayers of her womb, their very existence an affront to her Self. "It felt," she once told me, "like being possessed." She had thought that she couldn't bear children, hence: me.

The adopted daughter, "The Chosen One" (they used to tease me), who is here to wipe up. Back home for the first time since turning eighteen, taking care of Mom, postoperatively. No longer Virginia, but Vinci (like Leonardo). She waited for this surgery, like the way some kids' parents will wait until the kids are grown up to divorce, not wanting to split up the family.

What she split, though, was time, right down the middle, so that never again would there be a house without a Before and an After. What she split were the seams of her very skin.

He told me he'd felt "imprisoned" in an "empty soul," "of which the very windows are shuttered," and I said, "So what? So you redecorate? Doesn't that smack of women's work?"

Later, she—*he*—tried again, via text: "I need to clip the wings of my vulvar butterfly, in order to be truly free," she wrote. I misread the word as "vulgar," which now I can see as the actual sentiment. I wonder, did the dazzling and dramatic installation of a new phallus, which continues to stain the bandages, give him what she had wanted? Does it rise up against erasure? Will it create the desired tension between historical conditions and the life that she—that he—wants to lead?

I think of the doctors' fine needlework; I think of my mother's face, breast, and arms.

I never knew she had a sacred heart.

DIAMOND LEWIS

YEARS AS MENTEE: 2

GRADE: Senior

HIGH SCHOOL: Brooklyn College Academy

BORN: Brooklyn, NY

LIVES: Brooklyn, NY

MENTEE'S ANECDOTE: *Jaime and I have grown tremendously in our mentee–mentor relationship. From going from complete strangers to bouncing off of each other's ideas and trading interesting new reads. Jaime is always there when I need her, whether it be for assignments for Girls Write Now, school, or scholarships. Our relationship is amazing and I know it will continue to grow over our teas and coffees at Starbucks.*

JAIME FULLER

YEARS AS MENTOR: 1

OCCUPATION: Web Editor, *Lapham's Quarterly*

BORN: Glens Falls, NY

LIVES: Brooklyn, NY

MENTOR'S ANECDOTE: *Diamond gives the best book recommendations. It's not anything she says; it's the sheer joy on her face as she launches into a very detailed description of the plot and how she felt during every twist and turn of it. By the time you get to the end, you might know everything that happens in the book, but you still want to go check it out from the library to see if you can get the same kick out of reading it as she had in explaining it. Spending time with her made me appreciate words much more.*

Hating on *The Hate U Give*

DIAMOND LEWIS

The Hate U Give is one of my favorite novels and I believe everyone should read it. The book discusses situations, both commonplace and infuriating, that young people, especially black teenagers, are facing today.

"I do not like or agree with this book."
  "Neither do I."
  "Let's ban it."

I imagine this is the conversation that accompanies the banning of books. What I don't understand, though, is that it is the reader's choice to read the book, an at-your-own-risk Choose Your Own Adventure. No one enjoys every book they read, and people can't ban everything they don't like. If so, there would be no dark chocolate, no tomatoes, no racism, and everyone would live in my perfect world, where the flag is pink, college is free, and *The Flash* isn't just a show on TV.

These conversations I imagine can't be new, given the history of barring students from novels in the United States. *Beloved* was violent, *The Autobiography of Malcolm X* was viewed as a how-to manual for crime, *The Catcher in the Rye* was simply "unacceptable," *The Great Gatsby* mentioned sex, and *Moby-Dick* "conflicted with community values."

The book that has me thinking about book banning in the first place is *T.H.U.G. (The Hate U Give)*. It was banned in Texas, specifically the Katy Independent School District outside of Houston, because of language deemed inappropriate for students. This school district has 70,563 students within grades K-12. Thirty-six percent of the students are white, 35 percent of the students are Hispanic, 15 percent are Asian, and 11 percent are African American. The district board isn't as diverse. It contains seven members; all are white. The use of curse words in the award-winning book is evident, but in the grand scheme of things, they are not used a lot.

I can understand why people are hating on *The Hate U Give*. This young-adult novel, which was published in 2017, is about a sixteen-year-old named Starr Carter who witnessed her best friend get murdered by the police after the two were stopped on their way home. After the incident, her two worlds, a private predominantly white high school and her own neighborhood, Garden Heights, begin to collide. Williamson High School is full of affluent and snobby students. Garden Heights, on the other hand, is an impoverished predominantly black community. The only similarity the two settings have is that Starr does not seem to fit in either. In her own community, she is known for bagging groceries at her father's store and for going to a fancy school outside of Garden Heights. When at school, she is not "white" enough to fit in, and code switches often. As she starts to feel these fault lines, the #BLM (Black Lives Matter) movement becomes real to her for the first time.

From that summary of the book's plot, it's impossible not to think that language was perhaps just a scapegoat for the ban, and that the real reason for keeping the book out of schools was because it confronts realities about racism that our country has spent centuries trying to ignore. The book is suffused with the real-world problems and situations that have always been present in America. Banning these books from schools doesn't make these issues disappear; it just gives students less room to understand them.

Banning books mutes the voices of the characters within.

Though fictional, each character in *The Hate U Give* carries a specific lesson. For example, Khalil, the character killed in the book, is judged based on his community and race. People who knew him through news chyrons called him a thug and automatically assumed that he was in a gang, exposing the negative connotations that come with an individual's race. If this sounds familiar, it's because this is exactly what happened with Trayvon Martin.

Many students have no firsthand experience with the problems in *The Hate U Give*. Given how difficult it can be to find young-adult books featuring a cast of predominantly people of color, the book also offers unaware readers a chance to see what a world with white privilege offstage—or at least one where white privilege is acknowledged—looks like. Some students reading will never deal with what Starr went through, but they would be able to have some type of understanding when finished. That is a worthy thing for a book to do, not something worth punishing with a ban.

When I read the book I could not put it down. It was the first time I read a book with a female, black main character who was not pregnant by the end, or whose only role in the plot was not to become another negative teen statistic. Starr was a character I could relate to. I loved that.

But the book banning will probably not stop here. I expect *Dear Martin* by Nic Stone will be targeted next; after I read both this and *T.H.U.G.*, the books have become one big story in my mind. It may be because they touch on similar problems. Either way, I'm waiting for *Dear Martin* to spark in popularity. I dare someone to try and hate on it.

The History of Hating on Books Like The Hate U Give

JAIME FULLER

This piece jumps off from Diamond's column on book banning to glimpse at a story that feels familiar once you read her piece. Sometimes it takes much longer than a moment, or two decades, for a lesson to take root.

In 1998, a high school English teacher in Maryland was forced to defend teaching her students that the past is sometimes uncomfortable—and that the best voice to share that with ninth-graders might be one that sounds like their own. "It's one thing to read about segregation from a history textbook, another to read it in a teenager's young voice. It's much more vivid." Her school district had banned *I Know Why the Caged Bird Sings* by Maya Angelou, first from being taught at all, and then only in the ninth grade. One of the parents who complained told *The Washington Post*, "I kept waiting for her to realize all white people weren't bad. The book ends, and I'm thinking, 'Didn't this woman ever realize that white people aren't Neanderthals?'" The reaction does little but prove that the book, after all these years, still felt uncomfortable enough to provoke, perhaps the best argument teachers could ever hope to encounter for why it would be valuable to sit down with young readers and help them see the many shades of nuance in Angelou's words before they, too, found their critical reading skills calcified by the world.

The book topped most lists of banned novels of the '90s. It kept getting banned. In 2006, an English teacher, in Wisconsin, again had to defend the book: "I felt as a teacher of the book that the students were mature enough to handle the concepts of the book and look beyond the images portrayed to a deeper meaning and the effects of what Angelou went through. What better place to discuss adversity than in a classroom setting?" Three years later, Angelou was asked about another attempt to ban her memoir: "I'm always sorry that people ban my books," she said. "Many times I've been called the most banned. And many times my books are banned by people who never read two sentences. I feel sorry for the young person who never gets to read." As Diamond says in her piece, "Banning these books from schools doesn't make these issues disappear; it just gives students less room to understand them."

JADE LOZADA

YEARS AS MENTEE: 1

GRADE: Sophomore

HIGH SCHOOL: High School of American Studies at Lehman College

BORN: New York, NY

LIVES: New York, NY

PUBLICATIONS AND RECOGNITIONS: 2018 Scholastic Art & Writing Awards: Gold Key; *Affinity Magazine*

MENTEE'S ANECDOTE: *Over chia-seed muffins and skim-milk lattes, Carol has challenged me to give voice to the ideas in my head. We share more than a love of journalism and storytelling; we bond over the parallels between our generations. With her, I have not only improved my writing, but I have learned that the most pertinent words will not keep everyone comfortable, including myself. Carol has given me the opportunity to delve deeper than ever before into these ideas of race relations as I live them. Each piece with Carol is an analysis of myself, our world, and its future.*

CAROL HYMOWITZ

YEARS AS MENTOR: 1

OCCUPATION: Author and Journalist

BORN: New York, NY

LIVES: New York, NY

PUBLICATIONS AND RECOGNITIONS: Fellow, Stanford Longevity Center; *The Wall Street Journal*; *Bloomberg BusinessWeek*

MENTOR'S ANECDOTE: *My weekly meetings with Jade have been deeply satisfying and fun, and I'm grateful to Girls Write Now for the chance to work with my mentee on her journalism, poetry, and other writing. Jade is teaching me so much about what it's like to be a Latina teenager and high school student today, and I'm continually struck by her talent, wisdom, and diligence. When she shared her feelings about growing up in a neighborhood that has morphed from mostly Dominican to white—with bodegas converting to upscale coffee shops—I suddenly saw my community with new eyes.*

On Being America

JADE LOZADA

I wrote this piece as I considered the nature of my American identity in comparison with those of the more privileged people I have encountered throughout my life.

"So, like, where are you from?"

"New York."

"No, what are you?"

"American." I'm not sure why I say this. We both know what he's trying to ask and there's nothing wrong with it.

"You know what I mean."

"My mom was born in the Dominican Republic, and my dad's family is Puerto Rican."

"Oh, nice. I'm Korean."

"Cool."

Neither of us is ashamed, that is for sure. In fact, my ethnicity feels validated by explaining it to another person of color. There is a grossly understated appreciation for each other's backgrounds that "cool" doesn't reflect. And in speaking to my classmate, I wonder why this doesn't hold true when I have this conversation with white people. I do not expect everyone to be able to distinguish between Puerto Rican and Dominican, but nevertheless my ethnicity is rarely understood. Does white America know what it means to belong to two cultures?

Their heritage seems to exist exclusively in sepia photos from the last century and the knowledge of a few garbled and unrelated words of "their" language at best. Ancestors, I am often told, hailed from brisk Irish bluffs, hamlets in the snow-capped mountains of Germany, and picturesque Italian villages hugging the sea. Inevitably, some married the Eastern European Jews whom their parents had slandered and, somewhere down the bloodline, but not too far back, a single Frenchman perhaps joined the party. After all, who doesn't want to be French?

But this predictable laundry list of nationalities refers to the past, not the present. Our original "melting pot" has yielded homogeneous populations in which percentages do not matter because surnames no longer connect to roots. White people blend in with each other. They do not have to worry about being the "other." They are not defined by who "came off the boat" because those are not the same people now making dinner. White people have the privilege of deciding who will know their background. And, as whites, that is when they seem to most fit under the umbrella of "American."

Perhaps I feel so reluctant to talk about my own culture with white people because explaining my skin makes me feel less "American." This is my fallback, and that of many people of color. When America does not work for us, we refuse to be "American." Suddenly, we are Latino, Asian, and black first, and we pretend that the country for which our ancestors toiled never meant anything in the first place. We are American with a hyphen, because, ultimately, the term was made for white people.

It is difficult to love a country that does not always love you back. It is unfair that our few recorded ancestors lived at the outskirts of society and that we have to learn of them as a bloc relative to the exploits of white men. Their faces and stories are merged into a single PowerPoint slide defined by what they did not have. It is daunting not to know who you have lost. And when some of your civil rights are younger than your grandmother, it is infuriating to have them threatened.

So why, then, would we deny ourselves the label "American,"

for which our ancestors suffered, just because we are being denied the privileges attached? A group is most powerful when it embraces itself. Once not long ago, the ancestors of today's white America were driven to the shores of the United States from Europe's darkest corners, and they were not considered unquestionably American, either. Rather than acquiesce, they redefined the term "American." People of color will only succeed today in our mission for social equality if we emulate our predecessors.

Betting on Teens in the Trump Era

CAROL HYMOWITZ

This is a short essay I wrote about being American in today's difficult political climate and what's enabling me to stay optimistic. It was inspired by Jade's piece on her views on being American.

"There goes *your* president again," says an Australian friend, after hearing Donald Trump advocate that the way to stop school shootings is to arm teachers. "What's happening with Americans that got Trump elected?"

It's a question I've heard again and again from colleagues and friends around the world, and one that confounds and embarrasses me. In fact, proclaiming my nationality when I'm traveling overseas or among foreigners is something I avoid. Because the America I believe in—a place which, for all its historical injustices and failings, has always embraced the quest to become a better, more "perfect union"—isn't the America I hear when my country's president speaks or tweets.

Elections? If they go against Trump, they're "rigged." Judicial review? If it's not in his favor, it's unfair or crooked. The press? Anything critical of him is "fake news."

I'm old enough to have lived through many dark political times. I was in high school when John F. Kennedy was assassinated and in college when student "Freedom Riders" risked and in some cases lost their lives fighting for voting rights for African Americans. Then came the assassinations of Martin Luther King Jr. and Malcom X, followed by riots in big cities and the trauma of Vietnam, during which young men I knew were wounded and killed in combat or went to jail because they opposed the war. Out of the antiwar and civil rights movements, the women's liberation movement arose—disrupting workplaces as well as marriages as women sought equal footing in their professional and personal lives. And still later came the 9/11 terrorist attacks at the World Trade Center, which ushered in an era of global terrorism and devastating wars in the Middle East.

Through all these upheavals, however, I never doubted that democratic institutions would prevail and that out of every struggle or tragedy would come at least a bit of progress and reinvention. Now the ideas and ideals that have long defined America, especially respect for the rule of law and honesty and decency in conduct toward others, are being threatened daily.

Yet for all the distress I feel about Trump's assaults on democratic principles, I'm increasingly optimistic. Americans, instead of passively accepting Trump's beliefs and behavior or staying silent, are voicing their opposition. This political activism began the day after Trump took office with the Women's March. I was buoyed when I joined this protest in January 2017 and again this year, and marched with my husband, stepson, and other men as well as millions of women. I was buoyed again when Americans from every region helped save Obamacare by relentlessly lobbying legislators.

What makes me most hopeful is the surging activism among America's youth. High school and college students have emerged as the leaders who are transforming the debate about two of the nation's most pressing issues: gun control and immigration. Survivors of the Marjory Stoneman Douglas High School shooting in Florida, within days of that tragedy, channeled their grief into fighting the gun lobby by giving impassioned speeches, meeting with lawmakers, and organizing the nationwide March for Our Lives. And young DREAMers are risking their personal residency status to fight for their right to citizenship.

Just like the mentees at Girls Write Now, these teenagers are informed, articulate, and brave. I'm betting on them to create a better future, and I'll be supporting and marching with them as they do.

OUMOU LY

YEARS AS MENTEE: 1

GRADE: Senior

HIGH SCHOOL: Urban Assembly Institute of Math and Science for Young Women

BORN: New York, NY

LIVES: Brooklyn, NY

PUBLICATIONS AND RECOGNITIONS: Scholastic Art & Writing Awards: Silver Key

MENTEE'S ANECDOTE: *Stephanie and I both have very particular writing styles and opinions, so in our time together we have learned to listen and learn from each other. She's pushed me to be a better writer in challenging my ideas, and now I'm way more open to criticism, which can be hard for any writer to face. Explaining myself and my views is now something I can look forward to.*

STEPHANIE GOLDEN

YEARS AS MENTOR: 4

OCCUPATION: Author, Journalist, Book Doctor

BORN: Brooklyn, NY

LIVES: Brooklyn, NY

PUBLICATIONS AND RECOGNITIONS: "We Need the Singular 'They,'" *Aeon.co*, 2018

MENTOR'S ANECDOTE: *This was our first year together, but since Oumou is a senior, we didn't have a relaxed period of getting to know each other. Our relationship was forged in the heat of college essays—a lot of them. We plunged right in and worked hard all fall. I discovered that Oumou has a philosophical mind, and her essays are deep. She's not just talented, but determined—a great combination for a writer. I'm so impressed by her willingness to think her ideas through and dive deep to bring up her own profound truths.*

A Stranger

OUMOU LY

"To be sane in a mad world is madness." I resonate with this as a Muslim. My religion is what allows me to see through worldly illusion and still have purpose.

I'm *Muslim first* before anything.

I have Allah to thank for that.

Alhamdulillah.

I know myself but society doesn't.
My beliefs and I are strange to society,
but society is actually strange to me.

You see . . .
There's race—this thing defined by *black* or *white*,
or funny enough by the land you come from if you don't fit
    those two colors.
'Something—ish' . . . 'something—ian' . . . 'something—ese,'
for those who aren't black or white.
This *thing* called race, pits black against white in an uphill
    battle, involving the whole world, which almost seems to
    revolve around it . . .

Then there's ethnicity—which actually helps us to be familiar
    with one another as humans, and gives us culture . . .

yet there's this certain darkness of human nature that oozes in
    like poison and attacks our hearts.
Because funny enough defiantly dividing ourselves by our own
    ethnicities and the cultures they produced just wasn't enough.
We had to go further . . .
causing division even with those we supposedly identify with,
    bringing about high and low status, or tribes,
and fair skin vs. skin that isn't so,
which presents itself in almost all things.
And the fairer and richer are always more valued.
Says who?

Hate, jealousy, greed, disagreement and the angst that trails
    behind . . .
It's all on us—
we are the human nature.

So you see, race and ethnicity and all these other social
    constructs just don't matter all that much to me,
because they're either made up or messed up.
Time is money, money is time . . .
Money makes the world go round.
It's so sad it's funny, then sad again when you realize . . .
How did we get here? . . .
How did we make up these constructs?
No—why did we—have to?

Where do these things get you?
I wanna know—*really.*
You take nothing when you leave this place,
So why get attached to it?

Black vs. white,

sexism,
one person, one group, over another,
any oppression . . .
why feed into it?
What—is—your—point?
We're all the same—in the same exam room.
Placed onto Earth where the test is life.

But I've seen for myself what the bad of human nature can do . . .
In those stares that try to burn through the hijab that
    encapsulates me.
The hijab that is more than a scarf that I wrap around—it
    covers my being and soul, protecting me . . .
in my look and talk and from any harm.
And again I've seen for myself what human nature can do . . .
In those stares that try to undermine the brown skin that is
    just another part of me, a black girl in hijab—but skin
    doesn't define religion.
My hijab is more—Islam is more.
So never mind the stares and sly remarks and ignorance of
    some . . . never mind the fear.
Those, they fear the truth . . .
but they'll never know it as long as they let all the bad of
    human nature take over them.
And as for me,
a stranger it is.

I'm *Muslim first* before anything.

Unfazed by those who class me with terrorism at the instant
    of their eyes meeting my hijab,
and my skin with less worth at the instant of seeing its
    brownness.

Unfazed by those who disregard other humans
at the instant of seeing
that they don't meet the standards put forth by those who
    abuse the bad of human nature . . .
the human nature that should tip more toward good on the
    scale, should it be what's best for you.

Those see me as strange,
but we're all the same.
Because when we leave this place we take nothing.

YOLO.
No.
You only live twice.
There's something better coming—
Insha'Allah . . .
It's that eternal peace we all strive to achieve in everything we
    do, unknowing that we can only reach it after we leave this
    place.
That can come to you.

Proud to be a stranger in this ironically strange world.
It isn't home and things are just messed up—made up.
I don't know how everything has come to be so far gone, but
    I do know something.

I'm *Muslim first* before anything.

I have Allah to thank for that.

Alhamdulillah.

#MeToo, Circa 1978

STEPHANIE GOLDEN

This poem, written in our Poetic Forms workshop, presents a #MeToo moment of my own from long ago, before we even had a term for such an experience.

Leashless,
snuffling the grass,
puppy gambols about.
Sunny weekend afternoon
at park.

Up comes
baby-faced cop,
younger even than me.
"That dog can't be off leash," he warns.
"Okay."

So young,
doesn't scare me,
though after I leash her,
shrug, walk off, he follows,
talking.

Why? What?
Wants to seem tough,
this baby policeman,

so frightens available girl,
or tries.

But fails—
I'm too naïve
to fear a policeman,
though he wants to see me scared, just
for fun.

Why not?
Girls are for that.

CIARA McKAY

YEARS AS MENTEE: 1

GRADE: Sophomore

HIGH SCHOOL: Harvest Collegiate High School

BORN: Brooklyn, NY

LIVES: Brooklyn, NY

MENTEE'S ANECDOTE: *Jaime has changed my life and writing in so many ways. She has helped me actually edit my work (I know I wouldn't without her) and she understands when writing is "Just too much right now." With her I have opened up about sharing my work and ideas. Our weekly meetings at The Bean will always be my happy place.*

JAIME MISHKIN

YEARS AS MENTOR: 1

OCCUPATION: Freelance Writer; English as a New Language Teacher

BORN: Trenton, NJ

LIVES: New York, NY

MENTOR'S ANECDOTE: *My favorite thing about meeting with Ciara each week is hearing about all of the amazing things she's doing—I'm always in awe of the number of books she reads each week (three or four!), the new recipes she tries, the essays she's writing for school, the podcasts she's listening to, and more. Over each cup of coffee we share, she inspires me through and through, and reminds me to be curious and brave.*

Sisters

CIARA McKAY

This poem is about my relationship with my older sister, and how she affects my life; it's about change, evolution, and finding myself. This is for you, Oona.

When I was 5
And you were 6
I always used to cry when you got in trouble
'Cause I didn't want to do anything without you.

Dad would say
"Oona can't watch the movie with you"
"She's in trouble"
But I would cry until you could.

When I was 12
And you were 13
I was fine with you getting in trouble
But I only liked *Doctor Who* because
You liked *Doctor Who*

And we could talk about it
For hours on end
Until I started to like it for myself.

Now I'm 15
And you are 16

Next year is your last at home
And I'm scared for you to leave
Because I'm not sure what living without you is like.

But I'm excited
To learn what liking *Doctor Who* by myself is like.

Blessings

JAIME MISHKIN

Every age greets us with new challenges. I wrote this poem thinking about my relationship with Ciara this year: two women, ten years apart, trying to navigate our lives and this crazy city.

Blessings, 10 years ago
May you stop straightening your hair.
May you stop shaving your arm hair.
May you talk on the phone with friends for hours and never
    hang up.
May you hug your mother and forgive your dad.
May you walk home from school very, very slowly.
May you go to the movies with your mom every chance you get.
May you suspend your eye roll.

Blessings, today
May you breathe.
May you wait.
May you . . .

Blessings, 10 years from now
May you sit down every day at your desk and write.
May you own a proper desk.
May you stop worrying about what people think of you.
May you be kind and gentle to yourself.
May you have a job with benefits.

May you go to social gatherings without hesitation.
May you make new friends.
May you keep the old.

NATALIE MOJICA

YEARS AS MENTEE: 2

GRADE: Junior

HIGH SCHOOL: Central Park East High School

BORN: New York, NY

LIVES: Bronx, NY

PUBLICATIONS AND RECOGNITIONS: Scholastic Art & Writing Awards: Gold Key

MENTEE'S ANECDOTE: *I think the first time I met Gabriella outside of the Girls Write Now office was the most important. I was terrified that she would be someone I would never be able to talk to or want to share my writing with. However, from the first moment we started speaking I quickly realized the opposite would be true. She is someone who cultivates my creativity and inspires me to work on writing more. She doesn't dismiss my opinions or input, and supports me in more ways than one. I owe much of the writing projects I'm working on to her.*

GABRIELLA DOOB

YEARS AS MENTOR: 2

OCCUPATION: Editor, Ecco/HarperCollins

BORN: New Haven, CT

LIVES: New York, NY

MENTOR'S ANECDOTE: *Natalie has led me to think differently about my writing by being willing to try new things herself. She is constantly pushing herself to broaden the scope of her work, and I'm inspired by her example. She reads widely and finds her material in so many different places. I feel pretty confident we could sit down and write about almost anything together . . . and that's often what we do.*

Self-Conscience

NATALIE MOJICA

I wrote this piece after finishing what is now one of my favorite shows of all time. As I've grown as a writer, I've realized how the nuances of relationships can be explored through prose, and, using inspiration from the main characters, I created this short story.

> "I'm the one that you could come to for guidance, bring you home alive when you was wildin'"

Living in the country is hard. It's too hot in the summer and too cold in the winter. You run out of blankets quickly; and before that, you run out of love. There's something cute about how they thought they could run away from everything. As if death didn't haunt you if you lived far away. The grim reaper knows no boundaries. Why did they think moving to the countryside would make anything better? It is only worse. When things die here, everyone is too tired to even bother digging graves.

He found comfort in her like hot chocolate on a winter night, or how men always find comfort in the women they think are easy to make homes out of. Why is it that a girl always has to be a home for you to love her? Why can she not just be a woman? I have never understood. Maybe they go looking for bodies to live in because their own houses are too cold. But now they have run out of blankets. He should've just bought a space heater and called it a day.

A concept: They are young again. Her smile is enough now.

The city is vibrant with colors so pretty they don't have names yet. But he pretends they do. She names all the flowers she finds after him. A normal day is boring. Insignificant. Uneventful. It involves him breaking the rules to be with her and her laughing, telling him he shouldn't, but grateful that he does anyway. These days pass by slowly. She doesn't mind being a home for him. She relishes the fact that she is there for him. Always. Even when they are apart they aren't. He picks up sticks and puts them in her hair. She calls him immature but keeps all of them.

Here's the thing about sticks: They break.

Here's the thing about flowers: They wilt.

The countryside has droughts. There isn't enough water for her to grow flowers for him anyway. Not that she would. Even if it did nothing but rain, it is already too late. She would just let them drown. Being someone's home is exhausting. Sometimes all she wants to do is collapse. Fall asleep and stay that way, let their love rest in peace, as she has never been able to let it do. But then. A flicker of light appears in his eyes. Always on the days that the sun scorches their skin. He will look at her and she will feel the admiration from his gaze. He says thank you for letting me stay in your house with his eyes. She says you're welcome with her lips. On these days her smile is still not enough, but it is close. So close he can ignore how hard living in the country is. How death is coming for them still, how he's not sure he wants to run away from it again. These days they are young. She looks at the weeds growing in their farm and thinks, *Maybe I can name something else after him.*

Born

GABRIELLA DOOB

One of the great things about writing alongside my mentee has been feeling free to experiment with new forms—and to think about the future. As my friends start to have children, I think about new generations and what it means to decide to bring a human being into the world.

The vertiginous headlong
making of a human being.

When do you decide?
Is it now?
Is it now?
Is it now?
Is this the moment that changes all?

Maybe now was the moment
And now it's gone by.
Maybe then was the moment
It will always be gone.
Maybe soon is the moment
It will never arrive.

The catapulting-into-unknowingness
Making of a human being

The breaking of a human life

into then and now.

You can't undo
You can only do
And into the space you didn't know was vacant
Bring a person whose name,
spoken at the chosen moment,
will always have the power
to shatter you.

BETSY MORALES

YEARS AS MENTEE: 1

GRADE: Senior

HIGH SCHOOL: Baccalaureate School for Global Education

BORN: Queens, NY

LIVES: Queens, NY

PUBLICATIONS AND RECOGNITIONS: Scholastic Art & Writing Awards: Honorable Mention

MENTEE'S ANECDOTE: *Boy, am I glad I met Stephanie. At last, an adult who appreciates my sense of humor. Though she's way more than that—she's become my friend that lives far away that I see frequently at cafés for girl talk . . . and girl write. From struggling to connect to Juan Valdez's Wi-Fi to buying overpriced snacks at the Brooklyn Museum, we have done it all. But we've mostly drank tea and chai lattes. Sitting in the dark atrium after Amy's Bread closed in the NYPL wasn't so scary, unless chairs were dragged around. This year will be unforgettable, thanks to her!*

STEPHANIE FLETCHER

YEARS AS MENTOR: 1

OCCUPATION: Editor, Houghton Mifflin Harcourt

BORN: San Pedro, CA

LIVES: Brooklyn, NY

MENTOR'S ANECDOTE: *Getting to know Betsy has been so fun and inspiring. I've loved hearing about her amazing dad, who takes her to their favorite restaurant in Chinatown and decorates their apartment every year for her birthday (this year a space theme!). Her sense of humor is a little snarky and always refreshing—she was able to laugh and write about getting bitten by a dog on vacation, even though she had to get rabies shots! Sometimes the state of the world can feel very heavy, but Betsy always makes me feel optimistic, and I'm glad to have her on my side.*

Generation F: The FIGHT IS ON

BETSY MORALES

The first (PG) F-word that came to mind was "Female," but I wanted to go beyond that. After brainstorming, my mentor, Stephanie, and I thought "Fight" would ignite a thrilling story.

> Woke
> /wōk/ adj.: being aware of the social and political envi-ronments regarding all demographics and socio-economic standings.

A white wall stood in the parking lot of the Museum of the Moving Image, trash blown around with occasional gusts of cold wind.

The white wall now had a camera in its middle. The words HE WILL NOT DIVIDE US were printed above it in bold black letters.

Walking by on a rather glum day, music emanating from the "abandoned" parking lot made me stop and investigate. An abundance of teens danced around one another, forming circles and raising their arms. HE. WILL NOT. DIVIDE. US.

The repetition of these words compelled me to walk over and admire a few feet away. Holding on to my bookbag straps, I pondered who this mysterious "HE" was. A familiar face wearing a red beanie and all denim motioned my friend and me to join the crowd. Not once did he stop chanting.

Drummers beat on white plastic buckets resting on the gray gravel, bringing rhythm to the scene. Students desperately chanted, as if our words could change the glum atmosphere haunting our country.

Walking into the crowd, it hit me. The date was January 20, 2017, a historical day—for worse. It was the day of Donald Trump's inauguration.

The faces of teenagers from all around the world stunned me, even more so to find that they were all from the two nearby high schools, mine included. As soon as I joined the crowd, we all became one, preaching that no matter who is in office, we will stand our ground and voice what we believe in: unity.

Busy teens scurried around the small area of the parking lot. A girl with radiant skin and a soft smile offered me a flower to place in my hair, to match everyone around.

Possibly the only individual older than eighteen danced inside the circles we formed. He chanted the loudest as he bounced from side to side.

"YEAH, SHIA!" a boy with hair curled as tightly as rings of iron wire screamed.

Oh my God . . . It's Shia LaBeouf!

HE WILL NOT DIVIDE US was an interactive artwork by Shia LaBeouf and collaborators Nastja Säde Rönkkö and Luke Turner. It started the day of the inauguration in 2017. Visitors became part of the installation as they repeated the phrase "HE WILL NOT DIVIDE US" for as long as they wished into the security camera.

The following days burst with all of our voices. Our generation was being heard, rain or shine. The rain dropped hard and cold; we all bunched in small clusters under colorful umbrellas. The movement in our bodies never stopped, always demanding change. No, I don't mean change of POTUS, which we would all love, but change in society—acceptance of all people as what they were, people.

Soon enough, Shia left the scene, left New York. The crowd's vitality depleted consistently. We'd then all walk by and think of the memories we shared, music, unity, love, and life.

Until, on February 10, 2017, the museum abandoned the project. The camera vanished, the words were simply painted over with more white paint. It was as if all our hard work and efforts were never exerted. Our footprint was erased. Days, weeks, and months passed by, everyone seemed to have forgotten those two weeks. Truly, that was unfair to the experience and all it had provided us with was a safe space where we shared a belief . . . Trump sucks big-time! But it also offered a glimmer of hope. In the sense that this generation—our generation—has so much more to give, and we should never be written off as dumb technology-absorbed kids.

It was once more a white wall that stood in the parking lot of the Museum of the Moving Image. Occasionally the gusts of wind reminded us all of our exuberant cries yearning for change.

Time Travel

STEPHANIE FLETCHER

Trying out new genres in our workshops inspired me to get outside my nonfiction comfort zone. Instead I wrote not just a work of fiction, but challenged myself even more for one that's entirely dialogue.

"I think we should do it."

"Perry, you know we can't. Forget the butterfly effect— you're talking the last two hundred years—all of American history—annihilated. If we go back in time, if we convince them not to adopt the Electoral College, the world we know is gone."

"Maybe. Maybe not. But look around! Look at where we are now! Whatever the alternative, it couldn't be worse."

Maya bit her lip and looked at her friend. Couldn't it? "You don't think we can still make it better, here, now?" she asked. "You don't think we can come out on the other side?"

Perry frowned.

"Germany came back after Hitler," Maya said.

"Hitler was defeated by military might. No one can defeat the U.S., and if they try, he'll nuke the world. He'll destroy it. Everyone. I mean, the real apocalypse."

"And if we go back, if we do this, who will stop Hitler then? What if America isn't powerful anymore?"

"I know, it's risky. But an America without military power might be a blessing. Think of Afghanistan, Syria, Nicaragua, Vietnam. Don't you think the world could be a better place without our meddling?"

"Maybe," Maya said. She pressed on. "But what about the end of slavery? What about President Obama? If Dubya hadn't won in 2000, would Obama have won in '08? That could all be gone. We could come back to a Confederate America, or a real-life *Handmaid's Tale*."

"Is that so different from where we're headed now?" Perry cried, flinging his arms wide. "If we're there anyway, we have nothing to lose."

His voice softened. "But think where we could be. The good timeline. Think of the world we could have."

Maya let herself see it—a utopian America. The good time-line. Clean, and healthy; kind people who value equality and community; an economic landscape where everyone has a fair shot; a political process where everyone has a voice.

"We can have that world," she said. "But not by going to the past. We make it by going forward."

ANGELY MOREL

YEARS AS MENTEE: 1

GRADE: Sophomore

HIGH SCHOOL: Manhattan Village Academy

BORN: New York, NY

LIVES: New York, NY

PUBLICATIONS AND RECOGNITIONS: Scholastic Art & Writing Awards: Honorable Mention

MENTEE'S ANECDOTE: *My mentor and I went to a book launch, which left me completely amazed. I learned a lot about being empowering and standing up for what I believe in. There were people from all ages and generations, but it was like everyone was thinking the same thing. It taught me to be proud of who I am—a Latina, a teenager, and a woman—and it motivated me to work hard and prove that I can do anything.*

KATE JACOBS

YEARS AS MENTOR: 6

OCCUPATION: Senior Editor, Roaring Brook Press/Macmillan Children's Publishing Group

BORN: Grand Rapids, MI

LIVES: Brooklyn, NY

MENTOR'S ANECDOTE: *Even though we are from different generations, Angely and I are a lot alike. Through our weekly meetings and our writing together, we are constantly learning about things we have in common. (Even our birthdays are only two days apart!) The biggest thing is that we both have sisters, and we've both experienced how the relationship with our sisters changes over time. The only difference is, mine has been going on longer.*

An Everlasting Bond

ANGELY MOREL

Me and my sister's relationship changed when she went to college, but it didn't change in an entirely bad way. This experience helped me mature and opened my eyes to how to cherish the moments when they happen.

My relationship with my sister changed when she left for college.

Before, we were really close, like a piece of gum, we stuck to each other. We had a sister connection that always drew us together like we were in sync. Whenever we got hungry, we knew we had to make a snack, go to the living room, and watch something together. Or when it was Friday and the house was quiet, we would put music on and start dancing to Anthony Santos, no questions asked. And whenever our mom screamed at us, my sister would defend us.

When my sister left for Princeton she said everything would be the same and she would call me every day.

That didn't happen.

Ivy Leagues are no joke.

Now we talk only sometimes because either she is studying or I am—it seems like it's just never the right time. We're always out of sync. When she comes home from school on breaks there is no dancing and watching movies all the time like before. She's always worrying about all the things she needs to get done before returning to school.

My mom doesn't scream at her anymore because my mom puts her on a pedestal—the daughter who got into a fancy college on a full-ride scholarship. And when I get screamed at I have to deal with it myself.

Living and sleeping in the same room for years made us inseparable, and not having that anymore has made us drift apart. But I still get excited and always count down the days till she comes home because even if we don't talk every day, she is my best friend. She still knows me in a way that no one else ever will. And I treasure the memories I do have with her. But things aren't like they were before.

I Could Never Love Anyone as I Love My Sisters

KATE JACOBS

My relationship with my sisters has had so many ups and downs over the years—this piece is about a time when it was at its best, and how that memory sustains me even when our relationship is more difficult.

My relationship with my sisters changed when they started high school. As kids, we had always fought, and as twins they had frequently ganged up on me. But when I was a senior in high school and they became freshmen, something flipped. We went to a large high school and a lot of the kids at our new school had a lot of money. It was a pretty overwhelming change, and I wanted to protect them from feeling insignificant, I think. And they looked to me for advice about how to navigate this alien place. Also, having twin sisters was novel, unique, and a little cool! I was proud of them, not embarrassed by them for the first time ever. I went to their basketball games, they came to my plays. We sang Destiny's Child songs on the radio together while putting on makeup in our bathroom. I drove them around with the car windows down and a breeze in our hair, our laughter carried away on the wind. We pigged out on sour gummy bears together, cried about the movie *Titanic* together, and made life hell for our parents together.

When I left for college, I made them picture frames with our picture and a quote from the 1996 *Little Women* movie: "I could never love anyone as I love my sisters."

It's been twenty years since I gave them that quote. And since then we've laughed and cried and fought. And we've loved—friends, husbands, babies. But that quote is still true—no matter how many others I love, I'll never love anyone else the same way I love my sisters.

AMINA MORGAN

YEARS AS MENTEE: 1

GRADE: Junior

HIGH SCHOOL: The Institute for Collaborative Education

BORN: New York, NY

LIVES: New York, NY

MENTEE'S ANECDOTE: *Lauren and I have been meeting in one of the flashier cafés in our neighborhood, which coincides with the idea of how much where I live is constantly changing. We couldn't have met here a few years ago, since this place didn't exist back then. I was recently in Nepal and I noticed their streets were lined with the type of family-owned businesses my neighborhood used to have. And although I sometimes miss those smaller shops, I also enjoy the change that gives color to what I write with Lauren and the stories I tell my friends and family.*

LAUREN SPENCER

YEARS AS MENTOR: 1

OCCUPATION: Assistant Managing Editor, *Woman's Day* magazine

BORN: Pasadena, CA

LIVES: New York, NY

PUBLICATIONS AND RECOGNITIONS: NYU School of Professional Studies Teaching Excellence Award

MENTOR'S ANECDOTE: *Writing with Amina has been so fun because not only have we tackled things that both of us were nervous about (I'm looking at you, poetry), but also because once we get rolling talking about women in the world today and our power, I feel energized. Our weekly get-togethers are filled with the good fun of exploring new topics and also appreciating that by living only blocks away from each other we have some of the same view out the window, but I always look forward to hearing how she sees it differently—or the same—as I do.*

It All Started With . . .

AMINA MORGAN

I have noticed the rapid changes occurring in my neighborhood and how the new generation of people have impacted the flow of the surroundings. The little things I used to not notice are now all I see.

I remember going to Twin Donut five years ago, soon after I'd moved to my neighborhood: Washington Heights. It was right at the entrance to the subway station, and my favorite thing to order there was their oatmeal, *avena*, which I'd take on the train with me to school. It was served in a to-go coffee cup and the consistency was more something you drank than ate with a spoon. It was well spiced and comforting and reminded me of when I was young. Whenever I walked in the door, the people who worked there were always friendly and smiled. Then one day a "Closing Soon" sign appeared, and soon after, the place was empty and blue wooden panels sprang up around it. Next a "Boston Market" sign popped up. At first I was excited because their food had always been a treat when I lived in New Rochelle, but when the Boston Market finally opened it wasn't as special as I remembered. That's when I realized how much I'd taken Twin Donut for granted.

This isn't the first time that a business has closed down because of how the neighborhood's demographic changed. It makes me wonder what came first: the real estate agents driving the change or the new people moving in? By making the neighborhood more "desirable" (and who makes that call?), do the business owners become less involved in knowing who lives there? It makes me wonder if you can have a personal connection only if it's a small family-run business. There used to be a lovely older couple who owned a florist shop on the corner of 158th and Broadway. The windows were always filled with lush plants, lots of living things. They didn't care much about keeping it neat and were good at what they did. Now there's a GNC (General Nutrition Centers) in its place. Where there used to be natural light, it's now artificially bright, and flower food is replaced by *whey* and *protein*.

Don't get me wrong, through it all I still love my neighborhood. When I walk out the front door of my building, I feel bittersweet curiosity as to what will come next. When the places I love close, I get a little nervous because change is good . . . in moderation. It's hard to know when a neighborhood might lose its identity. You can get to know a neighborhood by its people; however, it's up to the community to keep its values in sight.

Two Sides to Every Story

LAUREN SPENCER

Amina's observations about the neighborhood we share made me think about the nature of finding oneself through our own perspective from one generation to the next. She and I share a neighborhood, but with a few blocks and a couple of well-placed decades in between.

The first time off the A train at 190th Street in my new neighborhood gave me a sense of up and down. For one, I'd never realized Manhattan had so many hills—I was used to the flat, gridded plains below 125th Street—and rolling down a steep incline to my apartment made me realize how city developers had left this bit alone. I was also experiencing the vertigo of being out of a decade-long marriage and realizing that glorious freedom could mix with hard loss. My new building also reflected a tale of two worlds. On the west side was a sheer stone cliff topped by Fort Tryon Park, where a now-fancy restaurant sat. I couldn't actually afford to go to that restaurant, but it made me happy to know it was there.

When I exited the building out the east side, I was on Broadway, where salsa music vibrated the pavement. There was a health-food store that had been there, according to the lady behind the counter, for two decades. There was a tax place next to a bodega where a card table sat and men played dominoes. I was home. Not because I knew anything about dominoes, but because I felt community. No one knew me, but everyone still smiled. For the years I lived in that apartment, I grew to understand how to live in different sides of a situation, whether it was outside my window or inside my heart. I could get dressed up and climb the hill for a pricey dinner or slip on my flip-flops and cross Broadway for a *batida*; could plan my future as solo or make a date with a new possibility.

Recently I took a walk up in my old neighborhood, having moved a bit south a few years ago. A beer bar had replaced the tax place. The bodega was boarded and a sign teased a new restaurant coming soon. But the health-food store was still there and a card table of domino players was outside. A lot had happened in the seven years since I'd lived there but the core remained the same and I realized how the stories that form us are available in the streets we walk through every day.

AMINA MUKHTAR

YEARS AS MENTEE: 1

GRADE: Junior

HIGH SCHOOL: Benjamin N. Cardozo High School

BORN: Lahore, Pakistan

LIVES: Queens, NY

PUBLICATIONS AND RECOGNITIONS: Scholastic Art & Writing Awards: Gold Key

MENTEE'S ANECDOTE: *I find that I don't tend to give as much time to writing as I would like to, and being in Girls Write Now has given me time to write more regularly, especially in genres I haven't explored yet—namely, writing fiction and poetry have been new for me. I'm looking forward to more genres that are outside of my areas, especially magical realism. My mentorship with Leah has fostered into a friendship and we talk about a number of topics other than writing, including my friendship problems and school worries.*

LEAH ANDERST

YEARS AS MENTOR: 1

OCCUPATION: Assistant Professor of English, Queensborough Community College, CUNY

BORN: Fargo, ND

LIVES: Brooklyn, NY

PUBLICATIONS AND RECOGNITIONS: *Basic Writing Journal*; Stanford University Grant Recipient

MENTOR'S ANECDOTE: *Amina and I have had a great time meeting and talking about writing and attending Girls Write Now workshops, but we've also had a lot of fun doing extracurricular stuff such as going out to dinner and seeing a movie together (Black Panther!). I really enjoy the connection we have and the relationship we've built so far over the year.*

Untitled (Cheating Man)

AMINA MUKHTAR

This in-progress piece represents me branching out to a genre I haven't explored. It's unorthodox for a teenage girl to write about, but I wanted to get into the mind of a cheater.

My unsteady hand sent the salt shaker to the ground, thousands of salt particles sprawled over the polished, mahogany wood floors.

"Jesus," I muttered, stooping down to pick up the salt particles from the floor in disguised shame.

"Wow, honey, you can't keep a hold on anything . . ." my wife, Ruby, spitefully commented. Ruby and her snide comments are like a relentless BB gun, they don't hurt if you hit someone with its bullets one at a time, but all those little hits accumulate to an everlasting pain.

"Thanks for your encouraging comments, they're duly noted."

"Smartass, why don't you just get a sweeper and sweep up the salt, it's not like we're going to eat that now."

"You know what, Ruby, just let me do what I'm doing."

"Okay, sir."

As I proceeded to pick up every salt particle off the floor like a fool, I thought back to how I'd gotten in this situation—my job lost, the only emotional connection I've made in a long time turned out to be a complete sham, and my wife has no clue about what I'm going through.

I heard her before I saw her. Her laugh permeated the bleak office, through the dismal environment built by the forever unsatisfied employees. She walked with an air of vigor that was foreign to us. She caught the attention of me and those around me—not because she was beautiful or anything, but because she was the first new employee that the company hired in over a year. Working in a small company, you don't see many different faces, and, working in an accounting company, you don't see many lively faces. Everyone who was working already had their life sucked out of their soul. Coupled with that, we worked in the heart of New York—Syracuse. Or at least that's what people who live in Syracuse call their city to make them feel better about their mediocre existence. Not to shit on Syracuse, but there are definitely more exciting places to live in New York.

Anyways, cut back to the new employee; she was being shown around the office as I was filing taxes. I tried to catch her eye several times, to get her to acknowledge my existence, but she was too busy trying to stay interested in what our manager was telling her. Though it was obvious that her thoughts were drifting away from her conversation, our manager was quite blasé to the same blank, expressionless look people get when talking to him. Though he is one of the sincerest guys in the office (and the one who gets you fired), he isn't the most enthralling.

Frustrated that she wasn't returning any of my hopeful glances, I decided to "get some water" and conveniently bump into them. As I started to get up, my palms grew sweaty and I unexpectedly started to second-guess my decision. What if I sneeze on her and inflict my snot on her? What if I touch her boob by accident and she thinks I'm a pervert? What if I trip on something and tumble into her, sending her flying across the room? What if I actually do get the chance to introduce myself but my breath smells like rotting garbage puked in it and she never wants to talk to me again?

Grabbing a mint and cautiously making my way toward her, I began to realize how laughable I sound. She's just a young woman who is new to our office and wants to be acquainted to her workplace—no need to be intimidated. Besides, I have a wife whom I've wholeheartedly tolerated for the past fifteen (or is it sixteen?) years.

I've made that joke to her once and she found it hilarious, which she finds everything to be. She's never been one to get easily offended and approaches life with a very coolheaded attitude—something that I've always loved about her.

That night I lay in bed, battling desperately with my mind to stop racing with images of her. Ever since I talked to her this morning, my mind keeps on drifting off to thoughts of her— how her mellifluous voice perfectly complemented her generous eyes, how everything she said seemed to be from a place of intellect and importance, how she managed to keep you entertained the entire time she talked, your eyes never wandering somewhere else . . . God, I'm doing it again. It's not like I fell in love with her, but she was a refreshing change from my dreary life, one embedded in routine and restrictions. You can't do this and you shouldn't do that is all I am told. Wasn't it Plato or Locke who philosophized the concept of free will; well, where's mine?

Flash Non/Fiction/@FlashNarratives

LEAH ANDERST

I don't normally write narratives or fiction, but I was inspired to try when Amina began working on a short story. These are some of the flash narratives I've posted on Twitter.

At church with her Catholic friend, staying behind during Communion, Kim wondered whether that wafer came from Jesus's thigh or breast.

Unrolling the crisp bills in his pocket, Sean tried to contain his excitement. His broken pinky finger notwithstanding, his first day driving for Rex had gone well.

She did her best work around 11:30 a.m., after she'd finished two cups of coffee and had a proper bowel movement.

Bill lately spent his weekends wandering the aisles at grocery stores and home-goods stores. He had very little room for new things in his studio apartment, but his day as a contestant on @PriceIsRight was fast approaching.

The pharmacist blushed and swallowed when she asked whether he carried non-applicator tampons.

Caitlin paused at the bathroom door, unsure whether she heard someone inside respond to her knock. The coffee shop was loud with tourists. She pushed the door open and stepped in without seeing the barista crumpled in the corner.

He'd really wanted to kiss his boyfriend after his game-winning #homerun, but they'd have to wait until they were both out of their uniforms and back at the hotel.

Qian and Sara both reached for the last veggie wrap; the professional development day had been long.

Mark finished reading the novel recommended by the guy he met from Tinder last week. He wished he was attracted to him.

MILENA NARANJO

YEARS AS MENTEE: 2

GRADE: Senior

HIGH SCHOOL: The Renaissance Charter School

BORN: Jackson Heights, NY

LIVES: Queens, NY

MENTEE'S ANECDOTE: *I am a senior in high school and will be going off to college very soon. I wouldn't be able to say this if it wasn't with the help of my mentor and friend, Andrea. She's supported me basically throughout high school. The best memories we have together, in my opinion, have to be all those times we sat in her office crafting through my personal statement and supplements for schools. She literally sat there with me week after week for hours, editing and listening to me talk in order to get it the way I wanted it to be.*

ANDREA CUTTLER

YEARS AS MENTOR: 2

OCCUPATION: Talent Booker, *Late Night with Seth Meyers*

BORN: Los Angeles, CA

LIVES: New York, NY

PUBLICATIONS AND RECOGNITIONS: *Vanity Fair*; VanityFair.com

MENTOR'S ANECDOTE: *Milena is a senior in high school, and much of the fall semester was spent toiling over her personal statement together. Writing, editing together, revising apart, rewriting together, repeat. It was a joy to work with her on something meaningful, just a small piece of a much larger application that will impact the rest of her life. The biggest thrills would come as we'd sit together and, slowly but surely, she'd make an edit of her own work before I could even get there. Those moments were so precious and made me so proud of all the work we've done together.*

61 Years Apart

MILENA NARANJO

This writing piece is a reflection of the relationship that I have with my grandmother. We have our disagreements but I appreciate her because, despite our differences, she has made me the woman I am today and made me grow a greater appreciation for all of the women around the world.

I am a seventeen-year-old Latina on my way to finishing high school and attending college. I am a seventeen-year-old Latina and I travel around the city to take college courses. I am a seventeen-year-old Latina who can't stand the thought of staying home, unproductive. I am a seventeen-year-old Latina who loves to spend time with my friends and go to the movies.

My grandmother, when asked what she was like at seventeen years old:

When I was seventeen, I had my first child. When I was seventeen, I wasn't allowed outside of the house unless accompanied by your grandfather, abuelo. *I had to wake up very early to harvest* cebollas *(onions). When I was seventeen, I had to be a good wife and have a* seco de pollo *ready for abuelo when he came home from work.*

That is why I encourage you to stay home, too. Be ladylike. Learn how to cook, stop going out every day, and help your mother do laundry.

I was born in Jackson Heights, New York, in 2000. My grandmother was born in Cuenca, Ecuador, in 1939. We are sixty-one years apart. In Jackson Heights, I have bits and pieces of the whole world at my hands. People from every country on the planet roam each block. I grew up around advanced technology and countless resources, which have played a role in shaping the kind of person I am today. I attend school with a vast library and laptops all around. I walk to the train station to take the 7 to explore my city. None of this was available in Ecuador in the 1930s. We grew up in two completely different generations with different societal expectations.

In hers: Women had to be perfect housewives to appeal to their husbands and not ruin family reputations. But even though it's 2018, I still get pushed by my grandmother to act as if I'm part of her generation. The old generation.

In mine: I get to wear what I desire. I get to cut off all of my hair and dye it purple if I want to. *God Forbid!* That would be a sin in my grandmother's eyes. She'd remind me it's devil-like, and that no man will ever lay his eyes on me. *Mija esas cosas son del diablo, no de una señorita.*

The role of women in my generation has changed immensely because we are contributing to the job fields that were once dominated by men, which is having a direct impact on today's society. Years ago, my grandmother's contribution to her society was very controlled by men.

She and her sisters spent their days crafting and decorating hats as a source of income. Meanwhile, when it came time to sell the goods, the men were in charge of negotiations, always keeping the pay. But the women never complained because at least they were fed by their husbands at night. And though it wasn't enough, they remained silent because it wasn't worth an argument.

Today women like myself have the opportunity to play major roles in different areas—business, politics, medicine, and publishing. The roles of women in my generation have changed from that of my grandmother's because we're educating ourselves. We are concerned with our communities and the destiny of future generations. Issues like generational poverty, LGBTQ rights, and public policy are arenas we're exploring so that we can advocate for them in the future.

I am graduating from high school in June of this year, and will pursue higher education in college, something my grandmother was not able to accomplish. She attended elementary school up until the fifth grade because her parents were convinced that she didn't need an education and should help them harvest vegetables instead. Because of that, she had to depend on *abuelo* her entire life.

I want to depend on myself. I want to live a life full of freedoms. I want to go out to dinner with my friends on weekends and still be *ladylike*. I want my grandmother to teach me to cook because I'll need it in the future for myself. I want to wake up early to buy *cebollas* and cook *seco de pollo* for my friends, my partner—or whoever *I* choose.

Despite the differences between my grandmother and me, I've never judged her. Sixty-one years ago, she couldn't stand up for herself. It's difficult for her to adjust to an ever-changing society where women are independent. It's difficult for her to understand that I am part of that change. I admire her for her strength; it's what keeps me grounded and motivates me to become an advocate for the next generation of both men and women who will come after me.

2018

ANDREA CUTTLER

A brief pondering on the power of our mentees, the current moment of our society, and how our past will shape our future.

2018: What a time to be a woman! It's terrifying and exhilarating, frustrating and glorious. Everything is spinning, whirring, charging, ahead.

But we can't move forward without looking back. Milena and her grandmother, sixty-one years apart. Milena and myself, sixteen years apart. We are both products of Latin American immigrant mothers who came to the United States in search of more. More for themselves, more for their families, more for us. We learn from them, we are grateful to them, we are inspired by them.

And yet . . . we're doing things a bit differently. Shaking it up just a little, living life on our own terms. Figuring out what we want and going after it. Seeking out meaningful ways to change the world, to speak up and speak out, to advocate for change. We are empowered.

All should beware the next generation. With the females of Girls Write Now at the forefront of what's next, everyone else around should take pause, and take note. These women, their minds, their ideas, and their voices are the key to the success of our collective future.

SARADINE NAZAIRE

YEARS AS MENTEE: 1

GRADE: Junior

HIGH SCHOOL: High School for Math, Science and Engineering

BORN: Port Au Prince, Haiti

LIVES: Brooklyn, NY

PUBLICATIONS AND RECOGNITIONS: Editor of school magazine, *Dr Dragon*; Certified Green Belt; Pencil member; Mount Sinai St. Luke's intern

MENTEE'S ANECDOTE: *One of my goals this year was to get to know all the cafés on the Upper West Side, where Laura lives. Every week we have our meetings in a different spot. So far my vote for first-prize pastry goes to Maison Kayser on 76th and Broadway. We also met at the movies once and saw* The Shape of Water, *a high point. I loved the film. Laura did not. Writing (and revision) is definitely hard work, but my mentor and I have a good time together.*

LAURA GERINGER BASS

YEARS AS MENTOR: 2

OCCUPATION: Author

BORN: New York, NY

LIVES: New York, NY

PUBLICATIONS AND RECOGNITIONS: Author of *The Girl with More Than One Heart* (Abrams, 2018); Girls Write Now Mid-Year craft talk speaker; Graduate student mentor at Stony Brook, Southampton, in the Fellowship program for Children's Literature

MENTOR'S ANECDOTE: *It has been inspiring to me to work with Saradine on "Tomorrow." One of her goals when she joined Girls Write Now was to write about her childhood memory of the earthquake in Haiti. It's been a privilege to help her do that. Informed in part by our open way of working together, I've developed a "Be Your Own!" writing workshop with prompts based on my new book* The Girl with More Than One Heart. *I hope to travel around the country this year to schools and nonprofit organizations, helping teen girls stand strong, speak out, and tell their stories.*

Tomorrow

SARADINE NAZAIRE

Every day, people around the world are impacted by life-changing events. At the age of nine, I experienced my first. A 7.2-magnitude earthquake forced my family to adjust to a new normal and rattled my whole world.

On New Year's Eve 2009, in Port-au-Prince, Haiti, my mother and I sat in our living room. I was nine years old. She was listening to prayer on the radio; I was reading a book. All of a sudden, we heard a rumble, and I felt the ground shake underneath me. It wasn't longer than a second, but my mom also felt it and started to pray. "If there's an earthquake tomorrow, that cabinet will crash," she warned. I wondered if what she said was true. I went on reading.

The morning of January 12, 2010, my brother, stepsister, and I went to school as usual, came home, finished our homework, and ate dinner. After dinner, having no chores, I went out to the terrace behind our house to relax. At 5 p.m., the earth started to rumble, lightly at first, then more and more strongly. I remembered what my mother had said: *"If there's an earthquake tomorrow . . ."*

I ran into the living room to see if the cabinet would crash. That decision almost cost me my life. Within seconds, the foundation of our house shook, the cement cracked, and it wasn't just china that crashed all around me. The wall in the hallway crumbled above my head. I saw my mom and stepsister running.

I tried to hold on to my mom's dress, but my hand slipped. I was buried!

Terrified and sure I was about to die, I prayed and begged God to help me. I crouched under the fallen bricks like a frog frozen before taking a leap.

How long will it take for the ceiling to fall down? I wondered. *Will the ground shake again?* My mom and stepsister were both outside, yelling for help. I didn't hear my little brother's voice. He must still be inside the house.

"Jesse?" My voice was muffled. "Jesse?" I called out louder.

"Saradine? I'm here," he answered, sounding smaller than his seven-year-old self.

"Are you hurt?"

"I don't know," he said. "Are we going to die here?" I was pretty sure that we were, but he wasn't crying and I didn't want him to start.

"No, someone will come. Let's pray so they come sooner."

"Okay."

"Let's pray out loud . . ."

"*Notre père qui es aux cieux, que ton nom soit sanctifié, que ton règne vienne, que ta volonté soit fait sûre La terre comme aux Cielle . . .*" It was Psalm 23, the only prayer we knew by heart.

He stopped and I panicked. "Jesse? Jesse!"

"I'm here."

"Why did you stop?"

"I forgot the rest."

At that moment, I felt the pain of someone's feet stepping on the debris on top of me. I cried out. Hearing my voice, the man backed up and called out my name. Another started to pull the blocks where my voice came from, relieving the weight on my back. He pulled me out. The whole world looked gray for the few moments that I stood still to get my balance. The man, I now realized, was one of my neighbors. He hurried me out of the building, my brother following. We were rescued!

We lost everything: our house, our furniture, our money. We lived in tents with our neighbors in fear that the next aftershock would be worse than the original. For five months, we ate, drank, slept, and healed together. We had survived. I missed a whole year of school. In 2011, at age ten, I came to America.

Today, I remember that day when every part of my life that was stable and familiar crumbled around me. I hear my mom's voice: *"If there's an earthquake tomorrow . . ."*

Six years ago, I spoke only Creole and French, having just arrived in New York City from Haiti. Prior to that move, I had lived a peaceful life; my only concerns were getting my homework done and what we'd have for dinner. If you had told me then that I would be here now, a part of *this* tomorrow, I'd have called you a liar. That is, if I understood you at all.

I've been granted the gift of a tomorrow.

When people say goodbye they often say "There's always tomorrow." Not always, I say.

Only Me

LAURA GERINGER BASS

My mother came to this country from Russia when she was three years old. There had been trauma before she arrived, tragedies I knew nothing about except by growing up in the force field of her fears. I pieced a narrative together from scraps I overheard when the adults sat around telling stories. This flash is an archeological remnant then, passed down to me from my immigrant grandmother and mother.

Mama told us about her Russian uncle who ran away from the Cossacks during a pogrom in Kishinev, fleeing over rooftops, fleeing finally to America, where he lived to be ninety-nine. She told us about her other uncle, who was not as lucky that night and so never came to America.

Mama told us about her baby brother who died of influenza and so also never came to America. She told us how the officer at Ellis Island asked "How many children?" and her mother had wept and couldn't speak and so Mama, afraid he would be angry and send them back to the Cossacks, pointed to her four-year-old self, at her fast-beating heart, and said in Russian, loudly, "Me. Only me!" and her mother slapped her and was sorry after and Mama was sorry, too.

Mama told us about her uncles, the one who escaped the Cossacks and lived and the one who did not and her dead baby brother who had been handsome and so much sweeter and better than Mama and as she told her stories her voice rang hollow and her words sounded foreign as if spoken in a language we would never be old enough to understand.

FAITH OKUNUBI

YEARS AS MENTEE: 1

GRADE: Freshman

HIGH SCHOOL: The Young Women's Leadership School of Queens

BORN: Queens, NY

LIVES: Queens, NY

PUBLICATIONS AND RECOGNITIONS: Published a poem in the school anthology 2016–2017

MENTEE'S ANECDOTE: *When I first came to Girls Write Now I was scared. As time went on, I grew more comfortable, but still not comfortable enough. This year I was too quiet. I wanted to share my pieces, but I just didn't. I think I am capable of doing a lot more and I would like to show it.*

ELENA COLN

YEARS AS MENTOR: 1

OCCUPATION: Advertising Manager, Columbia University Press

BORN: Moscow, Russia

LIVES: Queens, NY

PUBLICATIONS AND RECOGNITIONS: Translated contemporary science-fiction novels for publication in Moscow, Russia

MENTOR'S ANECDOTE: *Faith is one of the most hard-working people I've ever known. I cannot picture her without a heavy binder full of assignments, papers, and schedules that she carries everywhere with her. Faith opened up my eyes to what the life of a teenager in New York City is like—it is a lot of work and a lot of pressure! I do hope that Faith continues on the path of self-discovery through writing and writes more for pleasure and fun.*

Faith

FAITH OKUNUBI

My mentor and I were discussing the Generation F *theme and how it is perfect for me because my own name starts with "F." So this piece is all about me: a few things about Faith.*

Let's be honest, I have an unusual mind. You might be thinking, "Okay?" Or, "Doesn't everybody?" No, mine is different. I take stories from movies and pretend I am playing instead of an actor or actress. I do this every day until I find a different scene to play. That's how I overcome boredom. People say I watch too many movies because I don't know what's real and what's fake. In class, I'm always asking "why?" questions. My teachers get annoyed with me because: number one: I'm wasting class time; number two: if they can't answer the question I will ask more "why?" questions; and number three: I ask things at the wrong time. You know what's weird? I have always been special. I was born with childhood apraxia—my jaw couldn't read signals my brain was sending so I would react by crying until the age of four. Growing up was especially hard. If I didn't have my sister with me I don't know what I would have done. Kids would call me names and laugh; oftentimes I will run to the bathroom and cry. I stopped doing that when I was about ten or eleven. That is when problems started to happen. A lot of guys were noticing me because I reached puberty fast. But this one guy I thought was The One. He started to notice me in church. I got so excited, but I was naïve. Then it got to a phase where I didn't like him anymore, but that phase didn't last long. I was still thinking about him until like three or four years later. I developed the passion for writing at a very young age because it was my voice. I loved writing short stories as a kid. In second grade, when we had writing assignments, I used to write pages and pages. I remember writing a story about Cinderella. I don't know how people don't like to write and read. When I find a book I like, I just dive deep into it and never put it down. But when I grew up that passion just fell. Also I love to cook. Food Network is my favorite channel. When I get to my own place I can't wait to start trying out new recipes. Also, I love making people laugh and smile. Apparently I'm funny but I don't see it. I like to bother people. I like how pen glides on paper.

Frustration

ELENA COLN

This piece was part of a FREEwrite exercise my mentee and I did just for FUN at a lovely coffee shop in Long Island City, and it was by far my most FAVORITE session. Dedicated to my dear FRIENDS, Emiko and Dan.

He strolled into a café feeling bored. It was one of those dull days when rain just hung in the air, soaking the whole world gray. His freelance assignment had ended some time ago; his mornings felt empty now, making him fidgety and vaguely dissatisfied with everything.

The café was dark, illuminated with a few sparse lights. The barista, a young woman in her early twenties, chewed gum and blew out tiny pink bubbles, popping them gently. Her blond hair was cropped super-short and tinted pink. He reflected idly on her pinkish hair and pink gum bubbles, the only blotches of color inside the café filled with brown and golden hues. The girl was plain-looking; she stared blankly into space, lost in her thoughts or, perhaps, simply absorbed in the rhythm of chewing and blowing out the gum. That vacant stare annoyed him somehow, and when he ordered coffee, he was aware of sounding hoarse and unpleasant.

The girl did not seem to notice or care about the tone of his voice. She stared just as blankly at the milk jug and turned his coffee off-white (he preferred it dark). He handed her exact change, and she shifted her body away from the counter, without saying a word.

The place was empty. He looked around and noticed a sign in the corner: "Pick a question. Start a conversation." The last thing he wanted was to start a conversation, especially since the only other human being inside the café, the barista, seemed totally uninterested in the world. Yet he felt a strange compulsion to check out the conversation starters. He moved toward the sign and leaned forward, trying to make out tiny white letters on small black rectangles, struggling not to spill coffee as he took the first sip. "Who would you have a conversation with if you could pick anyone from history—and why?" he read. He found the question surprisingly difficult to answer. "Who, indeed?" he wondered, and felt a few hot drops of coffee slide down his chin.

"Who, indeed?" said a female voice behind him; his shoulder muscles clenched, and he spilled more coffee on his hand.

When he turned around, he found himself staring down into the dark, alert eyes of a petite woman standing very close to him. (When did she come in? He did not hear the café door open, did not recall a gush of cold, wet air.) She was dressed for the weather, in a long silvery raincoat cinched at the waist with a wide belt that accentuated how slim she was; carmine boots hugged her slender ankles. She held her dripping umbrella away from her body and used the free hand to push her long black hair away from her forehead. It was obvious she was expecting an answer, a faint smile hovering on the very edges of her mouth. He could not take his eyes off her mouth. Her lipstick matched the color of her boots (or vice versa?), and it seemed to glow bright in the dim light of the café. A tiny smudge in the left corner of her mouth where she had pressed on her lipstick a bit too hard irritated him, and his mind went blank. All of a sudden, he felt wary and almost hostile toward her. The woman sighed, gave a tiny shrug, and turned away to place her order.

GABI PALERMO

YEARS AS MENTEE: 1

GRADE: Sophomore

HIGH SCHOOL: Eleanor Roosevelt High School

BORN: New York, NY

LIVES: New York, NY

MENTEE'S ANECDOTE: *My weekly meetings with Kate have allowed me to grow and find my voice as a writer. Our conversations about our love for '90s music and being a teenager in different generations has encouraged me to incorporate my interest and beliefs into my own writing. One piece that I would not have written without Kate's help was my intergenerational memoir. In these past five months, I have enjoyed getting to know more about Kate and bonding more with her.*

KATE MULLEY

YEARS AS MENTOR: 3

OCCUPATION: Playwright

BORN: Boston, MA

LIVES: New York, NY

PUBLICATIONS AND RECOGNITIONS: World premiere of new musical *Razorhurst* at Luna Stage; "The Year Before the Civil War," *The Dionysian,* Issue 004

MENTOR'S ANECDOTE: *My weekly meetings with Gabi have made me examine the similarities and differences between being a teenager in the '90s and today. We are both diligent procrastinators and cynical optimists. We talk about music and TV, the things that inspire us about the worlds we live in. Our check-ins have grounded me during busy and stressful times and fed me when I have felt creatively empty. Gabi has become surer in her voice this past year, and it has been a joy to be on that journey with her.*

10 Years Later

GABI PALERMO

My piece is about my friends and I meeting after ten years. It explores how my friends and I have changed and stayed the same after high school.

She never thought that she would be nervous seeing them again. They used to meet at Brookfield when they were in high school, so why would it be different now? Gabi hadn't seen Zuri and Stephen in six months, and that was a long time considering they used to meet up every week in high school. They had just graduated from grad school, and Gabi felt like she was the only one who had no idea what she was going to do with her life. As she waited on the steps in Brookfield she thought about all of the times she waited for Zuri and Stephen on these exact steps. Brookfield hadn't changed, it had the same stores that were meant for the rich people, and it still had that same smell of money and success. Zuri met Gabi first (as usual, Stephen was late). When they saw each other, they became those annoying-ass people from high school who used to scream when they hadn't seen each other in two hours. They hugged each other, and couldn't stop telling each other how amazing they looked. Gabi always thought Zuri was a goddess, but Zuri never saw how beautiful she was. Zuri always thought the same about Gabi, but she could not see how amazing she was, either. They saw things in each other they didn't see in themselves. After two hours waiting for Stephen, he finally showed up looking the same as he did in high school. He wore the same glasses, faded flannel shirt, and jeans that his mom bought for him. He was six-three and towered over Gabi and Zuri. He gave them the usual uncomfortable hug. Stephen didn't sit down because he was hungry as hell. "Let's go to Shake Shack," he said.

Before ordering, they had to check their accounts to see if they had enough money, because after ten years, they still were broke. They realized they had money, and ordered the same thing. When they got their orders, they decided to go to the park behind Brookfield. "Let's hope we don't see any annoying-ass children," Zuri said, even though she knew that they used to be the annoying-ass children and probably still were even though they were twenty-six years old. As they walked through the park, Gabi pulled out her speaker and played Frank Ocean. They didn't care at all that this was TriBeCa. They all sang as loud as they could. Stephen was the worst singer, but hearing him try to sing made them all smile, so she didn't tell him to shut the hell up. Singing in the streets of TriBeCa took them back to high school when they used to do this every Friday even in freezing weather. While everyone else in their grade was getting high and drinking on Friday nights, they would sing and run in TriBeCa. As they walked to the park, Stephen said he wanted to go on the swings.

In high school, the swings were the one place they could actually catch up with one another. Going back to the swings meant feeling like they could go back to a time when life was a lot easier and they weren't in their twenties. When they got to the swings there was no one there. They could be alone.

"I really wish life was as easy as it used to be," Zuri said. "Medical school is really awful. I hate it. Everyone is so competitive, and I realized that I don't like dealing with bodily fluids, so I have no idea what I'm gonna do anymore." Gabi and Stephen were surprised by what she said because out of all of them she seemed like the one who had all of her shit together.

"I don't think any of us know what we're gonna do," Gabi said with fear in her voice. All of them agreed, and talked about how they took high school for granted. All of the times they spent complaining about the people in school, they never realized how valuable their time together was.

"If I could go back, I would have spent less time stressing and more time being a teenager," Zuri said. There was an awkward pause among them. No matter how much they hated high school, they had to admit that compared to now, their lives were better back then because they were all together. In order to lift up their moods, Stephen talked about the great memories they made when they were in high school. They remembered all of the times they went to thrift stores and made Stephen wait while they tried on clothes and all the times they went to get bubble tea and Stephen used to spit the boba at them. They reminisced about high school, and Gabi no longer felt like they were strangers. She felt like they had become closer now that they were more honest with one another about how their lives were going. And as they parted ways, she knew that they would still be close even ten years later.

I Lie Here

KATE MULLEY

Gabi and I talk about music and high school and expression a lot. For this poem, inspired by my conversations with Gabi, I took lyrics from three of my favorite Fiona Apple songs from high school and crafted an erasure poem.

I don't care
I say
You don't say
You care
And this mind
This body
Cannot
Forget

You let me
Know you
You don't know
When your gaze is
Too close
You set your spell
I wanted love
Once
And twice

Don't make it a game
Don't show your sorrow

Don't
Go

My pride
I understand I am too proud
(Like a fool)
My head's in the clouds
And what you seem
What you
Don't

I don't know
When I've been careless
I don't know
Where I can begin to be
Done
I know the next
Will
Help
But
I've got these lies you tell me
And I need to
Know

What I need is
Courage

But you don't understand
You say you give
And you lie
And you'll hold
My soul

I am
Too smart

You'll never understand why you cry

And I lie
Here

LESLIE PANTALEON

YEARS AS MENTEE: 2

GRADE: Sophomore

HIGH SCHOOL: Midwood High School

BORN: Brooklyn, NY

LIVES: Brooklyn, NY

MENTEE'S ANECDOTE: *Part two of a four-year journey through high school has proved to be particularly sporadic for both of our personal lives. Throughout the many changes, Lauren has encouraged me to keep writing a central anchor in my life. And much like my writing, Lauren has too become core to my development as a human.*

LAUREN HESSE

YEARS AS MENTOR: 5

OCCUPATION: Social Media Producer, The Metropolitan Museum of Art

BORN: Albany, NY

LIVES: Brooklyn, NY

MENTOR'S ANECDOTE: *Leslie never stops surprising me with her wit, accomplishments, and curiosity! She challenges me and makes me want to be a better person. With her packed high school schedule and my change of career this year, Leslie always made time and was ready to write, edit, and work hard. I can't imagine my life without Leslie as a mentee!*

Flight Departure

LESLIE PANTALEON

Generation F *speaks to all the strong generations of women before it that made it possible. This poem is about what happens after those kinds of women have passed.*

A great granddaughter.
In her eyes reflected the land that the old woman left years
   ago,
without family or a cent to her name.
Now the old woman has died, passed in a country in which
   she was not born in.
Passed in a country which refused to acknowledge her.
Her body not cold, before it boarded an airplane.
Now she is dead.
Now she watches over her great granddaughter, who gazes
   upon the old woman's motherland in awe.

On Funerals

LAUREN HESSE

I struggled with what to write this year, as we had to work on our anthology pieces separately and in different countries. Though apart, writing this and reading Leslie's piece made me feel more connected to her than ever.

My experiences with funerals have been sterile and generic, most in fake houses built specifically for honoring the dead with family and prayers from a local pastor that we did not know. We played a Leonard Cohen song for my grandfather, and graveside, a local National Guard officer whom we had never met presented a veteran's flag to my mother. I don't particularly remember any emotion, sad or reflective or joyful—I was more concerned with helping my parents and making sure we hadn't forgotten flower arrangements or a check for the funeral director.

I once sat shiva for a best friend's grandmother. Grandma Sara used to invite us over for dinner, where she made salads and roasted salmon, or we would meet her at Lord & Taylor to give her an opinion on sensible yet stylish semiorthopedic sneakers. Her funeral wasn't at a funeral home but rather a fancy funeral *parlor* on the Upper West Side. Afterward we went to the family's house and I ate too many bagels from the Second Avenue Deli.

And as I write this you're at the vigil for your great-grandmother, your family's matriarch, in Mexico. You and I have only emailed twice in weeks and you prefaced the note with "This email will be poorly punctuated because many English punctuations do not exist on this keyboard." You said Mexico was not what you expected but that the burial had given many peace. I realize I know nothing of your culture's traditions around death except for my visions of grand altars and a few key facts from a children's movie about Día de los Muertos. I feel naïve, I feel sadness, and I feel my own culture (or lack thereof) that I have taken for granted.

I wonder if you left a hot chocolate, like the ones you bring to share in our pair sessions, at her altar. I wonder what colors the flowers are in the town your family is from. I think about my parents not talking about death, and if we did, the moment was fleeting. You have nine days to help your great-grandmother cross over and to celebrate and reflect on her life. I wonder if this has helped you—helped your family—more than a sterile service and hearse processional through town helped mine. But the one thing I don't have to wonder about is how much you will teach me about your time away, about your culture, about your food and celebrations, and about your family as soon as you're back in Brooklyn.

RIA PARKER

YEARS AS MENTEE: 1

GRADE: Sophomore

HIGH SCHOOL: Harlem Children Zone Promise Academy II

BORN: New York, NY

LIVES: New York, NY

PUBLICATIONS AND RECOGNITIONS: Scholastic Art & Writing Awards: Honorable Mention; *YCteen*

MENTEE'S ANECDOTE: *One memorable memory with Amy was when we chose from a pile of folded papers with a word to write something based on that word. One time when we did this, the word selected was "milk." Usually I have ideas ready but that time my mind went blank and I was so frustrated. As it happened, that word brought us closer because it was challenging writing about milk. I think it actually made me more comfortable sharing pieces of works that I may not be proud of and more comfortable talking about issues happening in the media with Amy.*

AMY FLYNTZ

YEARS AS MENTOR: 6

OCCUPATION: Founder, Amy Flyntz Copywriting LLC

BORN: Bridgeport, CT

LIVES: Brooklyn, NY

MENTOR'S ANECDOTE: *Getting the email that Ria had been selected for a Scholastic Honorable Mention was something I will never forget! Getting to know Ria and her writing has been an honor. She is so informed, so passionate, so talented in her writing—and her ability to write across genres has been a source of inspiration for me. While I love talking to her about current events and social justice, I also just really enjoy getting to know her as a young woman. I keep telling her that one day, she will rule the world!*

Invalid Address

RIA PARKER

This poem was inspired by the definition of "dead letter mail" and being underappreciated as a black woman. This represents Generation F *because we refuse to be silent and will fight for change.*

JULY 4, 1983

Dear History,
You asked me how it was to be a
black woman in America.
I answered challenging
and you wanted me to elaborate but I
 didn't because the list is longer than
America's list of debts.
But here is my summed-up elaboration to your question.

Being black in America is having your
whole history placed on a pull-down projector screen for
 everyone to see
But on the screen it only contains struggle, injustice and
 persecution and being
told that this pain is
equivalent to your existence and only that.
But the funny thing is
You can't talk about it because it is an uncomfortable topic.

Being a woman in America
means not being able to
talk about certain subjects like
sexual assault and periods
in school, the workplace
and even your own home
  because this also makes people uncomfortable.

Being a black woman in America
  is knowing that your opinions aren't valuable to everybody
    because you are in a body where your gender and race is
    supposed to be silent.

Being black is having your
own people swallow the slavery mentality poison that says if
    you have any
Eurocentric features then you are automatically beautiful.

Being a woman
  is having your
own gender hate you because we live in a hegemonic
    patriarchal society
  in which we think
we are each other's competition.

Being a black woman
  is knowing that you will have derogatory terms from both
    ends fly at you like a plague and somehow magically
survive it.

Being black in America
  is having laws

pinned against you
such as being excluded from living in certain areas.

Being a woman in America
 is having laws be created by men who most likely won't ever
    get pregnant nor get periods.

Being a black woman in America
 is knowing that because you are
both black and a woman
 your body isn't yours and is only meant to be hypersexualized
    and fetishized.

Being black in America
 is knowing that you can be prosecuted or lynched even
    though you're innocent.

Being a woman in America
 is knowing that if you
say no to a date you can be murdered.

Being a black woman in America
 is knowing that both of these things can happen to you but
    there will be no Amber Alerts because to them you make
    up the bones in the cemetery.

Being black in America
means trying to figure out
how to make sure your children aren't
 afraid of the system
even though it's against them.
 In this country being black means you will push your child
    into adulthood before the rest of the world can.

Being a woman in America
is teaching your son and daughter
different things as they
grow older because it was how you were also taught. It means
that you are to be
emotionally abusive to your daughter so she can "mature."

Being a black woman in America
is knowing that someday you may have
children and will have to choose between ripping out their
hearts before they are three to protect them or have this
country destroy them like they did to you.

Being black in America is having somebody shoot the starting
pistol indicating it's everybody's time to run. And when
you start running you know the bullet will hit you at some
point even though the pistol doesn't contain bullets.
Being black in America is having an invisible bullet on you
before you're even born and you just hope that like many
others the bullet doesn't become real.

Being a woman in America is knowing that history kept hidden
the women that helped advance the feminist movement.
Being a black woman is screaming
Ain't I a woman
when it comes to movements in the black community and the
feminist movement that you decide to create the womanist
movement
So your voices can be heard.

Being both a woman and black is knowing that it is 100
percent illegal to be both but never silencing your voice
when it is needed the most.

There are so many unheard black women voices when it comes to struggle and injustice but also accomplishments that they never got to share with the world because of your history.

Sincerely, Ria

P.S. Being a black woman is to be in rage all the time because you are disrespected, unprotected, and neglected but despite this I wouldn't trade my resilience I'd encountered for the world.

***Invalid address*

Fire

AMY FLYNTZ

Overwhelmed by the constant attacks on our democracy and the egregious assaults on the environment and our civil liberties, I have sometimes struggled to find my place in the resistance. This piece was inspired by the theme Generation F: fire, fearlessness, and finding my voice.

My acupuncturist, Paul, sits across from me in a folding white chair and leans forward to examine the red rash on my throat.

"And my lips are so dry," I explain, "they're peeling."

I've been around enough "alternative" healing modalities to guess where he'll go with this. It's why I've chosen to see him for a second appointment instead of heading to another dermatologist. I want him to give it to me straight, but with a spiritual chaser. His eyes meet mine and he starts to grin. He knows that I know what he's about to say.

"Throat chakra!" we squawk in unison, and I laugh, my hand reaching up to stroke the scaly skin in the hollow of my collarbone. It's good to laugh with him. The last time I was here, I spent an hour fighting back tears. My body has been covered for months in red, itchy patches of various shapes and sizes from my neck to my ankles, and I refuse to accept that the only response is a shrug and a squash-sized tube of steroid cream from a doctor who can't, or won't, try to find the cause.

"So," Paul says quietly. "Your throat chakra is trying to tell you something. What do you have to say that's not being said, Amy?"

I scratch at my throat and swallow the hot lump that has

begun to form in the back of my mouth. Fire is one of the five powers that Five Elements acupuncture is based on, and Paul has told me that right now, my fire is excessive. It's no wonder my skin is dry and itchy. I need more joy in my life. My Qi needs balancing. Who isn't in need of joy these days?

"Amy?"

I think of everything I want to say—have to say—that I'm not saying. I think of the kids in Florida who were just gunned down in front of their classmates. I think of DACA and fracking and pervasive sexual violence against women. I think of the systematic incarceration of black men and their deaths at the hands of police. I think of my uterus, and the choices I've had access to that might soon be outlawed. Fire? Yes. I've got plenty of fire.

"Everything," I answer. "I have everything to say."

Paul nods. "Good," he says. "Let's get started."

REBECCA PARTAP

YEARS AS MENTEE: 1

GRADE: Senior

HIGH SCHOOL: Queens High School for the Sciences at York College

BORN: San Fernando, Trinidad

LIVES: Queens, NY

PUBLICATIONS AND RECOGNITIONS: Scholastic Art & Writing Awards: three Silver Keys

MENTEE'S ANECDOTE: *Over the past few months, my mentor and I have contended with the college applications process and wrestled deadlines left and right. It was exhausting, but ultimately incredibly rewarding. Countless drafts of my personal essay left me with a better understanding of my identity. Girls Write Now has really fostered my love of writing and newfound self-understanding into artistic endeavors with direction and purpose. I now have a portfolio full of works in a plethora of genres, all pieces I am truly proud of.*

NOELLE DE LA PAZ

YEARS AS MENTOR: 1

OCCUPATION: Assistant Acquisitions Editor, Teachers College Press

BORN: San Francisco, CA

LIVES: Queens, NY

PUBLICATIONS AND RECOGNITIONS: VONA/ Voices fellow; *Ano Ba Zine*; *Newtown Literary*

MENTOR'S ANECDOTE: *At the beginning of the year, Rebecca and I set out to tackle the college application season with organization and purpose (check! and check!). Now, as we sit back and watch the acceptance letters roll in, I am in deep admiration of all her hard work, and truly inspired by the ways her creative voice continues to open up and shine through as we explore different genres and dig deep into memory, family history, language, and the rich landscape of what it means to be daughters of diaspora.*

Harbinger

REBECCA PARTAP

This piece is an excerpt from a short story inspired by duality and contradiction. Fantasy has always been my favorite genre to both write and read, so this piece was a joy to create!

Asha tugged at Anjali's silk skirts pleadingly. "Please don't leave again, Ani! You're always disappearing in the night!"

"I'm sorry, Ash, but you know I have special responsibilities. We'll do something fun tomorrow." Anjali smoothed back her little sister's hair before handing her off to the nursemaid.

Anjali made her way to the dining hall to attend to her subjects. The common folk that flocked to see her fell to their knees and stretched their hands toward her, all hoping to be blessed by their resident saint. The long banquet tables were lined with *diyas*, and flowers of every hue were strewn across the tabletops and floors. The heady perfume of petals and spices wafted through the air. Anjali padded through the aisle of worshippers every night, touching the foreheads of those whose souls called out to her. Something in her could feel pain and sickness in others, and her own magic rose to heal them. A simple touch was enough to bless illness away.

Satisfied that her little sister and worshippers were taken care of, Anjali turned her mind toward the events to come. She made her nightly pilgrimage to the Holy Grove in her private gardens. The haven was forbidden to all, even her dear sister Asha. Anjali came to an enclosure of trees surrounding an altar and a perfectly round, reflective pond. She placed a flower she'd crafted upon the stone altar and knelt before the water. She whispered in an ancient language, the ground humming with the energy of her words. Once her spell was set, she rose to her feet. She turned away from the pond and looked up at the moonless, star-speckled sky above her. Then she took a breath and allowed herself to fall backward.

She fell into the clear water without disturbing its mirrorlike surface. As she sank further into the darkness, she felt herself change. Her sage-green dress deepened to black, and her baby's-breath crown turned to one of foxglove. More disturbing than her sartorial changes were the shifts she felt within her. The rot and poison she kept locked within herself bubbled to the surface. Her powers itched at her fingers.

Anjali emerged from the pond, bone-dry and hungry. She looked upward and saw a pitch-black sky illuminated by a single blue-white moon. She made her way through her gardens to her obsidian palace. The heavy doors swung open as if by their own accord.

Anjali drifted to her study, where a leather-bound ledger sat upon her desk. Its pages were covered in names, all written in black and accompanied by red-ink checks beside them. There were seven new, checkless entries since the night before. She mentally recorded the names and set off toward the first name on her list.

Elenore Hutchinson. Using the name as a tether, she passed rows of small, quiet homes before coming upon the one she knew undoubtedly held Elenore. Anjali gave the door three swift knocks, the trademark call of the Harbinger of Death, a signal that allowed families notice to compose themselves for her entrance. The door opened to reveal a small, pallid woman. She wordlessly stepped aside to let Anjali within. The dimly lit abode was host to several children, who arranged themselves in a line, breaths bated.

Anjali saw no sense in making the affair any longer than it need be. "Elenore." She stated the name with no explanation, for they all knew what was coming.

The girl could not be more than thirteen, her eyes deep blue and full of life. A dreadful mix of excitement and disgust ran through Anjali. She put the feelings aside and beckoned the girl forward.

"Elenore Hutchinson, you have been marked for death. You may say your farewells." Anjali had delivered those words countless times, learning to swallow her emotions from shaking her voice.

Elenore eventually disentangled herself from her family's embrace and sat before Anjali. Her power singed at the prospect of exercising itself on this girl. She gently cupped Elenore's face in her hands. Elenore's lip quivered, but she did not cry as Anjali often saw grown men do when faced with death. She almost regretted having to take this girl's life. Almost.

Anjali closed her eyes. She was washed in coldness as she spilled her magic into Elenore. She envisioned the heart ceasing to beat, blood stagnating in the girl's veins. Only when Anjali felt Elenore's body go slack in her hands did she open her eyes, gently slumping the lifeless body back against the chair. An acolyte would arrive soon to collect the body and see to the burial. Anjali nodded briefly to Elenore's sobbing mother before leaving. She put a mental check next to Elenore's name before setting off for the next person on her list.

When the first rays of light began to illuminate the sky, Anjali was exhausted. She returned to the pond, placing a lock of hair from one of her victims upon the altar. Taking one last look at the slowly lightening sky, she fell backward into the water.

A Ravenous Upturning

NOELLE DE LA PAZ

Rebecca and I are inspired by the Fantastical and Futuristic possibilities of Generation F. *My piece was sparked by the photography series "Home" by Gohar Dashti, which explores abandoned homes reclaimed by nature.*

A quiet but ravenous upturning is under way. The walls of this old house are awash in the vibrant cicada green of emerging moss. The iron gate is rusted orange, its filigree woven with vines. The windows blink, the house heaves wearily (or in relief?), having shucked off its responsibilities to people and their soft, tender bodies.

Unencumbered by a roof, the hardwood floors enjoy a view of the night sky. The stars are visible, for what used to be a bustling city full of electricity and lightbulbs is now aligned once more with the comings and goings of the sun.

The people, soft and tender, have gone, their softness and tenderness hardening along the way. Gone, too, are their buttons and their gadgets, their stubborn wrangling of the thing they called time. All the minutes have been set free from the no-longer-ticking clock in the dining room. Westerly winds chip away at the house's last paint job—a sort of lemon chiffon—exposing the bubblegum pink underneath, and the many colors that came before.

Once, I lived here—a different life, ages ago, when I was as flesh and bone as any other daughter. I scan the damp terrain of what used to be the living room, and a sudden memory wells up in me. The old river. I wonder, will it come back? But, alas, it has since gone home to the sea. I remember laughter, like the sound of bells—was it ours? The neighborhood buzzing with children, the slap of jump rope, the bounce of leather ball. But before the memory can make sense of itself, it disintegrates.

I watch a wildcat creep along the blackberry bush down in the clearing below. A dead branch falls onto the decaying piano in the corner and clunks out a few low notes, like a wet cough. The creature startles and darts away into the grove of growing cypress trees. This house is sturdy underneath me. The bones of its steel foundation endure, the brick and concrete remain. The rest is reclaimed, transformed. Fallen trees are arms, bathtub and sinks are ponds where frogs lay their eggs, and the backyard becomes the front, the center, the expanding heart overrun with manzanita shrubs, the unruly heartbeat of this new age.

There must be a reason I've been called back here.

Imperceptibly, my armor begins to soften.

SABRINA PERSAUD

YEARS AS MENTEE: 2

GRADE: Junior

HIGH SCHOOL: Richard R. Green

BORN: Queens, NY

LIVES: Queens, NY

PUBLICATIONS AND RECOGNITIONS: "Salt on Old Wounds," *Chime for Change*

MENTEE'S ANECDOTE: *I came back for my second year at Girls Write Now because of the bond I have with Stacie. We find out every day that we are more alike than we think—whether it be our tendency to procrastinate through our writing or the struggles we both faced with self-identity. Stacie challenges me to explore new writing techniques and she helps me develop a writing style that I am proud of. This year has been full of laughs, writing, coffee and chocolate, and meaningful conversations that go on for hours. She helps me develop into the writer I strive to be.*

STACIE EVANS

YEARS AS MENTOR: 5

OCCUPATION: Policy Analyst, NYC Mayor's Office of Workforce Development

BORN: New York, NY

LIVES: Brooklyn, NY

PUBLICATIONS AND RECOGNITIONS: *The Rumpus, Bitch Magazine*

MENTOR'S ANECDOTE: *I'm having such a wonderful time working with Sabrina. This has been a year of learning for me—finding new ways to get us both thinking about writing . . . and actually writing! (I still have a lot of work to do in this area.) I am still so amazed by how much Sabrina and I are alike, even as we are so very different. It all makes for a lot of laughter when we get together. I am looking forward to another fab year working with her!*

Fighting for My Full Self

SABRINA PERSAUD

This isn't about my parents. This isn't about their failed relationship or a broken family. It's about their daughter, who takes after both her mother and her father.

I am soft, sensitive like my father, yet I am still tough, a strength I got from my mother. Sometimes I'm told that I'm the spitting image of my dad. I can't pinpoint an exact feature that mirrors him, I never could, but it was my all-around appearance that reflected his. I see a lot of my mother in my eyes: a shape that wasn't almond or round that was under a thick, low arched brow.

You know all that they say about opposites attracting each other? My parents started off that way. A trait that he missed was always something she had, and together they placed jigsaw pieces down on the table to complete the puzzle. But what happens when chemistry is thrown aside and puzzles are put away and you come to realize that all the science in the world couldn't explain why you'd grown to hate everything you fell in love with.

They both had something that the other was missing. That missing piece is what drove them apart in the end. But then there's me, my mother and my father's daughter. I am the puzzle that they put together and I carry all of those traits with me.

What happens if I start to despise the person they made me into?

I always knew who I was. Sometimes, it feels like I've always been the same person. I was aware of the contradictions of my being, but I chose to ignore it—or at least half of it. Both of my parents have their fair share of admirable traits. My father is a charming man. I remember when he'd pick me up from my babysitter and we'd walk home together. He'd always stop to say hello to someone and ask them about their life. I remember wanting to be like that. The first hardworking person I ever met was my mother. She'd spend all day taking care of children, working until her bones ached and continuing on even after that. When you're young, there are some things you just don't realize, but I understood at six years old what a mother's sacrifice was. I strived to be that kind of woman.

While I claimed the characteristics that I wanted to have, I denied the ones that I didn't—even though they were already in me. My father is an emotionally driven man and I am the same way. He was the one who taught me that hearts were meant to be worn on your sleeve. I didn't see the problem with being "so sensitive." I saw it as being in tune with my own self, and I saw beauty in it. But there were days when he'd use those emotions to justify something that he'd clearly done wrong or avoid taking responsibility for his actions. It was easier for him to cry than apologize; I'd never seen something uglier.

At the same time, no one guards their heart as much as my mother does. Even after knowing her my whole life, I still try to pry in, get her to open up to me. Truth be told, she is a stubborn, reserved woman. It's strange seeing the way I act around my parents. When I'm with my father, I am my mother blocking him out and building up a wall as he tries with his best efforts to tear it down. With my mother, I am my father desperately trying to get to her, to no avail.

I had this misconception that if I ignored the parts of myself that I didn't like, they would automatically go away. I spent a long time lying about who I was for the sake of who I wanted to be perceived as. There's nothing wrong with striving to improve yourself, but there is a problem when you neglect who you are. I wanted to be a kind person and I wanted to have a good heart, but in the process of being that person to everyone else, I constantly fought with myself. I wondered if this was what my parents went through: the moment where you're fighting fire with ice and get nothing but burnt and frostbitten in the end.

Here's the thing. I didn't realize it gradually; instead, it all came crashing down like a tidal wave. I do not hate the person that I am. I couldn't hate the person that I am. It's true that I take after both parents, who are very different. But I am the piece they put together. No matter how odd it may seem, or how conflicting it may be, it's just right. While I'm my mother and my father's daughter, I will always be my own person before anything. I feel the most like myself when I openly embrace every part of who I am—the softness and the rough edges, the tranquility and the frustration, the loud and the quiet. What is the point of fighting with yourself when you're on both sides?

My Un-Quiet Self

STACIE EVANS

Sabrina and I had a lot of ways to fill in Generation F . . . *FIGHT, FORMIDABLE, FEAR, FOUND . . . and finally: FULL. I thought I was going to write about using my writing to fight. In the end, we both wrote about finding/coming to terms with our full selves.*

I grew up mouse-quiet, mouse-meek, a go-along-to-get-along girl, a "good" girl, a seen-but-not-heard girl. I was silent when I should have spoken. This isn't a thing to be proud of, and I'm not proud of it.

Writing ended my silence. I wrote things I didn't say out loud, told stories I never told: the first time I was called a nigger, the night I was raped, the acceptance of my inability to have children. And when I wrote, I found I had more to say. And more . . . And more. Silence stopped being my default position.

I am anything but silent today. My written voice has been loud and sustained. The steady drumbeat of devaluation and death that has been the storyline of black and brown communities calls up my voice again and again and again.

I recently wrote a piece for a reading with the theme "Backslide." I struggled with the theme at first, uncomfortable with the negative connotation that came to mind when I thought of the word. Desperate, I went to Google, hoping to discover an obscure meaning that would offer positive inspiration. I was surprised to find page after page of religious websites. I clicked on the first one, and what to my wondering eyes should appear but definitions of backsliding that resonated powerfully:

Revolt

Refuse to harken

Rebel

Suddenly, backsliding looked like something to which I could and should aspire. Biblically, of course, it's all bad—backsliders were folks who "refused to harken" to religious rules. Okay, fine. But is that always necessarily bad? Questioning authority—speaking up instead of keeping silent—can be exactly the thing that saves your life.

I thought about quiet, go-along-to-get-along me, and all the ways the stress and damage of my silence has manifested in my health, in my bad relationships, in my fear of embracing my anger, and all the ways silence was a way of denying who I really was, of hiding.

But no more. I have become a proud backslider. I have—to paraphrase my favorite of the religious definitions—refused to harken and turned a backsliding shoulder and made my ears heavy that they should not hear. I have become my own authentic, un-quiet, angry, rebellious, refusing-to-harken self.

One. Hundred. Percent.

ISIS PITT

YEARS AS MENTEE: 1

GRADE: Senior

HIGH SCHOOL: The Preparatory Academy for Writers

BORN: Queens, NY

LIVES: Brooklyn, NY

MENTEE'S ANECDOTE: *There was a time when I thought about quitting the program because I was overwhelmed. I met with Jessie and we talked it through. She made me feel really comfortable and did not judge me. She did not put any immediate pressure on me to figure things out. It was in that moment that I felt that I had made a friend.*

JESSIE PASSANANTI

YEARS AS MENTOR: 1

OCCUPATION: Group Account Director, Griffin360

BORN: Fair Lawn, NJ

LIVES: New York, NY

MENTOR'S ANECDOTE: *An evening at Bowery Poetry took our friendship to the next level. It was Isis's first reading ever, and my first SLAM. We were spontaneously selected from the crowd to judge the night's readers, which involved rating the performances on a whiteboard and holding it up for tally after each performance. It was exciting, invigorating, and a little nerve-racking, given the sudden responsibility. It brought us closer, not just as a mentee and mentor, but as two friends experiencing and interacting with the spoken word in the city.*

Becoming Cinnamon

ISIS PITT

It's normal to feel insecure throughout life. It becomes unhealthy when those feelings fester inside and influence your actions. Generation F *is empowered to not let their insecurities define them.*

If I am to be honest
I am made of dishonesty,
as everything I am
everything I say
is to be taken with
a pinch of salt and a spoonful of sugar.

Salt.

I've made a habit of
presenting myself in a negative light
before someone gets the chance to;
before I can feel the
harsh glare of scrutiny.

I am a firm believer that
only I am allowed
to ruin myself.

I've made a habit of
exaggerating what I believe;
makes me unfavorable,

minimizes the qualities
I love about myself.

Sugar.

I learn to sweeten
the sound of my voice
for strangers
in the hopes of
fitting into the stereotype
of what it means to be a woman,

how to shed my skin
in favor of another's.
I find comfort
in becoming what
makes others happy.
I live for them
instead of myself.

Cinnamon.

but I've grown tired of the voice
that never seems to be satisfied
with the changes I make
to who I am
who makes me question
if I ever knew her in the first place.

The period of
hating myself
will not be the death of me,
it will merely be used as an example

of all the wrong ways
to treat a mind and body.

I am learning to accept
the girl whose reflection
stands before me in the mirror,
how to be patient with her thoughts,
feel at ease with her mannerisms.
She is whole on her own.
She does not need fine-tuning or tinkering
in the hopes of impressing strangers.

We meet again

JESSIE PASSANANTI

We are taught that loving ourselves is sinister. We are asked to change. Generation F is abolishing these expectations by loving themselves wholly, by living their own truths—even when it is difficult.

We meet again

You've changed,
I say to my soul
standing naked in the river.

What a wild me
to have escaped from my chest
to have planted her feet in the riverbed
with hands stretching up and up
toward the sun
like a palm.

Am I allowed to love her?

From here
my heart slams harder
against the trunks of trees.
Doubt balances on the edge of a leaf, then falls.

I love her more than anything.

I am the banks that watch
water carve paths unto itself.

A river cannot flow without walls.

I lean in for a kiss,
sunlight dripping from our shoulders,
water surging past our feet.

STEPHANIE QUINTERO

YEARS AS MENTEE: 1

GRADE: Junior

HIGH SCHOOL: The Academy of American Studies

BORN: Queens, NY

LIVES: Queens, NY

MENTEE'S ANECDOTE: *The day that we went to go get a bagel during one of our pair writing sessions, we talked about one of my poems together, and it was such a deep conversation that I really enjoyed. We were working on my poem called "Thought Bubbles of an Eight-Year-Old" and discussing some really strange, existential thoughts about dreams and being outside of your own body, all of which had arisen from working on it together.*

JULIA LYNN RUBIN

YEARS AS MENTOR: 2

OCCUPATION: Author

BORN: Baltimore, MD

LIVES: Brooklyn, NY

PUBLICATIONS AND RECOGNITIONS: My debut YA novel, *Burro Hills* (Diversion Books, March 2018)

MENTOR'S ANECDOTE: *One beautiful fall day, after getting a bagel together and discussing poetry, my mentee and I went searching for colorful chalk, and then walked to Washington Square Park. Together, we wrote one line each of one of her poems on the ground as onlookers walked by and observed and read, and it was one of the coolest things I have done.*

August

STEPHANIE QUINTERO

This is a collection of poems that I wrote while I was in my first year of Girls Write Now. It speaks to the experiences of girls my age through feelings.

RAW AND NAKED
raw and naked.
imperfections are let loose
but he takes them all in with love and hunger.
her moans crack through walls
while the world is fast asleep.
their intimate moment not so intimate
anymore.
he finds pride in having her, and she is absolutely careless,
enjoying every second flirting with danger.
they share a connection that seems unbreakable
but is completely shattered under her eyes
when truth decides to spill over.

BRIGHT ROSE
I held on to a bright red
rose
the thorns made their way into
my veins
as I bleed for days and years
and somehow I was still alive
I removed the thorns with my teeth

while my teeth turned old
I was bruised
the kind of bruise that lasts
forever

LAYERS OF BEAUTY
you are covered in layers of beauty
beauty that shines bright enough to blind
weak eyes
layers of beauty that cover a scarred
canvas of skin
skin so scarred that you are confused
when you see your reflection
do the layers of beauty define you?
or do they speak out loud enough to show
the world what a great liar you are?

Your hands are on foreign skin
Your eyes are on unknown lips,
Your eyes are searching blindly
Do not question your mind
Darkness has washed over you
And now you find pleasure
Inflicting pain that multiplies

THE THOUGHT BUBBLES OF AN EIGHT-YEAR-OLD
The feeling of uncertainty was familiar
Because the questioning had begun from
A very young age
Dominoes six feet tall in a dark place fell
Equally
One tumbling as the others continued
The godly figures of hands putting together

A human being
Made much more sense than two people
Coming together to create a child
The spirit of the physical body floats
But is it just the mind itself?
What is the point of living if we live to die?

PEN AND PAPER

Can descriptive words explain a feeling?
The pen maneuvers in a sensational way
As the fingers grip on to the pen tighter
The ink stays on the paper forever
A multitude of worlds will read this
And live in my world
Yet others will feel foreign
But one day
All worlds will collide
And that will be the end of all living.

ALLURE

Every word carved invisible scars
As time
Overly carved my skin
I became numb
A living body with an empty soul
Time reached out
Begging me to undress my confidence
Begging me to flavor self-love
On my tongue
Begging me to murder my insecurities
That were carved deep within me
With my hands.

THE MOON

As the sun falls asleep
Her true self awakens
Her skin is bare
Her emotions stripped raw
She is no longer proud
And no longer pretends
She is exposed.

High up,
I am caressed by confidence.
Growth lies under my feet
And dances its way up,
Through my curves.
The sun glows
On my vibrant caramel skin,
That belongs to the sand
On my fingertips.
My eyes glow
And the future awaits,
On the waves of the ocean.

Mother

JULIA LYNN RUBIN

This is a piece of flash fiction I wrote one morning after waking up from a very vivid dream. I edited this piece with my mentee, and together we puzzled over the ways in which it fit within the theme of Generation F.

The house was flooding. It was breaking open from the inside, water pooling at the edges, leaking into every nook and cranny, every crack and crevice. She'd tried to stop the water from seeping in through the pores of the walls and floors. They'd all tried paper towels and newspapers at first, when it was just leaks, just little dribbles of liquid. A broken pipe, perhaps. Something benign. Fixable. It was an old row house, stacked against its neighbors like a thick slice of deli meat, with its predictable design and stout, simple layout. It was at least fifty years old, if not older. Things happened. Especially in old houses. But as the hours wore on, the leaking got worse and worse, and they found themselves scrambling—all five of them, the mother, the father, the two sons, and the one young daughter—and the dog, of course, the dog was frightened, barking its head off and running around as if the world were on fire. And the mother found herself covering her face with her hands and murmuring and crying out, shuttling the dog and the children out onto the street, and it was then that they realized the entire street was flooded, all of the row houses cracking open like raw eggs, the water steadily rising under their feet. And they had to get out, they had to, because the floodwaters were drowning the house, and no matter how hard they tried they knew they couldn't stop the water.

And so it came to be, long after the family had been taken away on an emergency boat to some other place, long after the mother had cried and mourned and moaned for her house, for her many things—her home that she'd built and labored over and loved, all those photographs and irreplaceable objects that feel so permanent before you lose them. After the children had stopped crying and the mother had stopped blaming herself for something she could not have stopped, there existed a long night, a still night, a black sky with burning silver stars, and beneath the stars there was a great water, long and expansive, like an ocean, murky and deep. A submarine hung below the surface, examining the sunken row houses, a soft *blip-blip* coming from the great machine, and there was no light but from the moon and stars, and everything else in the world was silent.

RAIBENA RAITA

YEARS AS MENTEE: 1

GRADE: Senior

HIGH SCHOOL: Stuyvesant High School

BORN: Queens, NY

LIVES: Queens, NY

PUBLICATIONS AND RECOGNITIONS: Scholastic Art & Writing Awards: Honorable Mention and Silver Key

MENTEE'S ANECDOTE: *My time with Daryl has been amazing. I love just talking with her; we have talked about everything from Shah Rukh Khan to her job to our families. Over the past few months, she has really helped me grow as a writer as well, through free writes with story dice, taking time editing my pieces, and just talking about my ideas and the projects I want to work on. I always have a bunch of ideas bouncing around my mind and sometimes I don't know how to put them into words, but bouncing ideas off Daryl always helps me clear things up.*

DARYL CHEN

YEARS AS MENTOR: 1

OCCUPATION: Ideas Editor, TED

BORN: New York, NY

LIVES: Brooklyn, NY

MENTOR'S ANECDOTE: *From the first time I met Raibena and she told me what Harry Potter house she would be (Gryffindor is too predictable, so either Ravenclaw or Hufflepuff), I knew we were a great match. Like many in* Generation F, *she is full of fiercely held opinions, and that, combined with her overflowing imagination, has made our writing sessions a joy. I never know what idea she will come up with next, and I cannot wait to find out.*

Lockdown

RAIBENA RAITA

Just like how the Vietnam War defined the '60s and the Cold War defined the '70s, terrorism defines our generation.

On October 31, 2017, there was a terror attack in downtown Manhattan, on the West Side Highway bike path. On November 1, 2017, *The New York Times* published a front-page article by Benjamin Mueller, William K. Rashbaum, and Al Baker, with the subhead "'Cowardly Act of Terror,' Mayor Declares." Mayor de Blasio classified it as an act of terror because of the supposed affiliation that attacker Sayfullo Saipov had with ISIS and, most important, because of the words he yelled out (*"Allahu Akbar"*) as he carried out the attack.

I was there when this tragedy occurred, in art class at Stuyvesant High School. When a lockdown was first declared at 3:05 p.m., my classmates and I shrugged it off. We thought it was just a drill, so we continued with class. We were on the tenth floor, the farthest from the chaos occurring below us. We didn't even realize there was anything wrong until, through the window in front of my desk, we saw the stretch of the West Side Highway covered with bright red and blue lights. My classmates and I immediately took out our phones, frantically surfing the Web to find out what had occurred right under our noses.

For the next couple of hours, as we were stuck in our classrooms until the lockdown was lifted, my classmates and I looked up article after article and shared them among ourselves. There was a constant stream of new information. We read about how the attacker had slammed into a school bus and then pulled out two guns; later, those guns were found to be fake. The story kept changing and we kept researching, terrified, as the body count increased.

At 5:00 p.m., the mayor and other city officials held a press conference concerning what had occurred two hours before-hand, and my class silently watched it, still unable to leave the building. I was passively listening, not entirely focused on the screen in front of me. Then a reporter asked, "Do we know if the attacker yelled out '*Allahu Akbar*' or anything of the sort?" After the mayor confirmed he had, everything—the conversa-tion and its tone, the way people viewed the situation and the perpetrator—shifted. The headlines of every article changed "shooter" or "deranged driver" to "terrorist," and experts on CNN began exclaiming that this was a confirmed terrorist at-tack because of the phrase that had passed through the lips of the criminal.

As I watched CNN after the press conference, the feeling of wanting to go home hit me hard. But I couldn't. Instead I sat at my desk, silently crying, the Eid *salwar kameez* that I had worn as a princess costume for Halloween suddenly unbearably heavy. For me, this was a terrorist attack when I first found out about the atrocity. This was a terrorist attack as the death toll kept rising. This was a terrorist attack before I knew about Saipov's affiliation with ISIS. For the media and the rest of the world, however, this wasn't a terrorist attack until they knew that he yelled "*Allahu Akbar.*"

Nowadays, while most people don't believe every Muslim is a terrorist, it's generally accepted that every terrorist is Muslim. That's why the Las Vegas shooter who killed dozens of people was not called a terrorist and was instead called a "gunman"; he was a white Christian, not a brown Muslim. While both events were atrocities, calling one a "shooting" and the other a "terrorist attack" changes the dynamic of how we see the events. A shooting is tragic, but a terror attack is seen as something more personal—it is seen as an attack on your country.

When people equate terrorists with Muslims, it allows them to discriminate against Muslims. This is why despicable policies such as the travel ban exist and why people support them. Our belief of who a "terrorist" is needs to change; when we resort to such terrible stereotypes, it separates us from one another.

The lockdown was finally lifted around 7:00 p.m. Each floor was cleared and dismissed one by one; I was one of the last students to leave the building. I met up with Fariya, a sophomore and a family friend who lives near me, and her two friends, and we all went home together. When we were two-thirds of the way to the City Hall R/W train station, my mother called me back, having missed my three phone calls to her. I explained to her that I was out of the building with Fariya and her friends, and I was on my way to the train station. She asked me if the attacker was Muslim; I hesitated before answering affirmatively. "You three girls stick close and keep your heads down, okay? Be careful," my mother instructed. This wasn't the first time my mother had told me to do this, but it was one of the first times I agreed with her.

How superiority is born

DARYL CHEN

My mentee and I have both been profoundly shaped—in different ways, of course—by being the children of immigrant parents. In this piece, I wanted to explore this heritage and touch on how I see Generation F *responding to parental influence.*

Perhaps it starts with an offhand remark from your parents about how certain classmates of yours are "ordinary" or, even more damning, "average." It's only later that you realize all of those classmates are white.

Week after week, they make comments about picky Jewish coworkers, lazy black store clerks, fat white diners, and so on. Since your parents speak to each other in Mandarin, these digs go unheard by the people they're referring to, but you understand them. You don't detect any prejudice or hate in their voices; instead, "Puerto Ricans are poor and loud" is said in much the same tone as "The sky is blue." Their remarks are small and offhand, but like a single drop of water that keeps striking a stone, they wear you down.

It's not solely about race. "Housewife" is one of the worst words they use about a person—it means terminal idleness and lack of ambition. "Secretary," you learn, is a few rungs up from "housewife"—it's above "waitress" and "gossip," but below "administrator" or "graduate student."

Occasionally you get confused about who's winning. As your family piles into the station wagon after dinner with your parents' friends and the seat belts click, your father and mother launch into how ill-behaved their children are and how carelessly the dishes were prepared. The friends are Chinese doctors, just like your parents, so you realize that even among the best people, there are gradations. *Our family's food is better than everyone else's,* you think in the back seat, with a glow of pride.

As you grow up, you see the ignorance in your parents' biases. You make friends with people of all kinds—from other races and backgrounds and even ones who didn't go to college. *You are a different person than your parents,* you think. *You are a better person.*

It takes years before you notice yourself listening to coworkers, friends, family members, with the unamused tolerance of a deity who is stuck living with mortals due to a twist of fate. It's still more years before you step down from the throne.

You envy the self-aware girls and women of *Generation F*— they let the remarks that you absorbed roll off them like water on ducks and they speak up when they need to. And you even start to think, *Maybe they're better than* . . . before you stop.

SARAH RAMIREZ

YEARS AS MENTEE: 2

GRADE: Senior

HIGH SCHOOL: Scholars' Academy

BORN: Long Island, NY

LIVES: Queens, NY

PUBLICATIONS AND RECOGNITIONS: Meringoff Family Scholarship recipient

MENTEE'S ANECDOTE: *In my second and final year at Girls Write Now, I've learned to savor every moment of mentor meetings and writing workshops. I'm extremely grateful when I think about the dedication of Girls Write Now staff and my mentor, Erica, who has helped me become a better writer and person. Erica is the person I trust most with my writing—writing I used to hide under my mattress. I'm inspired by the girls in various workshops who have shown me the importance of community and lifting one another up, helping me to see what we are capable of.*

ERICA SCHWIEGERSHAUSEN

YEARS AS MENTOR: 2

OCCUPATION: Adjunct Lecturer, Hunter College

BORN: Harvard, MA

LIVES: Brooklyn, NY

MENTOR'S ANECDOTE: *In our second year working together, Sarah and I allowed ourselves to loosen up a little. I've loved watching her continue to lean in to her strengths as a writer—especially her sense of humor! I'm inspired by her candor and vulnerability, and her willingness to confront challenging topics head-on. And I admire her ability to laugh at herself—which we find ourselves doing just about every week.*

An Anxious Child of God

SARAH RAMIREZ

Over the past year, I've become more aware of my anxiety and its control over my life. For me, writing about it was the first step to confronting it.

I spend a lot of time being anxious about my own anxiety. So when my Sunday school teacher, Ruth, announced one day that we were going to talk about anxiety, I thought to myself, *Finally*.

"What is everyone worried about?" Ruth asked the class.

"College . . . where I'm going to end up," one girl said.

The person next to her nodded. "My future in general." I agreed; I often feel nervous about the uncertainty of the future. Sometimes, I feel like I'm entwined with this anxiety, and I let it define my identity, because without it, I wouldn't know who I am.

My turn came. "How people perceive me?" I said, feeling unsure if I should be sharing something so personal. Immediately, I felt self-conscious. Ruth came up to me, put her hand on top of my head, and looked into my eyes. "Sarah, you are beautiful and intelligent, and I love you," she said. My hands were trembling. I was touched, but my initial feelings of self-consciousness lingered.

All the usual anxious thoughts rushed through my head. *I shouldn't have said that. Why did I say "perceive"? I could've just said "see." Now I look pretentious and they'll all think that I think I'm smarter than them. I should've given the same answer as everyone else, about the future, I mean, it still would've been true.*

"Anxiety is holding people in this very room back," Ruth

said, as if she had read my mind. I felt like her words were meant for me. Listening to her, I realized that all my life anxiety has held me back from attaining a full relationship with God—one where I can depend on him completely. My anxious thoughts have also held me back from seizing various opportunities, because fear of embarrassment and failure always overpowered anything else.

I've been in the Christian church my whole life and I am surrounded by faith-filled people, not only in church, but in my family as well. I've seen the evidence of having a strong faith in my mother's life. In 2008, she was diagnosed with breast cancer and was supposed to undergo a double mastectomy. But when the surgeons scanned her one last time, the tumor had disappeared. In the face of this scary diagnosis, she put everything in God's hands and was calm doing so. "My God is bigger than cancer," she said confidently. Her faith was formidable. My faith is weak in comparison. It wavers when any hint of a problem comes my way. I want to be optimistic, but it's hard to stop imagining possible worst-case scenarios. People oftentimes use the words "joy" and "optimism" to characterize me, from friends to supervisors and teachers. However, when dwelling on negativity, there is no sight of this beloved joy. It's stolen from me, and I can't see myself in this same light. I become unrecognizable.

But since that day with Ruth in Sunday school, I've been working on it. I've found refuge and guidance in the Bible. Recently, I was reading the book of Romans when I came across these words: "Do not let sin control the way you live . . . Instead, give yourself completely to God . . . Sin is no longer your master." I read the verses over and over again, replacing the word "sin" with "anxiety." Suddenly, I could see the oppressive role of anxiety in my life. I'd made it into my master, too paralyzed by fear to stray away from it.

These verses remind me that God is my true master who has

come to liberate me from my anxiety. It's comforting to know who I belong to—a sovereign God who has infinite power over anxiety and total authority over my future.

I'm realizing that as a child of God, I must surrender the things I can't control over to Him, having faith that He will take care of me. Instead of grounding my identity in anxiety, I'm grounding it in being a precious child under God's perfect love.

Be Safe

ERICA SCHWIEGERSHAUSEN

I was struck by the line in Sarah's essay: "Sometimes, I feel like I'm entwined with this anxiety, and I let it define my identity." Her writing inspired me to explore the roots of my own anxiety.

After my brother died, I fixated on the fact that I hadn't told him that I loved him. Had he known? I was five years old, and I convinced myself he was gone because I hadn't adequately appreciated him.

After he died, I started taking inventory of everything I was grateful for. At holidays and birthday parties, I counted my blessings in the bathroom. Sitting on the toilet, I told myself how lucky I was to be so happy, to be having so much fun, to get to eat cake and open presents and play games and have friends. Forcing myself to appreciate what I had felt like a protection against losing it. Even if it didn't last forever, at least I would know that I hadn't taken it for granted.

I can't hang up the phone with anyone in my family without saying "I love you." Sometimes, it embarrasses me, but I need to say it. I need to say it in case.

I am constantly imagining what might happen: car accidents, plane crashes, falling onto the subway tracks, illness. Before I go away for the weekend, I whisper to my boyfriend, "Be safe," as if these words might allow me to control the uncontrollable.

A therapist tells me this is an exhausting way to live, in a constant state of agitation and worry. I nod as she says this, imagining all the productive ways I might repurpose the mental energy spent anticipating catastrophe. But I'm oddly attached to my anxiety. I know it's not rational, but I imagine it as control— as a protection against the worst. I'm still scared of what might happen if I let go of it.

PILAR REYES

YEARS AS MENTEE: 1

GRADE: Senior

HIGH SCHOOL: Baruch College Campus High School

BORN: New York, NY

LIVES: New York, NY

MENTEE'S ANECDOTE: *I have lived in New York all my life, but I have never been as reliant on a subway map as I have this year—the subway map that I've hidden in my iBooks to avoid embarrassment. I must seek it out weekly; Amy, my mentor, and I meet at different cafés each week. Amy's laptop always has at least twenty tabs open at any given time. She multitasks: schedules vacations, shops for her friend's birthday gift, sends emails back and forth to her boss. Somehow, she fits me in to all of that. I couldn't feel more special.*

AMY ZIMMERMAN

YEARS AS MENTOR: 1

OCCUPATION: Entertainment Reporter, *The Daily Beast*

BORN: New York, NY

LIVES: New York, NY

PUBLICATIONS AND RECOGNITIONS: Runner-up Los Angeles Press Club Award (Arts and Entertainment Feature); upcoming publication in *Fourth Genre: Explorations in Nonfiction* (Lyric Essay)

MENTOR'S ANECDOTE: *This year, questions of gendered power imbalances have dominated my writing, reading, and mentee meetings. During one particularly illuminating conversation, Pilar told me about instances of everyday sexism and harassment she had experienced, and how she came to terms with these incidents and the boys behind the toxic rhetoric. I'm so inspired by young women like Pilar, who have the intelligence and the framework to analyze these experiences, and the vision to imagine something better. Getting to know Pilar has put a face on the things that I am fighting for and given me a new friend to fight beside.*

My Grandmother's First Period

PILAR REYES

I wrote this piece at my first Girls Write Now workshop this fall. It is about my grandmother, who continues to be an inspiration to me, and always finds her way into my writing. She and I are both Generation F.

My cousin Zoe got her first period in the summer of 2008. My relatives and I were at my great-aunt's farmhouse in Lancaster, Pennsylvania, when we got the call. I didn't know much about periods at the time because health class didn't start until fifth grade, and I was still four years away from my own defining moment as a woman, anyway.

I sat at the head of the table, not because I was the most important, but rather because it was the seat closest to the stove, on top of which sat the eggs I was scrambling. My grandmother sat opposite from me at the other head—however, as the leading matriarch she *was* rather important, with or without eggs to monitor—her body turned out, legs crossed, one arm resting on the flat linoleum surface.

From her plaque-ridden brain cells somehow rose an anecdote of her own first period, which she began to describe in vivid detail. My eight-year-old mind was not mature enough for this discussion, and I sat there squeamishly, legs tapping uncomfortably, with millions of questions in mind but zero balls to ask them.

She was walking through a field when she felt the warm blood trickle down her leg (that's how I imagined it; however, it was probably through the busy streets of Manila). As the oldest of four siblings, with each in tow, she had no frame of reference as to what to do, no one to ask help of or even for a tissue. Confused and embarrassed, she led her pack back to the house, where her mother's explanation awaited.

I remember being shocked by the ending to my grandmother's story, the not-so-grand finale. I knew period talk was, and still is, taboo, but did her mother think that never warning her meant that she would never experience it? That by keeping her in the dark meant she would somehow be pardoned from this natural phenomenon?

Compared to my grandmother's story, Zoe's—which was already filled with horrors about clots and tampons—seemed like a dream. However, I didn't truly appreciate it until I was twelve and experienced my period for the first time. I was lucky to have friends who carried buckets of pads with them, but what I truly had taken for granted was the preparation I had received in the years leading up to that moment. I was blessed to come home to boxes of pads, tampons, and liners that had been sitting at the top of my medicine cabinet for years, "just in case." I was blessed to have a health class that taught me not just *what* periods were, but *why* we got them and *how* they worked. I was blessed to have a mother who embraced the awkwardness to give me "the talk"—multiple times—as early as she could. Most of all I am blessed to be raised in a country where girls are educated about their bodies, and I hope to live to see the day when that ideal spreads across the pond; how can a woman love her body if she doesn't know about all the amazing things it does?

memory exercise

AMY ZIMMERMAN

Inspired by Pilar's piece and by Pilar, I recalled fragments from when I was around her age—moments when I felt myself becoming aware of my body, or when I grappled with what a woman was.

I remember the rainbow-sprinkle cookies that looked better than they tasted every single time, I still buy them for myself sometimes—to prove something?

I remember sitting in the park the night before Thanksgiving, it felt like we would never have to go back to school

I remember my polka-dot push-up bra from Target

I don't remember my first cigarette

I remember the doorknob falling off the door at the party; music cut for an announcement: "Did anybody take my knob?"

I remember winter in the city like it was the only season

I remember the exact time the McDonald's by my high school switched from hash browns to french fries: 10:37

I remember visiting my great-grandmother and hating it and knowing that I was supposed to hate myself for hating it

I remember the shop teacher flirting with me and knowing that I wasn't supposed to know that

I remember visiting my grandparents on Long Island, so much grass and fresh air I felt like I was about to fall off the planet

I remember trying to wear a tie to school one day but I got too embarrassed and hid it in my bag before homeroom

I remember always having the messiest uniform

I remember walking my dog with my mother on the West Side

I remember the Upper East Side on a Sunday night, far from home, black velvet sky and muffled paws on pavement

I remember the smell of thirty girls straightening their hair in one walk-in closet

I remember the feeling of a boy grabbing my ass through a pair of Abercrombie & Fitch jean shorts—before then I didn't know I had one

I remember eating so many SweeTarts my taste buds stopped working

I don't remember losing my virginity, I just remember the noise around it

I remember the story of your hurts like they are mine but I have others

I remember time stopping on the highway into Manhattan

I remember refusing to get out of the car

EMILY RINALDI

YEARS AS MENTEE: 2

GRADE: Junior

HIGH SCHOOL: Susan E. Wagner High School

BORN: Staten Island, NY

LIVES: Staten Island, NY

MENTEE'S ANECDOTE: *This year has brought about some challenges. Despite one of us traveling anywhere and everywhere writing (is that a dream job or what?!) and the other simply trying to survive junior year, it hasn't always been easy to have our weekly catch-ups . . . yet Molly and I still find a way. Whether we are thousands of miles apart in different time zones or in a local café, every week we get the chance to chat, write, laugh, occasionally drink some overpriced coffee, and write some more.*

MOLLY McARDLE

YEARS AS MENTOR: 2

OCCUPATION: Freelance Writer, *National Geographic*; *Travel + Leisure*; *GQ*; *Rhapsody*; *Oxford American*

BORN: Washington, DC

LIVES: Brooklyn, NY

MENTOR'S ANECDOTE: *I've heard other mentors talk about this phenomenon: The more time you spend with your mentee, the harder it is to find time to write. Emily and I can't help but talk about everything and anything. It's always the highlight of my week, whether we're chatting over a cup of coffee on Staten Island or laughing on our laptops via Skype. The writing still happens, by hook or by crook, and when it does it is astonishing. That's why pieces like this one—confident, funny, smart, swift, and surprising—are the highlight of my year.*

The Burgundy & Gold Stitched Chair

EMILY RINALDI

This piece represents Generation F *because in today's society the older generation tends to underestimate the younger one, when in all reality we are the change, whether or not those who come before us see it.*

A majority of my adult life has been spent sitting in a burgundy-and-gold stitched chair in a secluded office on the corner of some sketchy block in Houston, Texas. Being one of the only reliable psychologists in town, I have heard it all. From petty boy problems to fourth-graders' rape stories, I have comforted people through some of their darkest times right from that chair. Not only do I comfort those who seek my help, I help them battle their demons, and I must say, I am pretty darn good at it. Every single time I have some sort of game plan and pretty quickly, too . . . or at least a diagnosis. Then one day Alex Marshall came along.

The star athlete on his football team with a beautiful girlfriend and a large group of friends: a typical high school teenager. He began coming to me two weeks ago on Tuesdays and Thursdays, when he began hearing voices and having "thoughts that seemed to be coming true." Initially, I thought it was schizophrenia, but he didn't show any "normal" symptoms, so I was skeptical. The following weeks, he just became more of an impossible puzzle. I was getting pieces, but none seemed to fit. He told me last Tuesday that his dream vividly happened in real life. Apparently, a kid on his football team got diagnosed with skin cancer and he dreamt about it. I figured it could perhaps be a coincidence or all in his head. He also said he had these "visions" and when he had them he would go into paralysis mode. He mentioned that he's had sleep paralysis, and it was similar but this was real. He had a vision in the shower one night about receiving a test back and the next day it happened in real life exactly like the dream, everything down to the questions they got wrong. At this point I figured it was completely in his head but what exactly was IN his head? Schizophrenia? Too many football concussions? The fact that I couldn't figure it out was irking me, but I was determined to—even if it was the last thing I did.

Then he came in on Thursday for his second appointment of the week. Earlier that day there was a massive terrorist attack in a church in Rome, Italy. He came in, sat down, and said he had another image of the attack. He said he caused it. He wouldn't go into details about his image because "he never wants to relive that again." (Taken from my notes.) The rest of the session was silent. I thought he was making it up or having really bad schizophrenic or anxiety-induced false memories. But still, nothing seemed to add up. Until last night around six p.m. he texted me asking the nearest time he could come in. I told him that I had off and was in the office so he could come by whenever he needed to, free of charge. About five minutes later I heard a voice.

"I had an image." I looked up and across from me was Alex Marshall. He was shaking as the words left his mouth.

"What happened?" I asked.

"I was called down to the main office in physics saying that I was going home. I went down and this FBI agent posed as my uncle told me I was going with him and the ladies at the desk didn't even question it. He said to come with him and I went outside and into his car and he didn't say a word to me and then my phone went off with a loud alarm. Like really loud. Like

Amber-Alerts-on-steroids loud. I looked at my phone as I read: 'INCOMING MISSILE: YOU HAVE APPROXIMATELY THIRTY MINUTES TO FIND SAFETY.' I looked at him and he said, 'We are getting you to safety with your family; we know your secret, you won't be harmed.' Then the image ended," said Alex with tears welling in his eyes and his face as pale as a ghost.

"Alex . . . it's just a thought, it won't happen," I tried to reassure him.

"I know it sounds ridiculous and like I'm losing it, but I'm not."

That is the last conversation he asked me to record to prove he "wasn't losing it." I didn't believe him. Quite frankly, I thought he was losing it. Then this morning I was sitting in my chair after my patient had just left. And then alarms on my phone started and they were loud. Like really loud. Like Amber-Alerts-on-steroids loud. "INCOMING MISSILE: YOU HAVE APPROXIMATELY THIRTY MINUTES TO FIND SAFETY" was displayed on my phone. Now here I am, in the basement of a secluded office on some sketchy block of Houston, Texas, writing perhaps the last thing I will ever write. Maybe the FBI will find this. In the meantime, I am going to complete his diagnosis, which might be the last thing I do. Alex Marshall, seventeen, can actually predict the future.

Joy Girls in Salzburg

MOLLY MCARDLE

I've traveled, and written about travel, a lot this year for work, all while writing with Emily via Skype and text and email. She's shown up—obliquely—in my travel writing, too.

Our mothers' mother, Nana Fitz, used to call Nora and me the "Joy Girls." The moniker appeared without explanation at the end of her life, around the time Nora and I entered our twenties. I relished it as a signifier of our allegiance, as a sign that we—unmarried and ambitious, avid travelers and social planners par excellence—could be joyful because we insisted on it as a right. In a certain light, Joy Girl could be a critique, connoting immaturity, selfishness, flippancy. But Nana said it with a hint of wonder, as if she couldn't quite believe the kind of girls we were able to be, or the women we were becoming. She said it having been a Joy Girl once, too.

On-screen on the original *Sound of Music* tour, a group of nuns shake their heads in similar disbelief. "How do you solve a problem like Maria?" they ask as we drive away from the abbey, following the Salzach River out from the old city center. The young novice's faults are many: torn clothes, tree climbing, singing in the abbey, tardiness, overenthusiasm for meals. "She's a headache," one nun complains. "She's an angel," another insists. The Mother Abbess, in a bit of musical theater wisdom that both lifts up and breaks my heart, equates them: "She's a girl."

Like nearly everyone else on the tour—the second full bus

dispatched this rainy off-season morning—Nora and I have loved *The Sound of Music* since we were girls. Gorgeously shot on location (there's a reason we've all come to Salzburg), set to unforgettable music (try getting it out of your head), both romantic and antifascist—what's not to like? As adults we've loved doing *Sound of Music* things together: going to an outdoor sing-along and braiding our hair in a vaguely Alpine manner, seeing a stage revival when it came to our hometown and echoing the words under our breath. I love that Nora and I share this, but I love it even more because, in addition to its beauty, it speaks some sort of truth to me. Maria, when she spins in that Alpine meadow in the movie's iconic opening—hungry, happy, heedless—is the ultimate Joy Girl.

DALEELAH SALEH

YEARS AS MENTEE: 2

GRADE: Junior

HIGH SCHOOL: Baccalaureate School for Global Education

BORN: New York, NY

LIVES: Queens, NY

PUBLICATIONS AND RECOGNITIONS: Scholastic Art & Writing Awards: three Silver Keys

MENTEE'S ANECDOTE: *As intersectional feminists, Liv and I almost never run out of things to talk about at our pair sessions. There's seemingly a new injustice each week. A recurring topic we discuss is how we can implement change within our communities. It's often easy to feel helpless in the face of systemic oppression. However, there are many actions that can be taken as a means of resistance. One of the most powerful forms of resistance is marches/protests, and Liv and I were able to take part by attending the Women's March together. It was really empowering, and an amazing bonding experience.*

LIVIA NELSON

YEARS AS MENTOR: 2

OCCUPATION: Web Designer

BORN: Ridgefield, CT

LIVES: Queens, NY

MENTOR'S ANECDOTE: *I'm so proud that Daleelah chose to share "The New National Anthem," because it's so representative of our best pair sessions. When we meet up, we often spend the first half ranting and raving about the headlining social justice issues of the week, and Daleelah has incorporated many of those topics into this poem. This work also came out of a single pair session, where we sat down not knowing how we would tackle the Poetic Forms assignment, and left with a finished sestina. And even better, it won a Silver Key from the Scholastic Art & Writing Awards!*

The New National Anthem

DALEELAH SALEH

None of us are free until all of us are free—the national anthem
is not only hypocritical, it is a lie!

O say can you see: America,
land of the free
if you have enough money,
and your skin color's the right shade,
you can pay your way out of prison,
home of the brave.

tell me, was it really that brave,
sending soldiers over
from America to Iraq,
to bleed red, all in the same shade,
or was it just a way
to make money?
either way, both sides are prisoners,
the war on terror
leaves no room for freedom.

the Emancipation Proclamation reads,

"All persons held as slaves [. . .] are and henceforward shall
be free."
but this great nation of America
was a system founded on white supremacy,

holding people of color as prisoners
no matter the shade.
but weren't we so brave?
to thrive despite
only being seen as a way
to make money.

and immigrants are only acceptable
when they save employers' money,
doing under-the-table jobs
essentially
for free.
we corrupted
the countries within Latin America,
then threatened to
build a wall
to ensure imprisonment.
so risking everything to cross the border
is the definition of brave,
and yet there's a constant fear of being detained
if your skin isn't just the right shade.

under the harsh sun of imperialism, there is no shade—
in North Dakota the need for water
is superseded by the hunger for money, and
Standing Rock protectors continue the fight of generations
before them,
standing fierce and brave.
once upon a time, indigenous people could roam this land
freely.
then Columbus Sailed the Ocean Blue, 1492,
discovered America,

and what was once a haven
now serves as a prison.

and in our America,
women's bodies often serve as their prisons.
because you are a girl, you must never take up the spotlight,
always stay in the shade.
and your body has no value
unless it can be objectified
in the name of making money, so
daring to look in the mirror without flinching
makes you brave.
because haven't you learned by now?
things such as freedom
aren't so easily attained
in a society built on oppression.

America: hypocrites proudly wave
gleaming red white and blue shades,
o'er the land of the free
and the home of the brave.

We Can Do Better

LIVIA NELSON

I was so inspired by Daleelah's poem that I decided to write a poem to support it. I usually write prose, and I was scared to address this topic, but Daleelah gave me the courage!

And let me also add: I am the "right" shade
But when I look at my race, I feel so ashamed.

How can we claim any national pride
With our history of slavery, internment, genocide
We say "My ancestors weren't part of all that, so I'm good"
But just because we didn't cut down the trees doesn't mean
    we live in the woods.

No refuge could save the hireling and slave
From the terror of flight, or the gloom of the grave.
Our National Anthem still dares have these words
But maybe it makes sense—past and present are blurred.

Stop pretending, dear white people, that this isn't our problem
Or that injustice can be viewed in a present-day vacuum
Racial inequality goes back to our country's roots
To pull yourself up by your bootstraps, you have to have
    boots.

And I'm not just calling out southern whites
Neo-Nazis, the KKK, or the alt-right

I'm talking about white people who claim to be on the left
Then turn our backs on our fellow citizens and all the ways
    they are oppressed

While we sit comfortably in our Connecticut homes
In our downtown offices, on our unearned thrones
In Silicon Valley and our Ivy League halls
Pretending there isn't blood on our hands, in the walls

And using our privilege to take the cowardly route
Saying "This is just how things are," shrugging, opting out
Hiding in our bubble, that lily-white cocoon
That allows us to ignore all the elephants in the room.

But if we can be neutral in situations of injustice
If we can justify our ignorance because it's just bliss
Then we are just as bad as our white predecessors,
And have chosen the side of the future's oppressors.

We need to be allies as a means to atone
Because Daleelah shouldn't have to fight this fight alone.

MARIFER SANTOS

YEARS AS MENTEE: 2

GRADE: Senior

HIGH SCHOOL: Inwood Academy for Leadership

BORN: San Francisco de Macorís, Dominican Republic

LIVES: New York, NY

PUBLICATIONS AND RECOGNITIONS: Scholastic Art & Writing Awards: Gold Key and Silver Key

MENTEE'S ANECDOTE: *My mentor and I live in the same neighborhood, Inwood. For one of our first writing meetings, we went to our local park. We saw and wrote about so many hidden gems in the park, from the culture to the beautiful view. Linda Kay Klein has taught me how to write from my own perspective about truth, about things that to the naked eye might not be poetic, and how even simple surroundings can speak to my own truth.*

LINDA KAY KLEIN

YEARS AS MENTOR: 1

OCCUPATION: Storyteller and Social Innovator

LIVES: New York, NY

PUBLICATIONS AND RECOGNITIONS: *Pure: Inside the Evangelical Movement that Shamed a Generation of Young Women and How I Broke Free* (Simon & Schuster, August 2018)

MENTOR'S ANECDOTE: *Marifer has welcomed me into her world through her stories. Stories of her family, her friends, her heartache, and her frustration. And so, though we've gone on all kinds of exciting field trips together—visiting book publishing and magazine houses, nonprofits that use writing to help people heal, and more—when I think of Marifer, the moments that stand out most to me are the small ones. Sitting in a coffee shop reading an intimate story I feel honored to have shared with me, or helping her think through how to address a friend's tragedy. It's those moments I'm most grateful for.*

Between Worlds

MARIFER SANTOS

This is a piece about my place in the world and how, as a member of
Generation F, I do (and don't) fit in. The piece is based on my fami-
ly's home daycare and my grandfather's illness.

Home smells like cherry lip gloss
Lip gloss for the impressionable elementary school girls
Diapers for the babies and bubblegum lollipops for the toddlers
Here is the place of alternatives
But cherry lip gloss is how they try to impress me

Home smells like menthol
Menthol like the witches' medicinal vapor rub to dress the sick
Diffused camphor and eucalyptus
Here is the place where there are no alternatives
but menthol is impressed upon his chest

Home sounds like tantrums
Tantrums like screams of frustration and crying outburst
Sometimes the bursts of laughter
Sometimes screeching claims and blames
Sometimes a scuffle of discoordinated jumping
Following, the downstairs neighbor's thumping on his
ceiling/my floors

Home sounds like an oxygen concentrator

Oxygen concentration like the wheezing and coughing of a
grown man
Sometimes like the outburst of gasping for air
Sometimes the faded tantrums
Sometimes the sound of the repeated mariachi song
Sometimes *the loud shuffling of dominoes and his victory chant*

Home tastes like movie popcorn
Movie popcorn, cheerios or oreos
Cafeteria trays with veggies, proteins and sweets
And here the food ends in crumbs and cups spill
These children use my home as a movie set production
At least there are snacks in this little home of mine

Home tastes like Caribbean cuisine
Caribbean cuisine like mondongo, mofongo or sancocho
Mountains of rice and protein and sweets
His own unshared cookies, cakes and candies
*And here in the wheel*chair his tastes are childlike
Replacing the cigarettes he smoked as a child

Home looks like scattered toys
Scattered toys like blocks, books and teddy bears
And here is the place of colorful alphabet mats and checkered
patterns
The ethnic dolls and the frugal child merchant with plastic
foods
And this framed holiday card of the previous and current
nursery kids

Home looks like a living room
A living room with a dying man

And here is the place of his faded alphabet and checked
memories
The native prayers to the children he surpassed in livelihood
And this holiday *card* from his now-adult kids

Home feels like ooey gooey slime
Ooey gooey slime like sticky, indestructible furniture
The feeling of the kids' confusion in a hanged-man game
To feel as if I am a kid again in this place of
Shatterproof vases and untied laces
Untangled manes and the sticky glue-dot remains

Home feels like living in asphyxiation
I am forbidden to see him choking out a cough of help
I do not find the hanged man pitiful or sick or weak
He is merely trying to grasp a few more breaths
with no fear of death

Where am I in this home?
I feel guilty for even asking that
But sometimes I feel lost between worlds

The Middle of Nowhere

LINDA KAY KLEIN

Working with Marifer on her piece, "Between Worlds," we explored questions such as "What is home?" and "Where do I belong?" together. The following personal piece was inspired by Marifer's beautifully structured response to these questions.

The road smells like hot dry dirt when you throw a pail of
    water on it.
Musky. It gets up in your nose. Then it dries up again quick.
The road smells sweet, like wildflowers candied in the sun.
Foul like manure. Fetid like the carcass of a deer. Clean like
    crisp, brown fields of wheat.

The road sounds like a hum, a long note sung on and on.
It sounds like quiet, like a hush, and yet, so loud you can't
    hear anything over it.
It sounds like rock-and-roll, country, and the oldies station.
Be-bop-a-doo-wop-a-doo-wop-*wow*.

The road tastes dry, like drinking from an empty canteen.
A few grains of sand you smack and smack.
It tastes like saliva rolling around in your mouth while you
    scan the passing signs for a gas station, a weigh station, a
    truck stop, a rest stop, a rest already, a stop.

The road looks like a scar. A hardened wound in the tender
    side of the land.

A man-made cut through her—patched, packed, padded, and
    ready to ride.
It looks like a snake. Wiley and prepared to pounce but settled
    by your steady hand.
It looks like restlessness. Like wild dogs. Bears. Moose. And
    you.

The road feels like freedom, like wind and feather and yes,
    whole bird even.
Like being stripped of the world's expectations in just a
    minute.
Like forgetting all the things they think you are and say you
    are and believe you are,
and that you, deep down, believe, too.

My mother grew up in a little town called Scobey, Montana.
    In high school, she moved across the state to Glasgow. And
    this afternoon in New York City, I read in the paper that
    these two towns had just been named the first and second
    "most remote" in the country.*

And finally I understand it: I am a child of nowhere. And not
    just any kind of nowhere, but the *middle* of it. No wonder I
    have never felt comfortable in the suburbs, or the country,
    or the city. No wonder, then, of course (!), my home has
    always been the road.

---

*Andrew Van Dam, "Using the Best Data Possible, We Set Out to Find the
Middle of Nowhere," *The Washington Post* (February 20, 2018).

CAROLYN SCHMIT

YEARS AS MENTEE: 1

GRADE: Sophomore

HIGH SCHOOL: Columbia Secondary School

BORN: Detroit, MI

LIVES: New York, NY

MENTEE'S ANECDOTE: *In a meeting when Amanda and I met to work on a piece, I remember having all these ideas in my head, but when I was to write them, I couldn't figure out where to start or what to say. I voiced this, and Amanda suggested using a page to write down ideas, details, questions, and connections I had. With my scrambled ideas written out, we were able to work and put them into a piece. While writing, Amanda balances her brain and her heart, and I am constantly learning new ways from her to approach my writing.*

AMANDA OTTAWAY

YEARS AS MENTOR: 1

OCCUPATION: Journalist, *Courthouse News*

BORN: Morgantown, WV

LIVES: Brooklyn, NY

PUBLICATIONS AND RECOGNITIONS: *The Rebounders: A Division I Basketball Journey* (University of Nebraska Press); *The Christian Science Monitor*; *VICE*

MENTOR'S ANECDOTE: *Carolyn has lived all over the world already in her sixteen years, whereas I didn't even board my first airplane until I was seventeen. I'm fascinated by her thoughtfulness and her view of the world, and I love learning from her about all the places she has called home, including Amsterdam, Switzerland, Israel, and now New York City.*

TO honour your roots

CAROLYN SCHMIT

*This piece was written for the Generations workshop, as an apprecia-
tion of my grandfather, but it became a much bigger project over the
past months as Amanda and I researched, wrote, and edited it together.*

You came here by sea. You stood on the railing of the SS *Himalaya*, looking down at all who came to bid you farewell. At least
fifty of them came, all of your cousins and your aunts and your
uncles and even the little boys down the street you'd played
cricket with. You left your whole world behind you that night.
You watched as the Taj Mahal hotel got smaller and smaller, and
then you watched it disappear. Your grandma was there; you
never saw her again. You used to be so close.

While growing up in India, you always wanted to leave your
little suburban neighbourhood, which was too small and slow,
too mundane. You wanted to leave when you, who taught yourself English, had ranked amongst the top English-speaking students in the Bombay state. When you'd work work work in the
fields like all the other boys and girls but all you could think
about was a world where you'd work work work, but not like
this. No more riding your metal bike to that same dirt field,
every morning, working under the same sun until evening. Instead you'd get into the subway each morning, amongst all the
other men and women in black and white suits, and then you'd
take a deep breath and stride into that tall building. Onto greater
things you'd always wanted to go.

You rode the SS *Himalaya* to London. Oh how your father would laugh if he saw you here amongst the English, them greeting you and attending to your bags. Only thirty years ago, he was temporarily jailed by the British for marching alongside Gandhi. Your father had always had stories to tell, and when he did, it was as if the winds would quiet down and the babies would stop crying and, for a while, everyone would just listen.

After departing the boat in London, you flew to New York City. In this "new world" of opportunities, New York was a world all on its own. Alone, you took a cab to the YMCA, and for three dollars a night, you stayed there. That first night, you had entered the Empire State Building and the elevator you rode up was filled with you, a Chinese couple, and a middle-aged Frenchman and it was humming with freedom so as soon as the doors opened you flung yourself out and you rushed to the edge and as you stood and looked out, it felt like you were still flying.

On your second day in this new esteemed world, it was raining, and when you smiled at a lady on the train, she clutched her handbag closer to her chest. Did she not know of the work your family back in India had done to earn their wealth? When people made fun of your accent you wondered, do they not realize you taught yourself English at the age of fourteen? "My elite status in India did not apply here in the United States," you wrote in your diary.

When I came to New York City, I came by car. I was fourteen, and I had my mom, my dad, my sisters. I had my cousins, a couple hours away. I had you, a couple hours away. My dad and I walked the streets that first night and I looked at all the different people. All the stories they must have to tell and cultures they must bring. People like you.

When you flew into your new life, you had no idea what it would bring. You had no idea the prices you'd have to pay.

Would you have left if you'd known? Your grandmother, your beloved grandmother who'd made you warm milk with honey under grey growling skies. Your grandma who made you listen to Bollywood music (you always have it playing in your home today). Your grandma who'd picked you up and tended to your scabbed knees and kissed them and then sent you back out to play. You never saw her again after boarding that ship. She sang to you a song that day. A prayer. She told you to sing it if you ever felt lonely, homesick. You scratched the lyrics onto a piece of paper and you sang that song to yourself over and over on that boat, till it was buried deep in your mind.

When you talk about moving here, you say you did it for us. I used to wonder if there really was that connection, because it was you who left your home and your family, in their house of brick and mud, on a boat that night. Now I realize that you exist as a bridge between two lands. That this story starts with you. That maybe, in a way, all of my stories begin with you.

To the Catcaller

AMANDA OTTAWAY

This piece isn't directly related to Carolyn's, but she and I—like so many women and girls—have spent a lot of time talking and thinking about harassment this year.

You wanted to know where I was going.
Well,
I'm feeling generous.

Last week when you whistled at me from behind
I was on my way to poop
in the Starbucks public bathroom.

Three days ago when you hollered
at my hips I was going to borrow some tampons
for the blood in my grungy underwear.

Yesterday when you told me
I wouldn't be able to run away I was en route to a wart-
    removal kit
and some toenail clippers.

Today it's my turn to talk.

Tugged skyward by moontides
pinned earthside by gravity
women stride, shift, stomp, eat

space. We are a flesh requiem,
we are ancient torchbearers and eternal life-breathers
and we are all of these things bound up in skin and blood and
   bone,
like yours.

I am in a carnal orbit of my mother's creation,
like you.
I am skin and phlegm and sinew
like you.

I am a bloody, belching, hungry, lusty, defecating, ephemeral
   lump
of flesh and stardust,
like you.

MAEVE SLON

YEARS AS MENTEE: 3

GRADE: Junior

HIGH SCHOOL: Harvest Collegiate High School

BORN: New York, NY

LIVES: New York, NY

PUBLICATIONS AND RECOGNITIONS: Moth GrandSLAM

MENTEE'S ANECDOTE: *I spent all of last spring to early fall in a creativeless headspace. I was distracted by school and friend drama and found it impossible to write. At our meetings, Vivian and I were able to find a way to write through games and strange prompts. And even though they were silly, it was something more than a blank page. Vivian is always there to help with a yummy cup of hot chocolate and the motivation to never stop writing.*

VIVIAN CONAN

YEARS AS MENTOR: 6

OCCUPATION: Librarian, Westchester Library System

BORN: New York, NY

LIVES: New York, NY

MENTOR'S ANECDOTE: *Maeve has taught me how to look—really look. At artwork in the garden of the Cathedral of St. John the Divine. At the way the darkness changes after the winter solstice until one day the sky seems lighter. She has taught me that the link between just talking and writing is not always direct. What seem like random digressions percolate inside her and can lead to a piece a month or two later. I have also learned that you can order online from Starbucks so your drink is waiting for you when you arrive.*

Snow That Grows

MAEVE SLON

This story was inspired by an application question asking what my magical object was. Not sure what to write, I searched my room for an object, when I remembered the Christmas I spent in Indiana.

My two brothers and I grew up in the city. Despite our slightly large apartment, from the time we were babies to when we were in our teens, we all shared a room and everything else. When we were little, we also shared the same imagination and believed in everything, from magical beings that came overnight—like Santa or the Tooth Fairy—to silly fairy tales. Each holiday added another being to our list.

My favorite was Christmas. Weeks before, the cold air would taste like mint and everything would feel lighter when my family and I walked around a city wrapped in lights and red bows. It was impossible to forget the magical day was near.

The winter I was seven, my family decided to drive from our New York City home to spend Christmas in Indiana. My mom had grown up there, but we rarely went back.

The house had belonged to my mom's grandparents, but once they died, it remained empty until my uncle moved in. On the drive there, I did not remember what the house looked like since I had not been there in a long time. While the car passed flat roads, malls, and cornfields, I drew pictures of what I imagined the house might look like. When we finally arrived, it was even bigger and more beautiful. My brothers and I, happy to stand again after the long car ride, could not believe our eyes.

Inside was even better. The smell of food filled the house, and Christmas music played softly as we all greeted one another. Everything about it was magical, like every movie and children's book was about this house. Snow grew feet from the ground, and there were enough bedrooms for the three of us to have our own rooms.

My brothers and I lived out a fairy tale for the days before and after Christmas, pretending the giant house belonged to us, pretending that we were royalty. On Christmas Eve, we were all ready for bed just as the sun dipped down into darkness. We put out cookies and milk for Santa, and we watched cartoons until we were forced upstairs to sleep. I lay wide awake in the giant bed alone in the room, looking out at the sky. I fell asleep watching the stars twinkle, shutting my eyes to hold all the excitement.

When I awoke, snow had fallen on the long tree branches and the ground was covered in a white blanket. The sun had barely risen and peeked through the skeleton trees that sparkled from the ice. Without another second, I threw the heavy itchy blankets off me, jumped out of bed, and tiptoed to my brother Nigel's room across the hall. I opened the door slowly and walked over to the bed and whispered in his ear, "It's Christmas." His eyes seemed to shoot open, and soon we were both wide awake, tiptoeing to see what had been left under the tree.

When we got to the stairs, we both stood there for a moment, afraid to see what might be. And then we ran. Down the stairs as our tiny feet made pattering noises against the carpet. And there was the tree, glowing in the center of the room, and underneath, packs of presents. I don't remember what we got— I don't think it matters. I remember only the magic that was in that house.

A few years after that Christmas, my family sold the house. I can no longer return, but it will forever be the most magical place in my memories.

American Dreamers

VIVIAN CONAN

This piece is dedicated to Nona, my grandmother, who was Generation F *without knowing what feminism was.*

Nona and Papoo, my Greek-Jewish grandparents, sailed to America in 1903 knowing no English. When their ship docked at Ellis Island, doctors determined that Nona's eyes were infected. Without explanation, an official put a chalk mark on the back of her coat and sent her to one line. Papoo was directed to another line. Finding an immigration worker who spoke Albanian, one of the languages he knew, Papoo learned that Nona was going to be deported. The man advised Papoo to rub the chalk off Nona's coat and bring her to his line. Papoo put his arm around his wife, and as they walked, he moved it up and down her back, removing the chalk. In that way, they entered America together.

Papoo sewed in factories and later built small multifamily homes in Brooklyn that are still in use today. Nona sewed in the basement at home. When an inspector fined her $25 for having factory machines in a residential building, Nona went to court to ask the judge how else she could work and still take care of her children. The fine was not waived, and Nona paid it. A few days later, she received a personal check for $25 in the mail. It was from the judge.

Nona and Papoo had eight children in America. One was my mother, who became an elementary school principal. At her retirement party, the PTA president gave a speech. "When Mrs.

Conan came to this school, our children did not read. *Now our children read!*" Another was my uncle. During WWII, he was an Air Force navigator who made quick in-flight calculations under enormous pressure, a job that today is done by computers. After the war, he became a math teacher.

My grandparents had fifteen grandchildren, all second-generation Americans. One is a family court judge. One is an economist who worked for the Federal Reserve. I am a librarian and mentor at Girls Write Now.

Though Nona and Papoo lived to their mid-nineties, it was not long enough to know all of their twenty-three great-grandchildren. These include a veterinarian, a humanitarian aid worker, the manager of a university radio station, and an engineer who did a college internship at NASA.

When Nona was in her nineties, she said to me, "Huh! They were going to send me back because of my eyes, and *still* I don't wear glasses!"

TASNIM TARANNUM

YEARS AS MENTEE: 2

GRADE: Senior

HIGH SCHOOL: Baccalaureate School for Global Education

BORN: Bogra, Bangladesh

LIVES: Queens, NY

PUBLICATIONS AND RECOGNITIONS: "Opportunity," *Girlboss* (October 2017); Scholarship for New York Road Runners Run for the Future Program (2018)

MENTEE'S ANECDOTE: *I am pretty proud of all the hard work I put into my essays and short stories. Having a mentor with whom I can share my love of chocolate concoctions while we discuss literature, politics, and silly stories has been a great experience. Being part of a community of supportive writers has also been a dream come true for me. Since I will be entering college in the fall, I hope to carry on the lessons learned from the Girls Write Now community, ranging from editing skills to collaborative working style.*

NAN BAUER-MAGLIN

YEARS AS MENTOR: 4

OCCUPATION: Professor (retired), Writer

BORN: New York, NY

LIVES: New York, NY

PUBLICATIONS AND RECOGNITIONS: Coeditor of six books; Author of "Mentoring at Girls Write Now," *Radical Teacher*, vol. 109, 2017

MENTOR'S ANECDOTE: *Usually we work at the 42nd Street library, but one cold January day, Tasnim suggested we meet at a French-Korean café. The shiny café was piled high with glazed and stuffed sweet pastries. While revising a college essay, we both happily munched on chocolate concoctions. Tasnim ambitiously wrote many college supplemental essays this year; with each completed piece, she became a better editor. After her first year with Girls Write Now, she expanded her horizons by training with the New York Road Runners Run for the Future program. I cannot wait to see all that she takes on in college.*

The Tale of the Wind Chimes and the Disgruntled Demoness

TASNIM TARANNUM

This piece was inspired by a painting of The Demoness of Tibet *at the Rubin Museum of Art, upon which I based the three female characters in my flash fantasy fiction story. The protagonist, Rose, is an Asian American girl who helps her grandmother run an Asian antiques shop.*

You can tell when someone enters by the sound of the wind chimes on the door. If it is a light, slightly airy sound, this person takes caution and does not want to disturb anyone whilst entering. If it is a more abrupt, robust chime, it's either a person in a rush to catch the train or a person who has stumbled here by accident to our antiques shop full of Asian merchandise. However, if it is a long, continuous string of chimes, it is probably the wind. The wind howls especially when the temperature drops in the middle of November.

They say the people of Hollow Township are warm-blooded folk; if only that extended to me. Armed with my fluffy red hat, layers of brightly woven and intricately tied scarves, and two pairs of wooly brown socks, I was ready to fend off any storm.

What I wasn't prepared for was the onslaught of chimes that came from a disgruntled human. I tried to muster up the courage after being shaken by her appearance. I smiled and politely asked her if she would like any help. When she blinked, instead of regular eyelids it looked like she had snakelike slits and green tints in her skin.

"Well, do you have any trinkets?"

When she smiled, she reminded me of a reptile. Yet she had more grace and stature than any human I had ever met.

"We have some in this chest, if you're interested." I pointed at an ebony black chest painted elegantly with gold symbols by my grandmother, who was a master of calligraphy. My grandmother told me she wrote the word "entrances" on the chest in Bengali, a language connected to my family.

"Yes, I am definitely interested." She suddenly appeared closer to the chest. It was jarring to see her move so abruptly. She threw the lid open, flicking trinkets over her shoulder. Soon there were no trinkets left, as she threw the chest away carelessly. With a cold smile, she materialized out of the shop, leaving me in a daze. Except for the trinkets on the floor that looked like a gold mine exploded and the slight ring of the chimes, there was no indication that anyone had been there.

When I kneeled down to pick up a coin, it disappeared. Whilst occupied, my grandmother appeared in a spring-green dress behind me. Considering how close our apartment was and the ruckus that occurred, I wasn't surprised that she came down. She assessed the situation with a smile on her face as the floor looked less like King Midas dropped by. In moving her hand, I glimpsed a part of her skin that looked discolored; the cause might be the burden of running the store. That's why I agreed to help out part-time after school and on weekends.

"You look like you had a lively morning. Don't worry too much or else you will get wrinkles just like your old man," she said, referring to my grandfather, who worried over the smallest things.

I peered at my grandmother's face. She had a few wrinkles

around her eyes, but what was striking were the faint swirls on the side of her face. I took in her posture and her face that closely resembled my aunt's. Her long fingers were covered in the same type of swirls that adorned my aunt's fingers. They both had fingernails that could cut your face into ribbons. When my aunt dressed as a demoness from Southeast Asia during cultural festivals, she painted her skin light green with flecks of gold. I later learned that my grandmother dressed up in a similar manner in her youth.

I recalled the stories about the Southeast Asian demoness that my grandmother often told me in between takes of her charcoal black pipe. Stretching out her legs toward the crackling fire, I would lay my head on the blue pillow as she told me tales of a culture that was still an integral part of our family. Remembering the warmth of those stories, my mind filled with pity for the demoness that was betrayed by her own people. They were scared of her strength rather than empowered by it.

When the last coin evaporated, I turned my attention back to where my grandmother had been standing. She disappeared into thin air. I assumed she went to the kitchen that connected the store to the rest of her apartment. Rather than finding her there, steaming beef ramen and a note was laid out. The note read, in my grandmother's perfect handwriting, "You did well on your first task, Rose. Congratulations."

I looked down at my hands to see glimmers of small green scales that felt rough to the touch. Puzzled, I took the ramen to the old-fashioned dining table and sat down for a hearty meal. The demoness my grandmother told me about was more familiar to me than I'd previously thought. I couldn't tell if I should be worried about the encounter with the green customer or brush it off as my grandmother would.

Baby Walking

NAN BAUER-MAGLIN

At the Poetic Forms workshop, I attempted to write a sonnet. Inspired by a recent video of my grandson taking his first steps at the beach, I wanted the poem to sound nursery rhyme—like.

D. C. Ace Marino,
such a cute bambino.
Crawling, crawling, eyes bright bebe
mouthing "Mama, Dada," maybe.

Afternoons she wheels him to the beach,
the Atlantic Ocean soon in reach.
Sand in his mouth, sand in his nose,
One day at fourteen months, he rose.

Giddy, wobbly, he rushes headlong;
unsteady, falling, laughing, sing-song.
"Careful, careful," she warns.
Waving sea shells, he yawns.

Domenick Christian Ace Marino,
More drunken sailor than bambino.

JANIAH TAYLOR

YEARS AS MENTEE: 2

GRADE: Junior

HIGH SCHOOL: Academy for Young Writers

BORN: Brooklyn, NY

LIVES: Brooklyn, NY

MENTEE'S ANECDOTE: *I always thought that getting a new mentor would be hard for me. Yet this year, my mentor really went beyond my expectations. She is extremely motivational and supportive with my work, and always inspires me to be better. I owe a lot to her, because I wouldn't be doing a lot of things such as entering contests without her, and I am extremely grateful to her.*

LYNDSEY REESE

YEARS AS MENTOR: 1

OCCUPATION: Product Support Lead, Squarespace

BORN: Cincinnati, OH

LIVES: Brooklyn, NY

MENTOR'S ANECDOTE: *Since we've met, I've been so impressed by Janiah's creativity, enthusiasm, and determination. We've experimented with so many forms this year, and it's all because of her willingness to try new things and go outside of her comfort zone. She's inspired me to take risks in my own writing and reminded me of how much joy exists in the writing process.*

Anxiety's Wildest Dreams

JANIAH TAYLOR

This is an excerpt from an essay. I've never written anything like this before. It's about anxiety and its effects on how people see their future. In this part, I go back to the point in my life where my anxiety started and go into how it defined my future.

Junior year is supposed to be one of the most stressful years in your high school life. Making it halfway through, still surviving this hellhole of a year, is a miracle. The expectation is truly high because this is the year you are "supposed" to decide what you are going to do for the rest of your life.

You ask yourself, "What do I *really* want to do with my life?" You never truly know, like you are picking a flavor of ice cream out of the array you are presented with. I've never had a doubt in my mind that one day I'll be a musician. Yet what society puts on mute is the fear behind pursuing your dream—the anxiety behind becoming something you're not even sure you can be. Although I know what I want, I am always doubtful of whether I can achieve it or not. The American ideal is to work hard in order to get to the top. It makes it difficult for people with anxiety to compete with people with more vigor and skill than you can handle. Yet some say just to brush it off and not let fear hold you back. But with anxiety holding the leash, it makes it easier to limit our own freedom.

Ever since I was little, my family and friends told me that I would do great things. The whole *dream big* idea was put in front of me like a plate of food because people saw that I had the skills and talents to be something great. I listened, but I don't think I ever believed in myself. From the perspective of a little nine-year-old girl, I wasn't quite grasping what people saw in me yet. Besides, what could a black girl from Staten Island do? I saw myself in the same place for a long time and I thought things would never change, because why would they change? But the next thing I knew, my family and I moved out to Brooklyn and my life was flipped upside down.

I still did everything I was supposed to, and that's what people saw. But on the inside, I was collapsing piece by piece. I stayed behind in a world I didn't know or understand. That year was when I first started feeling that I was truly alone in my problems and that everyone was too busy to hear about how I was feeling. From what I remember, I was deemed overdramatic. And though I had my moments, that's how people defined me forever. I didn't feel as though my feelings were accounted for, so I thought no one would ever understand me. Being that way made me take situations into my own hands, which changed my whole personality. Between fourth and eighth grade, I was aggressive and oftentimes got into physical and verbal fights. I kept things to myself, and every so often I would blow up because I could never hold in my anger. I thought that being violent was the only way to get people to not walk over me. It took me a while to realize that my anxiety took form in all of those fights. I thought the worst of it was over. But it only reshaped itself again.

Anxiety

LYNDSEY REESE

Janiah and I often talk about what it's like to deal with anxiety. Her wonderful essay inspired me to write about my experiences, too.

We go everywhere together, its fingers in mine. We walk into meetings, bars, cramped living rooms. We step out of the house, underdressed, without an umbrella, our keys on the kitchen table. I open my mouth and it speaks. We write and rewrite and erase. I look at a blank page. It says, "You're back where you started." I walk a long path toward forgetting, but it remembers. We stay up nights. We sleep in late. We repeat. I take a deep breath. Then another. I tell myself a kinder story. It listens. We find relief.

NNEKA ULU

YEARS AS MENTEE: 1

GRADE: Senior

HIGH SCHOOL: Queens Gateway to Health Sciences Secondary School

BORN: Columbus, OH

LIVES: Queens, NY

MENTEE'S ANECDOTE: *I arrive, fashionably late, to meet Jasmine at the Whitney Museum for one of our adventures. While the exhibits were stunning, what I treasured the most from that day was our conversation. I shared the details of my first love interest, she relayed the mixed feelings that came with moving into a new apartment, and we both ruminated over the lack of (at least) six-foot-tall men in our lives. By talking to someone who is eerily similar to me, I better understand the aspects of writing that transfer seamlessly across generations and the aspects that are tinged by the times.*

JASMINE STEIN

YEARS AS MENTOR: 1

OCCUPATION: Senior Creative Strategist, *The New York Times*

BORN: Novi, MI

LIVES: Brooklyn, NY

PUBLICATIONS AND RECOGNITIONS: *The New York Times; Entropy Mag; NoiseMedium*

MENTOR'S ANECDOTE: *Both Nneka and I write what we know. Regardless of genre, we write about the cities we have lived in, the people we know, the people we love, and the conversations we have overheard. I think the most rewarding part of our writing relationship is that we use our work to pull back layers of ourselves and open up to each other. No subject is taboo, and writing is the way to get at the things we are both scared of and hopeful for.*

A Contemplation of Love

NNEKA ULU

As part of a generation of blacksmiths that bend and shape the concept of love into various (sometimes twisted) forms, I look to my mother for advice. I understand the importance of looking at untouched metal, for it is impossible to shape any metal without first appreciating its untampered state.

Looking at the women in my life, I ponder their experiences constantly. They have all juggled the term "love" on their lips, yet none have convinced me of its sweet taste. In fact, none have recalled it as having been sweet. To them, love was not a euphoric feeling but a term that was either thrown around casually or banned from their vocabulary with such celerity that it made even Voldemort jealous. Love was not a pleasure but a means of survival.

My mother was twenty-three when she first met my father. They met in a hospital in Trinidad when my father delivered the news that her only remaining family member had passed. Her tears fell violently. They fell not only for her dead brother but for herself. She was now alone. Captivated by my mother's beauty, my father vowed to take care of her. After years of dating, they got married and moved to America.

At first glance their story seems like that of a fairy tale. A damsel? *Check.* Distress? *Check.* A knight in shining armor? *More like a suave nerd with a heart of gold and good money, but check.* I grew up believing that their story was romance to its finest degree, but it wasn't until recently that I started to question.

When my mother talks of my father, she praises him for being an amazing provider as well as being generous to a fault. Even after the divorce, they would still laugh and talk to each other. They would buy each other birthday gifts and exchange kind words. They have one of the nicest damn divorces I have ever heard of, yet something struck me as peculiar. My mother had never talked about loving my father. In fact, she had never even referred to him as attractive. She would speak of him with warmth and reverence but never love. Has she ever stated that she loved him? *Yes. Numerous times.* But to me, it appeared as though the sweetness of her love tasted more like water.

To dive more in depth, I will break down the nature of their relationship. My mother grew up in destitution softened by her beauty and piety. She had fair skin and long curly hair, and attended every Sunday Mass. She was the jewel of her small town and was treated with adoration despite her status. My mother had been shrouded in God's blessings and she knew it. On the other hand, my father grew up in a privileged family and held one of the more elite family names in the village. He was trained from youth to become a doctor and had the support of a hard-working father and diligent mother. He grew up the prince of the slums, enjoying a privileged life yet still scorned nonetheless. He was not the most attractive, nor the tallest, but he was blessed with a big brain and a big heart. God granted him success.

My mother said "I do" because my father was a doctor and could support her. My father said "I do" because my mother was beautiful and could guarantee him beautiful children. Both "loved" each other for their potential to the other. *Is that wrong?* One would swiftly admonish this behavior and call it a disrespect to "real" marriages. One would shake their head and say that they are making a mockery of love. I was one of these opinionated individuals.

I vowed I would marry for love, but as I grew, love appeared to me as cotton candy. It was something that was flashy and bright. It was something that was sweeter than nectar. It was something that disappeared as suddenly as it was created. When sweetness leaves too quickly, it leaves bitterness behind. I was bitter. I was bitter because I knew I was too young to be bitter.

I currently view love with a curiosity and zeal rendered when seeing an oddity of nature. Love is sweet, bitter, sour, and savory. These flavors add to its depth. Each flavor seasoned with a particular experience. Love is not limited to one person, and it can transcend into other forms. Love is a concept I have witnessed and experienced to some degree. However, numerous forms of love remain misunderstood in my eyes. I am studying love as if I were stargazing on a cloudless night. Love is still under my contemplation, and it may remain there for quite some time.

Red

JASMINE STEIN

"Red" is about grief and loss and coming out of that grief through partnership and love. It was inspired by a prompt to write a piece about color.

The sand was burning underneath the feet of Miranda and Lile. The red dirt flowed in between the cuts of their toes and they were unable to tell if they were in water or on land. They had traveled as far east as they could afford to, and they had intended to reach the end of the world. When they found it they just sat and watched the sunset. The sun looked like it was on fire. "But it always does," Miranda told Lile. "No matter where you are, the sun goes down slow at first and then all at once."

It wasn't the distant sun that lit up the sky and was fading down to leave them in utter darkness that confused them, but the hot coals of the earth below them that was shocking. "Have you ever felt sand this hot?" Miranda asked Lile. "Never in my life have I ever questioned the very stability of the ground we are sitting on as much as I do now," she told him. "I fear it might fall beneath us at any moment."

Red was the color of their skin. It was the color of their home they had left behind, and the color of the plane they flew east on. It was the color of the red-bean ice cream they ate on movie nights, and the color of the light that flickered on Bowery from the fading bulb that kept them up at night. And it was the color of the truck Noah played with the night he died, and now it was the color of the sand they were burning on.

LILY WALKER

YEARS AS MENTEE: 1

GRADE: Senior

HIGH SCHOOL: Lower East Side Preparatory High School

BORN: New Orleans, LA

LIVES: Brooklyn, NY

MENTEE'S ANECDOTE: *I have always loved reading magical realism, but when I began to write short stories I realized that I was more comfortable with realistic fiction. Although I have a diverse background, I tended to write about the same types of stories I saw on TV, which were repetitive and whitewashed. Amira's help has shown me how to create stories that are more magical and unique than I ever thought possible. Her knowledge of science in writing has been an incredible resource for my newfound love of writing science fiction, and exploring our mutual interest in magical realism has been a blast.*

AMIRA PIERCE

YEARS AS MENTOR: 1

OCCUPATION: Language Lecturer, Expository Writing Program, New York University

BORN: Beirut, Lebanon

LIVES: Brooklyn, NY

MENTOR'S ANECDOTE: *For years, I have said I wanted to explore young adult fiction but given priority to "more important" genres. Then I met Lily and loved seeing her light up as she told me about her current favorite series, The Lunar Chronicles by Marissa Meyer. Soon, I found myself at The Strand, exploring the YA section for the first time ever, and taking a few titles home, including Meyer's* Cinder. *That book—and everything else that has come with getting to know Lily—has opened up new possibilities for making meaning in my writing life, my teaching life, and my life life.*

Fake (an excerpt)

LILY WALKER

This is an excerpt of a short story I have been working on called "Fake." The piece takes place in a tech-oriented parallel universe and questions the authenticity of relationships and society's interpretation of mental illness.

I'd met him on a Sunday.

And at my favorite coffee shop, no less.

I spent all day at that café, nestled in a corner and scribbling tirelessly in a leather-bound journal. Perhaps for most, spending a lazy Sunday in a quiet café would be charming. Almost picturesque. But I felt the day's labor like a horizon carrying the weight of the sun at twilight, and the four lattes that I had consumed did nothing to calm my fervor.

Scratch. Erase. Tear. Scratch. Scrawl. Tear. Rip. Scratch.

By noon I was hyperventilating. For a brief moment I looked up, away, above the dancing letters on my page, and caught the barista giving me a curious look. Then, a smile. Bright white and alluring, a sharp contrast from the yellowish pages I wrote on. *The pages.*

Scratch. Erase. Tear. Scratch. Scrawl. Tear. Rip. Scratch.

By three in the afternoon my eyes were glazed over, and I was not sure if it was from the sickeningly banal task of writing for so many hours or if it stemmed from my genuine hysteria. I figured it was the latter, because soon I felt the tears fall. *Tears.*

Tear. Scratch. Scrawl. Tear. Rip. Scratch. Scratch. Erase.

By six I was a robot. I did not need to see myself to know

what I looked like. Deadened eyes. Glossy hair tied back and slipping out of its ponytail. Freckles. Tanned skin. Deadened eyes. Flushed cheeks. Glistening brow. It was hot. Hotter than it had been when I got to the coffee shop that morning. I looked over to the barista again and briefly registered that there was a different person in the place of the man with the glowing smile. A woman this time. I watched her pour milk into a mug through the stuffy air. It was hot.

Scratch. Erase. Tear. Scratch. Scrawl—

"Hey."

I startled. An unfamiliar man was sitting in front of me. Perfect posture. Crooked glasses.

"Hey," he said again. "I noticed you were writing something."

I stared at him. Of course he noticed that I was writing something. It was obvious. Mainly because I was *writing something*. "Yes."

"What are you working on?"

I said nothing. If I said something, I would crack like a porcelain doll. I would obliterate into dust. I would freeze so intensely that—

"Are you okay?" The man looked concerned now, whereas before he seemed almost . . . hopeful?

I looked at him then. I really did. He was something straight out of an ad campaign. His skin was olive-toned and smoother than mine. His hair was sandy and coiffed. His lips formed a perfect bow and pout. It took everything in me not to cringe at his irreproachable figure. He could have been eighteen or twenty-eight.

"What do you mean by 'okay'?" I finally responded. I closed my journal for good measure, in case his eyes drifted to the words. *The words.*

Scratch. Erase—

"I mean," he said, cutting me off from . . . what? I was so delirious that I could not remember if I had actually started writing again or if I only thought I was. "I mean, I approached you because I thought we were the same. But now that I see you, I wonder . . ."

"The same?" I questioned.

"The same," the man confirmed. "I saw it when I first walked in. Our eyes. They're the same. They're the eyes of our people."

Deadened eyes.

His explanation was strange. I rapidly deduced two possibilities: The first was that he was in some type of cult that sucked the souls out of its members until they looked like vacant-eyed sex dolls. The second was that he was hitting on me. Either way, the man was bizarre and timeless and, though he was beautiful, something about him was unnatural. I feared if I kept speaking with him my parents would next see my face on the side of a milk carton.

So I didn't. I continued writing. It didn't take me long to realize that the man was still sitting there, with his impeccably straight back and steady gaze and horn-rimmed glasses. When I glanced up at him beneath my lashes, he didn't seem bothered at all that I had ignored him. He quickly caught my eye before I could look away.

"It's the Super Bowl today."

"It is?"

"That's why there's so many people here. This place turns into a bar after six."

"I know *that*," I said irritably. This was my turf. My favorite coffee shop. I had just spent ten hours in this caffeinated death trap and this man had the nerve to tell me *that it turned into a bar at six?* As though I had not already included that in my plans for the day. As if I would have forgotten that crucial detail.

He recoiled. "Sorry. I just wanted to let you know. Because, um. You seem like you're still using this place as a café." He gestured toward my coffee.

"That's none of your business."

"I know."

"I'm dying in here."

"I know."

Maybe we were the same after all.

New Year, New Orleans (an excerpt from "The Other Guy Won")

AMIRA PIERCE

This is an excerpt from my essay "The Other Guy Won." Though based on events from my ordinary life, I want it to read like an adventure tale, its anxious female narrator finding power in a world she is compelled to build from an amalgam of fragments—past and future, personal and political, fantastic and real.

On the very last morning of 2016, Sam and I took our first flight together, from Brooklyn to New Orleans. That night, we ate oysters on Bourbon Street at a place called Desire, then walked hand in hand through the Seventh Ward to hear music at a club that had just opened on an otherwise dismal stretch of houses and vacant lots. It was called Po' Boys and the headlining act was two women in ghost-lace dresses who played violins and crooned folk songs. A drummer coated in tattoos and piercings inserted fragments of skull-thumping noise between their haunting feminine harmonies.

At midnight everyone moved outside to set off fireworks in the parking lot. I was afraid to light the Roman candle a new friend offered me but stood behind Sam as his flew with a *whizzz* and a *popp* and lots of smoke and light. It was 2017!

We kissed deeply, absorbed in the happy crowd of old and young bodies and haircuts and clothes and shining eyes, buzzing brains that pretended a fake future, professed a love of nature amid the chaos of the city, long limbs that told how fucked-up and beautiful we could be at once.

We were both innocent and grimy; it had rained that night and, as we would learn in the week that followed, New Orleans seems to have a way, even in winter, of always coating you in its weather.

For seven days, as we wandered that haunted, pulsing, breathing city, our new president-elect was absent from the conversations we had with each other and all the kind and crazy people we met. For seven nights and mornings, we rested in an old house that sighed with the changing weather. Our New Orleans bed felt like a magic carpet, like Sam and I were floating, swimming, gathering strength for the year ahead. I stared up at the ceiling fan and talked about Beirut and my family there, and Sam talked about wanting to go to Tehran to see his family, as he never had. I imagined we would go to those faraway places together, but I never said it. The fan whirred and groaned.

New Orleans was like a rainbow-colored shooting star that fizzled into the grayness of winter. Brooklyn that January felt dead like a cemetery, gray like a tombstone.

SHANAI WILLIAMS

YEARS AS MENTEE: 2

GRADE: Junior

HIGH SCHOOL: NYC iSchool

BORN: New York, NY

LIVES: Bronx, NY

MENTEE'S ANECDOTE: *This may be my second year with Girls Write Now but it was my first year with Julia as my mentor. From the day I met her at the Girls Write Now office she has been a bundle of inspiration, support, and excitement. I have learned so much with her. Whether during our tours through exhibitions at The Metropolitan Museum of Art, Poets House, and the New York Public Library at Bryant Park; or our conversations that start off simple and end up dripping with ideas. I swear, if our ideas alone could make books we would need to build a library to house them.*

JULIA CARPENTER

YEARS AS MENTOR: 1

OCCUPATION: Writer, *CNNMoney*

BORN: Atlanta, GA

LIVES: Brooklyn, NY

PUBLICATIONS AND RECOGNITIONS: 2018 Awesome Without Borders grantee; 2018 Shorty Award winner

MENTOR'S ANECDOTE: *This is my first year working with Girls Write Now, and I am so happy to have met Shanai. She inspires me so much—in how much she literally does (school! playwriting! so many extracurriculars!), but, more important, in how much she creates. She sends me poems constantly. She writes them at night, after school, on the weekends, whenever she is moved to jot something down in her Notes app. Her dedication to following her inspiration encourages me, in turn, to listen to my own. I am hoping in the coming year we continue trading work, sharing whenever it comes to us.*

Point A to Z; a map of me

SHANAI WILLIAMS

This piece is representative of me connecting the dots and reflecting on how my memories, my parents, and the impact they unknowingly leave on me affects, and will continue to affect, my life.

I am the by-product of a funny set of people.

I'm like my mother in the way that
I am in constant crisis;

"I didn't grow up with a family dynamic, so I don't know how to be any other way."

When the world is calm
We're the storm watch centers

On high alert
Because every calm we've ever encountered
Is the prerequisite to a storm;

I'm like my father in the way that
I am able to thrive in the aftermath.

"Make sure you keep an eye on your sister."

When everyone else is in panic
We're the lighthearted laughter

That reminds the world
That things are only as bad as you let them be,
That there is a lesson in every trauma.

"Hey, Mom, so I know it's early, 5:00 a.m., in fact, and you're at work, but I've been wanting to tell you something . . .

"It's nothing crazy—"

"What is it?"

"I have a girlfriend."

. . .

"I think you're just desperate for attention."

I never believed my mother and I could be anything alike
She didn't laugh like me
Or make jokes similarly

People said we looked alike
But I couldn't disagree more

Until I saw that she struggled too
With finding a home in others,
Did I realize we
Were more alike than I had chosen to see

At her lowest point
She is like me

I have been trying to explain the same dilemma

To multiple humans
In hopes of finding one
Who could just
Understand . . .

"Aren't I a good person? So why don't people stay? Is this what I deserve?"

And as my mother's voice cracked
Trying to express
The same pain

"They don't ask because they care, they ask because they want to know my business. I'm not stupid, because when I do trust them the one time I need them they aren't there."

I knew she was me.

I knew people saw what I wouldn't see.

"I swear looking in his eyes was the worst, he could make you cry on the spot even if he'd been telling you how beautiful you were."

I never believed I'd been living with my father my whole life
He wasn't understanding
He never paid much attention

My sister told me I could trust him
But I couldn't disagree more

Until I found myself telling my little sister the same thing
When she was struggling

I realized when I was battling internal conflict
My father was the beach that I could escape to

At my lowest point
He is my peace.

The first sign was the rustling in the living room. I'd stare into the darkness toward my bedroom door, expectantly. Then, there was his distinct cough, that was my cue to jump out of bed and head to the living room.

"Hi, Daddy."

"Hey, Daughter."

I'd watch him awhile, then walk through the kitchen past the shopping cart acting as a laundry hamper and into the hallway by the door. Pick up the black "work boots," as he'd call them, and retrace my steps back to the couch where he sat with the news now on. He listened to the traffic report as he got up to put on the rest of his uniform, a Jacobi hospital shirt and his black zip-up hoodie.

I placed the boots beside him, proud that I'd done so before he had time to ask.

"Thank you, are you going to go back to bed?"

I'd nod. "After you leave."

We'd walk to the door, my small feet following behind the thumps of his seemingly massive ones. He'd stop to reach down to hug

my little body and kiss me on the forehead. I'd kiss him back
on the cheek.

And as I held our apartment door open, smiling, he wouldn't get
past the first steps before I bid him parting words,

"I love you, Daddy."

I didn't see him watching carefully
As I tried to lick my own wounds
He knew when to butt in
More than I could admit
He understood . . .

And as my voice cracked
Failing to express
My pains

He spoke to me knowingly.

He'd always been there for me.

"It's amazing the things we forget."

I am

The sun
Sitting in a cave
Waiting to be discovered
By an unsuspecting few.

"You have become the highlight of my day,"

The night
Cascading over mountains
And valleys
They all know my presence.

"I miss seeing you on Saturdays,"

Like my parents.

"You look so much alike . . . even your voices sound the same."

And although

My easel
Has creaky worn-down legs
And my palette has dull colors

My canvas?
Is F R E E of stains
Smudges or other's
Previous marks

My mind F R E E
My perspective F R E S H

I am
The artist bound
To take away your breath.

But what you see
Is not what you get,

We are merely numbered dots

Each point
Has a connection to the next.

Connect them all
And what do you see?

Point A to Z; a map of me.

A talk with my mother

JULIA CARPENTER

I have thought a lot lately about the interior lives of mothers. When we first met, Shanai and I talked about women of different generations responding to #MeToo. After that, I called my mom to talk.

My mother grew up in a man's world.

When #MeToo hit headlines late last year, I thought about the women I know. Women forced out of jobs or careers. Women who found out the hard way what it was like to work in that world.

And I thought about my mom. When she was just nineteen, my mother worked at a restaurant where her boss sexually harassed her. One time he tried to push her and a friend into a car to go on a date—in the middle of their waitressing shifts.

When we talked about it, though, my mother did not call it "harassment" at the time. She had never talked about that boss or thought her experience unusual. She did not even know what the words "sexual harassment" meant.

"It was not something you even thought about," she told me. "You did what you were told. Back then, a lot of people felt that if someone complained, it was the woman overreacting."

She had never had a conversation with her mother, either.

My grandmother was one of two women admitted to her medical school in 1949. That is because she was bright and driven, yes—but also because the school only ever opened two spots for female applicants.

She met my grandfather there, and they had their first big fight when she bought a car—with her own money.

"I think it quite definitely was a man's world—if there was a problem, it was because you as a woman did something," my mom said. "I don't think it was very often thought that the man had overstepped his line."

Even when she graduated, my grandmother only worked part-time in an evening clinic. Her income paid for children's school uniforms and camp vacations.

When I asked her about my mother's time at the restaurant, and then about her own experiences with sexual harassment, she barely blinked.

She said something like that had never happened to her.

"I think harassment happens more nowadays," she said. I did not press her.

When I told my mother about that conversation, she rolled her eyes. What had I expected an eighty-nine-year-old grandmother to say?

"Look at the difference in generation that you and I can talk about this," my mother said. "I wouldn't have dreamed of even mentioning it with my mother."

But I grew up in a different world.

KAITLYN YANG

YEARS AS MENTEE: 1

GRADE: Freshman

HIGH SCHOOL: Hunter College High School

BORN: New York, NY

LIVES: New York, NY

PUBLICATIONS AND RECOGNITIONS: 2016 Scholastic Art & Writing Awards: Silver Key; 2017 Scholastic Art & Writing Awards: Gold Key and Honorable Mention; 2018 Scholastic Art & Writing Awards: Gold Key

MENTEE'S ANECDOTE: *In just one year of having been a part of Girls Write Now, I have learned so much about writing and gained so many experiences by being around others who share my passion. Meg and I have shared so many stories, and my experiences have inspired new ideas. Spending time with my mentor and the Girls Write Now community has allowed me to share my work in an open, accepting environment and challenged me to reach my full potential as a writer, creator, and person.*

MEGHANN FOYE

YEARS AS MENTOR: 1

OCCUPATION: Writer, Editor, and Author

BORN: Marblehead, MA

LIVES: Jersey City, NJ

PUBLICATIONS AND RECOGNITIONS: I am a regular contributor to women's lifestyle publications, including *Redbook, Good Housekeeping, Brit + Co, SheKnows, StyleCaster,* and Refinery29.

MENTOR'S ANECDOTE: *In working with Kaitlyn, my mentee, this past year, we'd start each session off with a five-minute free write, in which we'd download our days, current events, even characters in our lives. Through these free writes, I became acquainted with her world and the unique bravery of her generation in the face of so many challenges. This poem, inspired by our time together, represents the distillation of that courageous force she's shared with me.*

Raindrops and Coffee

KAITLYN YANG

"Raindrops and Coffee" illustrates the relationships between strong, resilient women that surround us. The poem focuses on the importance of supporting one another and cherishing the moments and memories we share.

Maybe it's
because my memory's been slipping or
because I've only heard your voice on a recorded message for a
    while now but
I'm afraid I've forgotten how you looked
outside the mirror

the photographs
that filled the scrapbooks we made during the day you got off
    from school
are still filed in the cabinet
beneath the bookcase
in the den
even without creaking down the stairs to
flip through the now-faded pages I can remember
the pittering-pattering against the windows and
you sneaking sips from the chipped green mug you made me
    for my birthday but
scrunching your face at the bitter taste though it was
a creamy light brown with milk and sugar
your smile with

the two front teeth slightly crooked beamed happiness
bouncing in your seat at the wooden dining table in
your favorite sneakers
navy worn into gray and a big toe threatening to poke out
proof of a hard-won race from
the edge of the schoolyard to
your classroom
your leggings torn at the knee
were another clue

the shadows
that danced along your cheek from a growing number of
    flickering dripping candles on your cake
looked to have gotten darker
and deeper each year like
layers of unhealed bruises
even without squinting my eyes to
see beyond the camera's flash I can remember
the pittering-pattering against the windows and
you brewing another pot of strong black coffee in the machine
    we bought at the flea market but
wincing as you poured a cup and dribbled some onto your
    fingers even though it was
the second time your shaking hands did it this morning
might be easier if you kept your heavy eyelids open
even though the overhead lights that dimmed until they
    disappeared with a fizz
may be to blame

and the reflection
in the murky puddle on edge of the cement path
that shattered and splashed from scrambling tires to
your stockings as you waited for the light to change

lasted only a moment but
even without running my finger over the scars
from pinching myself with the needle I can remember
the pittering-pattering against the windows and
you throwing open the door in tears and
crashing into your seat even though the stuffing of the
    cushion was already climbing out
shaking the table with a pile of books under the shortest leg
that chipped off after we balanced on it to change the
    lightbulbs
I didn't say a word but
handed you a cup of coffee
with a little sugar
you needed something sweet
you took the cup
downed it and
fell asleep at the table
the thread fought against slipping into the eye but
I stitched your stocking up

and the wait
by the bus stop
covered in a black umbrella
purchased after you read that
black is metropolitan in a magazine
hair straightened just that morning but
already curling up at the edges
when the bus pulled up by the curb
you stepped inside
shaking out your umbrella
handing the driver
crisp birthday money
removed from its neat folding in your wallet

you found a seat by the front
and waved to me but
by the time I waved back
the bus was no more than a cloud of smoke and
the rain stopped me
from running after you

and I can see the picture
of your face staring out the foggy glass window
of the café
so clearly in my mind
content to sip your black coffee
beside strangers and
go home to silence
fingerprint-covered tortoiseshell glasses pushed up
on your nose
a closed umbrella rested on the
chair beside you
dripping onto the
black and white tiles
nervous but feeling safe
behind a mirage

and the hope
that shone from your face to a reflection off a tall building
drew a halo around your head
that only I could see
chic mug in hand
swirling around your drink
in a practiced manner
studied the women sitting next to you in the café
teetering on bright red pumps
and slipping on the wet pavement

feet aching but smile in place
in your precious city it's just
have a seat
tell me about yourself
goodbye
you trudge out
shoulders slumped
tears hidden behind tortoiseshell glasses
you wrestle your umbrella open
the black one you brought with you on the bus
now torn but
bills to be paid and
there's not enough to buy a new one
then the wind blows and
flips it inside out
you drop onto the sidewalk and cry
I hope you can feel my hand
patting your shoulder
and pulling you up
for a hug

maybe one day
I will see you again and
perhaps you'll happen to be standing before me in line
I'll order coffee sweetened with milk and sugar while
you get yours black or
maybe you'll decide to catch a bus ride home and
surprise me with a visit
I might not recognize you at first
haven't seen you outside the mirror for a while
but I hope that we'll learn to remember each other
over raindrops and coffee.

One Two Z

MEGHANN FOYE

"One Two Z" encapsulates a conversation between the generations. It highlights the ways the young can often remind us to remove our blinders and see all the possibilities.

She comes in quietly
Beyond her fourteen years, an equanimity
She pushes her multicolored strands into a high messy bun
She sits, open to new ideas, open to feedback, open to wisdom
But she doesn't realize, her example contains it

A woman of forty, her low messy bun now gray
looking back and wondering
Why she waited, waited so long
To free her own voice, hear her own song
Her voice was always there, whisper-screaming the words

No, no, no, NO
The ones she never learned to say

The girl wields her pen, her pad, her shining confidence
Brave and bold, she names her emotions, her thoughts, her
     fears
One, two, three
The darkness only contains stars and dazzling galactic winds
It's just as bright with the moon
As the day that comes with the sun

Why not see what's there
She asks

But wait, but wait
What if, what if

So what if,
She smiles, doodling curls and cues with the same fervor
As dragons and flames

Aren't you scared, she asks, as the girl looks up to the right
Where the ideas are all held tight

No, not really
But what about the pain, the terror of friends turned foes
Armed, dangerous and menacing

Yes, of course
Yes, we are
But we know something your generation does not

What's that
That we are not alone
We have each other
And with that, if one of us falls,
The others are there, alongside them
To raise up their spirits, living or dead
Their hearts, their art,
We see it all,
It's easier for us to, than not

I had a voice, within me, but the only ones who saw
Were sitting in ivory towers

With judgmental pens, with "constructive" words meant to
   tear and shred
Or guns, meant to shoot those dead who spoke words of truth
To those who believed in different gods, different crowns,
   different books

But is that true? she says, laughing eyes
Weren't there also the sun, moon and stars?
They were catching every last unspoken word, until the world
   revolved to see it
Now, with the rain, and your pen, and these zeroes, they're
   ready to hear it
To feel it

Let it out, let it out
Share it.
Why not?
See if it might stick
This time

Maybe, maybe
Yes, yes, yes, YES
Okay

We're all here, waiting to see
Us girls of Generation F
Us women of the future
Of force, fire, freedom

Ready for us? One, Two, Z

EN YU ZHANG

YEARS AS MENTEE: 2

GRADE: Junior

HIGH SCHOOL: Stuyvesant High School

BORN: Hong Kong, SAR

LIVES: Brooklyn, NY

MENTEE'S ANECDOTE: *Our second year has definitely been filled with more completed writing—my mentor pushes me out of my laziness to at least write a little each time. More significantly, I have been able to develop a lot of my ideas, not even just the ones related to writing. Elizabeth is always willing to listen to me go on about my latest interest, as well as to provide her own insights (ever so helpful!); I feel that I have grown a lot as a person thanks to her.*

ELIZABETH KOSTER

YEARS AS MENTOR: 2

OCCUPATION: Creative Writing Teacher, West Brooklyn Community High School

BORN: New York, NY

LIVES: New York, NY

PUBLICATIONS AND RECOGNITIONS: "Modern Love," *The New York Times*, August 2014

MENTOR'S ANECDOTE: *En Yu and I are working together for a second year, and our bond has become stronger. Our meetings are longer, richer, timed writing sessions peppered with conversations about politics, literature, and existentialism. She is filled with insight and has an eye for the absurd, and it's a joy to work with her.*

The Sky over Our Heads

EN YU ZHANG

This piece explores the idea of freedom through the classic symbol of the sky, and uses quotes (italicized) from Gustave Flaubert's Madame Bovary.

As we all fiddle with our pencils, double-checking to confirm that they are of the No. 2 variety, that we have erasers, that our cell phones have been turned off, there is nothing more to be done than to wait for time to crawl past, so that our ordeal may be over.

Outside, the cloudless blue sky eludes us all, *as though flouting the whole world*, particularly our myopic mind-sets that we peer through.

Settling in, there were jokes thrown around about the *range* of activities that we were able to do upon completion of the exam when time wasn't called yet. Checking the test for perhaps the sixth time was an apt checkpoint, though sleeping, singing, and all other great, fun activities were prohibited.

I suggested looking out the window.

Of course, I never got around to it, spending my time repeatedly checking my answers.

The splendor of a poetical sky was full of mirth, laughing at me from the shadows of my vision.

It is early afternoon as my friend and I walk by the Hudson River, where "sunlight on waves [is] drowsy tinsel."* The glit-

---

*From David Mitchell's *Black Swan Green*.

tering beads scatter among the yellow-green waterscape as they are directed by the winds. New Jersey peers over from the other side, looking as undistinguished as New York has ever perceived it.

This part of the sky is an intense azure, unmarred by white, as the sun makes its descent. As we walk toward it, we move farther away from the section of sky so densely concentrated with gray clouds that sunlight could not filter through. Such was the divide between cloudy and clear, as we walked along its boundary.

To stare into the unblemished blue sky is to stare into the depths of infinity, for there is nothing in that blue that could be retrieved that the mind could attribute to solid form. It *held layers and layers of colors, denser deep down and lighter and lighter toward the enameled surface*, allowing us to *lose* ourselves *in those depths*.

There is a plane heading into those depths, out of our reach. We stare at it, straining our eyes, trying to hold that white dot within our sight. In the end, the plane still eludes us, becoming indistinguishable from the blue.

We blink some more and laugh it off.

How happy those days were. *How free, how full of hope. There* are *none left now.*

The sky from my room is a caged bird, its wide expanse contained by black bars and insect screens. The glass on one side of the windows is translucent, with patches of unidentifiable gray matter spread upon it thinly. My desk is placed right next to this view, alongside a much longer table jammed behind it, leaving only a narrow aisle for my chair. When the chair faces to the north there is the desk meant for work, with nothing on it; when it turns around there is the table with stacks of books piled upon it, meant for escape.

I sit on the ladder, despite its failing legs, reading, despite my obligations to my schoolwork. I *gave* myself *deadlines, which* I *would extend.*

Waiting for a new self *at the bottoms of pages,* I seek epiphanies from the novels, something to bring into my life. Schoolwork is never fulfilling. On some days I could be full of motivation, seeing the tedious tasks as just one step to complete the higher goal of education. However, most days this is not the case.

I can never seem to get myself to my desk to even start my work. I know that if I can take that first step, everything will be much smoother sailing. When I watch shows on my laptop my eye is constantly monitoring the clock. Somehow, even as I know of my duties, I can ignore them so easily.

Let *the succession of identical days* occur. There isn't much I can do about it, anyway.

I read on, not thinking about all those bothersome issues of reality. If *I've read everything,* will I find the better details of the world? Is there something intrinsically worthwhile in humanity I could cling to, something in myself, that could be discovered in novels, that allowed myself an excuse for my action?

But how can it be easy *to express an uneasiness so intangible, one that changes shape like a cloud, that changes direction like the wind?*

The sky holds so much beauty, indulging in my need to seek something beyond what modern life can offer. A cloudless sky's endless depths beckon to me, allowing me to become lost within them, so that I may cast aside the troubles that plague my reality. The ceiling of the world is a relic of the past; sometimes I imagine New York as it had once been, heavily forested, as the sky engulfs my vision. The night sky is my refuge, where

I am free to do as I wish for those scant hours of darkness, before society demands I enter again.

Such is the sky's comfort.

Photo Montage

ELIZABETH KOSTER

This piece, inspired by a distant trip to Nepal, is about our human need to share experiences with others, and the way in which social media has amplified this need.

On the penultimate day of our Himalayan trek, we were to ascend the 17,500-foot Gokyo Peak to see views of Mount Everest. Helicopters hovered over the mountain and carried hikers with altitude sickness to medical centers, while I lay in my sleeping bag with a fever, my body wracked with sweat and chills. *I almost saw Everest,* I imagined telling people, *but I was sick that day.*

You haven't been? People would ask. *Oh. You haven't lived.* (Who were these people I thought were going to ask me this? How many times has someone said, "If you were in Nepal, you must have seen Everest"? Zero.) But I had to go, regardless of how ill I already felt. At nineteen, I thought I could find myself through travel—having a photo of Everest seemed essential, as if it were a key that would unlock some unknown part of me. The peak was the last 500 feet of elevation gain, and so I crawled out of my tent, clutching water bottles and steadying myself.

A few minutes into the hike, my fingers and feet became swollen and puffy and it felt like liquid was pressing inside my skin, ready to explode. I bent over my knees, trying to breathe, but was only able to wheeze. Up at the top, I saw my friend engulfed in fog, and I dragged one foot in front of the other, my scalp tightening around my skull like a vise.

"Come, take a picture!" she said.

I staggered toward her, faded prayer flags snapping in the wind. To my right was Everest's jagged iciness, hidden by storm clouds. I got a shot of it and a part of my sluggish brain thought, *Saw Everest: check.*

I needed to place the glossy 4x6 into an album as proof, in the way people now post Facebook updates of their lives—their dinners, their cat videos—so they can elicit "likes" and comments. If we go on a trip and don't post photos, did the trip really happen? It's the urge to be heard, to matter, to live and have something to show for it. See? Can you see me? Do I exist?

To an outsider, the Everest photo might seem impressive. To me, the cloud-obscured peak conjures memories of nausea and wheezing, and of a then insatiable desire to experience without actually tasting.

MIN ZHENG

YEARS AS MENTEE: 1

GRADE: Senior

HIGH SCHOOL: Millennium Brooklyn High School

BORN: Putian, Fujian, China

LIVES: Brooklyn, NY

MENTEE'S ANECDOTE: *I was taking a short break from writing when I joined Girls Write Now, so I was extremely nervous when I met Julia for our first weekly meeting. However, we fell right into place. She had a list of prompts for me to choose from and a five-minute timer for each prompt. I have a habit of attempting to perfect my stories before I finish getting my ideas out, and through this warm-up, I find myself worrying less about what I could have done and focusing more on what I have done.*

JULIA WEISS

YEARS AS MENTOR: 2

OCCUPATION: Copywriter, Beyond, a Creative Agency

BORN: Santa Monica, CA

LIVES: Brooklyn, NY

MENTOR'S ANECDOTE: *One great memory with Min—and I promise you there are many—was when I encouraged Min to analyze the first two pages of* Harry Potter and the Sorcerer's Stone *as a writing exercise. Until then, Min had assured me that watching the movie was enough and that she didn't need to read the book. But, after those two pages, she was admittedly curious, and we took a trip to the bookstore to buy* Harry Potter and the Sorcerer's Stone. *Later, after parting ways on the subway platform, she sent me a text: "I read two chapters on the train. It's so good!"*

Found You

MIN ZHENG

Miyu is a high school student who's coming home after a late night of tutoring and hanging with her friend, Sam. She's never questioned a stranger's intentions despite the news being filled with kidnapping and murder cases. What does she do when she's in the middle of one?

The ringing in her head was getting unbearable. Miyu opens her eyes and finds herself sitting at one of the Thirty-sixth Street train station benches. It is currently nine p.m. and Miyu just parted ways with Sam.

"Ugh, why did I agree to take the R train? The D train isn't coming for another six minutes." Miyu sneers at herself before taking her phone out of her pocket to text-spam Sam of her cursed fate.

Her spam ends abruptly when a pair of shoes enters her vision. "Hi! Is this downtown or uptown? I'm not from around here." The man is wearing a dark blue North Face coat. His right hand clutches onto his black bookbag while his left hand rubs his neck shamefully.

"It's downtown," Miyu replies and gives the stranger a small smile.

"Oh, thanks!" the man chirps back with a grin that stretches to his eyes. He lingers in front of Miyu, who goes back to her spam.

After a moment of silence and a bunch of mock-hostile sent texts, Miyu's lips move again. "Are you heading to Manhattan?"

"No, I'm trying to go to Coney Island," the man quickly answers.

Miyu hums in acknowledgment and gives another friendly smile to the stranger before she puts on her earphones and zones the rest of the station out.

The man walks away to the end of the platform.

Miyu is texting Sam, who has arrived home, when she gets a text from her sister, Mio. "I'm on the bridge right now," the text reads.

"I'm at Thirty-sixth Street right now, do you want me to wait for you so we can go home together?"

"Sure."

By the time the short conversation is over, the man returns and proceeds to sit down on the empty seat next to Miyu.

"I'm not from around here," the man repeats from before, while leaning his face too close for comfort.

Miyu smells alcohol coming from the guy next to her. Her heart starts to race, panicking. She gives a nervous smile as an answer and scooches in her seat in an attempt to put more space between them.

"Have you been waiting for the train for a long time?" the stranger asks after a moment of silence.

"Yeah, I'm waiting for someone," Miyu replies quickly, rapidly texting Sam and Mio.

The guy seems to notice her discomfort and walks away.

Noticing the N train that goes to Coney Island passed, Miyu looks up, only to be startled by the man's glance in her direction while he passes by her. Miyu's hands start to tremble as she texts her sister again. "Where are you? Why are you taking so long??"

Miyu's eyes follow the figure in the dark blue coat closely as another N train arrives at the platform. She stands up from her seat and waits for the train to come to a halt. The figure quickly walks up next to her, waiting for the train to come to a halt as well. Miyu lets out a shaky breath and goes back to the seats. The man parts from Miyu and walks to the end of the platform again.

Miyu's train is about to arrive, and in her last attempt to figure out if she was being dramatic or paranoid, Miyu walks to the end of the platform.

The man follows.

The D train is entering the platform. The man is now ten steps away from Miyu.

The train doors open. She enters the crowded train. The stranger enters as well. Miyu takes a deep breath with her eyes closed. It is now or never. Miyu looks at her phone as she exits and runs to the next car as quickly as her shaky legs allow. She hides among the crowd in the car.

"Miyu!" a voice calls out. Miyu turns around in alarm and lets out a sigh of relief to see her sister sitting there.

"He was following me," Miyu says, her voice trembling. "He was following me."

Miyu peers at the open doors of the train, hoping they will close soon. Miyu holds her breath when she sees a familiar dark blue coat cross her vision. The doors close. Miyu scans his actions, the man looks like he is searching for something . . . or someone. The train leaves the platform and the man disappears from her vision.

Miyu slides onto the floor, leaning her head against the doors, and breathes.

Tears are streaming down Miyu's face when she jolts awake. Curling into herself, she clenches her thin white tee. Her heart pounds as she takes uneven breaths.

"It's just a dream," she whispers to herself. She takes a long deep breath, cold sweat is trickling down her neck. "It's just a dream," she continues to mutter, almost as if she is trying to brainwash herself.

"Oh, is it?" a voice from the corner of her bedroom calls out. "I found you."

She shivers, goose bumps decorating her skin. "It's not real."

Course

JULIA WEISS

I'm currently working on a poetry collection about women in the workplace, highlighting my experiences at a male-dominated marketing agency and beyond. This is one of the pieces from the book. I hope that the book makes its way into the world, and I hope future generations of women never have to endure the misogyny that those before them have encountered.

The woman behind me in the coffee line
says, "I can't handle today. Normally,
I can handle his micromanaging bullshit,
but not today. Don't get me wrong—I love
my job—but not today." I turn to see
two tall black women with flawless skin
and meticulously painted red lips.
I feel that way every day, I say,
loud enough for them to hear,
quiet enough for nobody else to notice.
Her friend frowns in response.
She beams. "We should've been strippers,"
she says, tucking her wallet under her arm
looking up as if contemplating that path.
"Really, we should've been strippers."
Now her friend is laughing. "No,"
her friend says. "No, that's not our motto.
Don't make that our motto."
The barista calls me up. I order my coffee,

they order their coffee, we walk out
of the coffee shop going in opposite directions
heading exactly the same way.

Generation F

PROMPTS AND WRITING EXERCISES FOR INDIVIDUALS AND GROUPS

At Girls Write Now, our mentees are part of a generation yet to be defined, a generation facing unprecedented challenges, freedoms, technologies, and choices. They are fighters and feminists, freethinkers and forces to be reckoned with. They are fitting in (or not), fed up, fighting back, and figuring it out in classrooms, cafés, and all across New York City. This year, our mentees and mentors explored what it meant to be members of *Generation F* through genres such as intergenerational memoir, poetic forms, column writing, and magical realism. As a community, we sought to redefine our feminist identities, find our voices, fight for essential freedoms, and face our world with fresh eyes.

Join us in the activities and prompts below, as we continue to define *Generation F* together!

—SIERRA RITZ, Senior Program Coordinator, and
NAOMI SOLOMON, Assistant Director of Programs

MEMOIR: Intergenerational Memoir

In these exercises, you will focus on how family members and members from other generations have shaped your life to create a memoir piece. This memoir should highlight a moment when your beliefs, life choices, or lifestyle led to a turning point in your relationship with someone from another generation.

PART ONE: Intergenerational Prompts

Think about someone who is from a generation older or younger than yours who has had an impact on your life, and answer these questions with that person in mind:

- What is a value you and this person share?
- What is a value you and this person disagree on?
- What is an experience you have had that this person will never have, or that this person has had that you will never have?

PART TWO: Creating Conflict

Think about a time when you found yourself on the opposite side of an intergenerational argument from the person from the prompt above. Craft a story around this conflict: How did it come about? How was the conflict resolved? Did anyone change their mind?

PART THREE: Changing Perspective

Now try writing a paragraph from the point of view of the other person in your story. Use this time to embrace their perspective and get a sense for their voice.

RECOMMENDED READING

Miriam's Kitchen
by Elizabeth Ehrlich

Reading Lolita in Tehran
by Azar Nafisi

Nasty Women: Feminism, Resistance, and Revolution in Trump's America by Kate Harding and Samhita Mukhopadhyay

Tomorrow
by Saradine Nazaire

POETRY: Poetic Forms

These activities center on utilizing poetic forms—sometimes considered outdated or old-fashioned—as a vehicle for addressing contemporary issues and sharing timely, relevant experiences. Explore and embrace the challenges and opportunities provided by these strictly defined poetry formats!

PART ONE: Getting the Rhythm

Start by picking one of the following to write about:

- A complicated idea or opinion that you're struggling with or have debated a lot
- A current event that is on your mind

Now try writing a couplet (two lines that rhyme and have the same number of syllables) that can be a part of your final poem.

PART TWO: Following the Rules

Next try building off of your couplet and create a sonnet. For reference, a sonnet is a poem that . . .

- is fourteen lines long, and is traditionally three stanzas that are four lines each, and ends with a couplet—so four lines, four lines, four lines, two lines; however, some poets split up the stanzas as four-four-six or other variations

PART THREE: Exchanging Formats

Take your original theme and write it into another form of poetry—you can try a super-short version, like writing a single cinquain (a five-line verse) or a few couplets, or try out one of the longer forms you haven't used yet. Many poets write stand-alone cinquains as minimalist poetry, like haiku!

JOURNALISM: Column Writing

Use the exercises below to inspire the early stages of your very own column. Column writing centers on the concept of developing a voice or theme that maintains consistency for readers over multiple installments while bringing fresh ideas, information, and insight with every installment.

PART ONE: The Big Idea

Start by picking one of the following as a focus for your column:

- A specific area of arts and culture—you can pick a category, a genre that exists across categories, or art created by a specific group of artists
- Current events on a local, state, national, or international scale
- Slice of life—a column that, week by week, introduces your reader to your neighborhood, school or workplace, personal life, or other social context you're a part of

PART TWO: Define Your Column

Now, thinking about your topic of choice and the voice you plan to use, write a brief (no more than three sentences) description of what your column will be about. Consider how you'll introduce your topic and voice/point of view to readers—what is most likely to get a new reader hooked on your column?

PART THREE: Future Thinking

With all of the above in mind, write teasers for three installments of your column. Your teasers should be three to five sentences long, and should describe what each column will be about.

RECOMMENDED READING

"The Land of the Large Adult Son" by Jia Tolentino

"On Being Way Too Hot" from Romaissaa Benzizoune's column *Hijabi in Plain Sight*

"Eliza Hamilton Was Not Helpless" from Amy Watkin's column *Women Who Should Be Pretty Pissed Off*

"Equality Begins with Changing Education" by Waeza Jagirdar

FICTION: Magical Realism

In these writing exercises, you will begin to build a believable world with magical elements that represent larger themes of a story. This is the basis for any magical realism piece.

A famous (and very short) example is this seven-word story "The Dinosaur" by Augusto Monterroso.

"Cuando despertó, el dinosaurio todavía estaba."

or

"When he awoke, the dinosaur was still there."

PART ONE: We've Got Issues

Start by writing about a social, cultural, or political issue that is important to you. Your story doesn't have to be about this issue explicitly, but this issue should be part of the general world/context of your story, and the magical element(s) of your story can act as a metaphor for this issue. For example, if your issue is government surveillance of people's cell phone and Internet usage, your magical element might be that after you turn eighteen, your thoughts start to show up visibly on your forehead, and only wealthy or well-connected people are allowed to wear hats or hairstyles that cover their foreheads.

PART TWO: Make It Magical

Next, think about what the magical element(s) of your world will be. There are lots of options! Remember to consider how this element may connect back to your issue, or act as a metaphor for it, and/or ultimately reveal a truth about the issue.

How do these magical elements relate to the issue you chose? How in the course of your story will these magical elements reveal a truth about the issue?

PART THREE: Tying It Together

Now think over the elements of your story so far. Write a one-sentence version of your story, in the style of "The Dinosaur." This version obviously won't include all the details of your final story, but it will provide a taste of your theme/issue and magical elements, and will introduce a character and/or a setting.

RECOMMENDED READING

"The Dinosaur" by Augusto Monterroso

Short Stories by Latin American Women: The Magic and Real
by Dora Alonso, edited by Celia Correas Zapata

"The Burgundy & Gold Stitched Chair" by Emily Rinaldi

About Girls Write Now

For twenty years, Girls Write Now has been a leader in arts education as New York's first and only writing and mentoring organization for girls. We match underserved teen girls and gender-nonconforming youth from throughout the five boroughs of New York City with women professional writers and digital media makers as their personal mentors. Our mentees—more than 95 percent girls of color and 90 percent high-need—are published in outlets including *The New York Times*, *Newsweek*, and *BuzzFeed*; perform at Lincoln Center and the United Nations; and earn hundreds of Scholastic Art & Writing Awards. One hundred percent of Girls Write Now seniors are accepted to college.

Girls Write Now has been distinguished three times by the White House as one of the nation's top youth programs and twice by the Nonprofit Excellence Awards as one of New York's top ten nonprofits. Reaching thousands of girls, Girls Write Now is a founding partner of the New York City Council's STARS Citywide Girls Initiative. Girls Write Now has received the Youth INC Innovators Award, NBCUniversal's 21st Century Solutions prize for social innovation through media arts, and the Diane von Furstenberg (DVF) People's Choice nomination.

Our annual anthology has received the Outstanding Book of the Year award by the Independent Publisher Book Awards, and has earned honors from the International Book Awards, The New York Book Festival, the National Indie Excellence Awards, and the Next Generation Indie Book Awards. The anthology has also received Honorable Mention from the San Francisco Book Festival and the Paris Book Festival.

Literary Partners

Alliance for Young Artists & Writers

Belletrist

Bustle

Chime for Change

Coach

Columbia University Artists/ Teachers Program

Comedy Central

Dutton

Diane von Furstenberg

Feminist Press

Fletcher & Co

Foundry

GIPHY

GirlBoss

HarperCollins

Houghton Mifflin Harcourt

Lenny Letter

Macmillan

MAKERS

McNally Jackson Books

Movado

National Book Foundation

Newmark Grubb Knight Frank

News Corp

New-York Historical Society

New York Women's Foundation

One Teen Story

Parsons The New School of Design

Pen + Brush

Penguin Random House

PIMCO Foundation

Riverhead Books

SparkPoint Studio

StoryBundle

The Wing

ThoughtMatter

Tin House

Urban Outfitters

VIDA: Women in Literary Arts

The Wall Street Journal

Young to Publishing Group

Youth INC

Girls Write Now 2018

Mikey Mercedes
Kaya Middleton
Gabi Palermo
Leslie Pantaleon
Yvonne Prieto
Daleelah Saleh
Maeve Slon
Jacqueline Thom
Nneka Ulu
Sabrina Wen
Sharon Young
Luljeta Zenka
En Yu Zhang

CRAFT TALK SPEAKERS

Amber Atiya
Romaissaa Benzizoune
Kyla Marshell
Aarti Monteiro
Samhita Mukhopadhyay
Brooke Obie
Camille Perri
Jia Tolentino

CHAPTERS READING SERIES KEYNOTE SPEAKERS

Naima Coster
Molly Crabapple
Kayleen Schaefer
Meg Wolitzer
Jenny Zhang

PHOTOGRAPHERS

Marsha Bernstein
Muneesh Jain
Maggie Muldoon
Jessie Roth
Richelle Szypulski
Paolo Villanueva

Anthology Supporters

We are grateful to the countless institutions and individuals who have supported our work through their generous contributions. Visit our website at girlswritenow.org to view the extended list.

Girls Write Now would like to thank Dutton for their help producing this year's anthology.

Girls Write Now would like to thank Amazon Literary Partnership, which provided the charitable contribution that made possible this year's anthology.

The anthology is supported, in part, by public funds from the National Endowment for the Arts; the New York State Council on the Arts, a State Agency; and the New York City Department of Cultural Affairs, in partnership with the City Council, the Manhattan Borough President's Office, and STARS Citywide Girls Initiative.